Alternative Schools
❧ A REFERENCE HANDBOOK

Other Titles in
ABC-CLIO'S
CONTEMPORARY EDUCATION ISSUES
Series

African American Education, Cynthia L. Jackson
The Assessment Debate, Valerie J. Janesick
Bilingual Education, Rosa Castro Feinberg
Charter Schools, Danny Weil
Educational Leadership, Pat Williams-Boyd
Migrant Education, Judith A. Gouwens
Multicultural and Diversity Education, Peter Appelbaum
Sex, Youth, and Sex Education, David Campos
Special Education, Arlene Sacks
Student Rights, Patricia H. Hinchey
Teacher Training, David B. Pushkin
Understanding Educational Reform, Raymond A. Horn, Jr.

FORTHCOMING
Literacy and Learning, Brett Elizabeth Blake and Robert W. Blake
School Vouchers and Privatization, Danny Weil

CONTEMPORARY EDUCATION ISSUES

Alternative Schools

A REFERENCE HANDBOOK

Brenda Edgerton Conley

A B C CLIO

Santa Barbara, California • Denver, Colorado • Oxford, England

Library of Congress Cataloging-in-Publication Data
Conley, Brenda Edgerton.
Alternative schools : a reference handbook / Brenda Edgerton Conley.
p. cm. — (Contemporary education issues)
Includes bibliographical references and index.
ISBN 1-57607-440-4 (hard : alk. paper) — ISBN 1-57607-441-2 (e-book)
1. Alternative schools—United States—Handbooks, manuals, etc.
2. Alternative education—United States—Handbooks, manuals, etc.
I. Title. II. Series.
LC46.4 .C66 2002
371.04'0973—dc21
2002014680

06 05 04 03 02   10 9 8 7 6 5 4 3 2 1

This book is also available on the World Wide Web as an e-book.
Visit www.abc-clio.com for details.

ABC-CLIO, Inc.
130 Cremona Drive, P.O. Box 1911
Santa Barbara, California 93116-1911

Manufactured in the United States of America

This book is dedicated to
Leon, Jr., Georgine, Marian, Leon III, Kraig, Keon, Danny,
Juanita, Khia, Erika, Claudette, Gene, Lowell, Garcia, Sid,
Angela, Michael, Trevor, Sydney, Bernadette, Mark,
Aaron, Melvin, Hattye, and Marquise.

It is with deep gratitude that I express my thanks
and appreciation for the love, support, and
encouragement you provide.
Your presence in my life is a blessing today and always.

⚬⬥ Contents

❧ Series Editor's Preface

The Contemporary Education Issues series is dedicated to providing readers with an up-to-date exploration of the central issues in education today. Books in the series will examine such controversial topics as home schooling, charter schools, privatization of public schools, Native American education, African American education, literacy, curriculum development, and many others. The series is national in scope and is intended to encourage research by anyone interested in the field.

Because education is undergoing radical if not revolutionary change, the series is particularly concerned with how contemporary controversies in education affect both the organization of schools and the content and delivery of curriculum. Authors will endeavor to provide a balanced understanding of the issues and their effects on teachers, students, parents, administrators, and policymakers. The aim of the Contemporary Education Issues series is to publish excellent research on today's educational concerns by some of the finest scholars/practitioners in the field while pointing to new directions. The series promises to offer important analyses of some of the most controversial issues facing society today.

Danny Weil
Series Editor

◆ Preface

This book has been written for a very broad audience. The information included here provides ideas for school administrators searching for alternative programs to support school improvement. A historical and present-day perspective on alternative programs is offered to school board members who want to be better informed about alternative learning options. Politicians will find content that helps shape agenda items for prospective political campaigns that are in the best interests of schools. And, above all, this book serves as a resource for parents who are seeking information to help them develop the knowledge base they need in order to make decisions about the most appropriate education experience for their children.

Brenda Edgerton Conley

Chapter 1
☙ Introduction

Progressive education, often called modern education or the new education practice, is defined as an attitude, a belief in experimentation, and a commitment to the education of all children and to democracy in the schools. It may be the most enduring education reform movement in this country, spanning about one hundred years thus far. Although progressive education waxes and wanes in popularity, many of its practices now appear so regularly in both private and public schools as to have become mainstream. The four dominant themes of progressive education are as follows:

1. A broadening of the school to include a direct concern for health, vocation, and the quality of community life
2. The application in the classroom of more humane, more active, and more rational pedagogical techniques derived from research in philosophy, psychology, and the social sciences
3. The tailoring of instruction more directly to the different kinds of classes of children who have been brought within the purview of schools
4. The use of more systematic and rational approaches to the administration and management of the schools

Alternative education programs come in many more varieties than they did perhaps two or three decades ago. In these earlier years, the term *alternative education* denoted programs for court-adjudicated youth, programs for advanced-placement students, and special education for disabled students. Indeed, prior to the charter school movement, the home schooling movement, and privatization, this denotation remained relatively unchanged and alternative school enrollees were disproportionately drawn from low-income, disabled, and minority communities.

Although public alternative schools have been developed in response to specific needs within their communities, most share some of the following characteristics:

1. Alternative schools provide an option for students, parents, and teachers—an option that is open to all within the community, so that alternative schools have a voluntary clientele. At the same time, the population of such schools should reflect the socioeconomic and racial makeup of the entire community.
2. Alternative schools have as their reason for existence a commitment to be more responsive to particular educational needs within the community than conventional schools have been.
3. Alternative schools usually have more comprehensive goals and objectives than their conventional counterparts. For example, in addition to developing basic skills and preparing students for college and vocations, they are concerned with improving a student's self-concept, developing individual talent and uniqueness, understanding and encouraging cultural plurality and diversity, and preparing students for various roles in society.
4. Alternative schools are more flexible than conventional schools and, therefore, more responsive to planned evolution and change. Having been developed in our age of accountability, they rely on feedback and formative evaluation in formulating and modifying their curricula.
5. Alternative schools tend to be smaller than comprehensive schools. The median enrollment in alternative public high schools is under 200. Because they are smaller, alternatives tend to have fewer rules and bureaucratic constraints on students and teachers.

When Joseph Gauld founded the Hyde School in 1966 in Bath, Maine, he did so because he believed that values are sadly missing from today's schools. He was determined to explore the new educational premise that every youngster is gifted with a "unique potential" that defies a destiny. What emerged from this "break the mold" solution was a new philosophy of education, built on the foundation of unique potential, focused on character development, and centered on the family. Gauld describes his experience developing an alternative school in his book *Character First*—an experience similar to that described by other organizers of alternative schools. The development of alternative learning environments is often based on the simple idea that learning experiences for children can be provided in many different ways. The experience at the Hyde School is best characterized as alternative with elements and characteristics of the progressive school movement.

Young people who for whatever reason are unable or choose not to succeed in such environments can now select from among an ever-increasing network of alternative educational settings. At one time, these alternative environments were considered merely a recourse for students who were at risk of dropping out of school or so disruptive they could not participate in a regular school traditional learning environment. In the last several decades, however, such schools have taken on many different names and descriptions. In some cases, they are now formally known as charter schools, magnet schools, accelerated schools, and the like. In other cases, parents have taken on the responsibility of home schooling as an alternative method of educating their children. Alternative programs now exist at all levels: elementary school, middle school, and high school. Many researchers agree that the number of alternative education programs in the United States has increased dramatically over the past few years, but the amount of resource information available about such programs is scant at best. As the public continues to express dissatisfaction with public schools, we will see many different forms of alternative schools and programs initiated throughout the country.

The alternative schools movement can best be explained in a political context, inasmuch as the value of schooling and the focus of its delivery vary according to the demands of the day. With respect to alternative schools, the 1960s might be considered the period of innovation; the 1970s, the age of accountability and improvement; the 1980s, the "Excellence Movement," which led to restructuring in the 1990s; and the twenty-first century, the era of competition, school choice, and reprivatization. The Clinton administration proposed programs to create pilot enterprise schools within empowerment zones, year-round community centers in urban and rural communities for the disadvantaged, and the Goals 2000: Educate America Act, which was intended to increase equity among schools without federal mandates. Throughout the 1980s and 1990s, in fact, education was a top national priority, becoming a major agenda item for the presidential elections of 1984, 1992, 1996, and 2000. In 1984, for example, thirty governors organized task forces on schooling, as did hundred of school boards. The National Governors' Association report, *Time for Results*, advocated a national board to certify teachers, performance and pay links, school choice, school buildings that remain open all year, and academic bankruptcy for schools and school districts not meeting standards. In 1991, the same group issued *Results in Education: 1990,* a report evaluating the results of earlier proposals for sweeping educational reforms.

Within a political context, it is virtually impossible to separate the alternative schools movement from school reform. Many alternative schools and alternative programs were developed in response to school reform initiatives. However, multiple definitions of the word *reform* must be taken into account if one is to understand what alternative schooling means in the twenty-first century.

There are probably as many different definitions of alternative education as there are alternative programs. Some writers view alternative education in an almost revolutionary context. For example, Ron Miller (1994) believes that alternative education is genuinely countercultural. He states that alternative education seeks to replace values and assumptions that have dominated Western culture, particularly American culture, over the past two or three centuries. Other writers, such as Jonathan Kozol (1982), view alternative education as a metaphor for values, visions, and ideals that ensure the psychological and intellectual survival of today's children. Many students who attend alternative schools view alternative programs as places where they have much greater freedom and opportunities for choices than in traditional schools.

In the late 1960s and into the 1970s, alternative schools proliferated across the United States. Earlier writings about alternative education describe it as an anomaly in public education—a phenomenon that was probably not even supposed to exist. Many researchers believe that the alternative schools movement simply cropped up out of nowhere and that there is widespread disagreement about the origin of alternative schools. Other writers trace the development of alternative schools to John Dewey and the progressive movement in education in the 1920s. Still others, in greater numbers, report that the genesis of the current alternative education movement can be found in the social revolution of the 1960s. Many would attribute the increase in alternative options to a decline in the number of private schools during that period. Others might say that alternatives to public schools sprang up as a protest against racially segregated schools. Such schools emphasized the basic subjects of reading, writing, and arithmetic, but they also included the history of African Americans, what the civil rights movement was all about, and how schools could be tied to community needs. Some of these alternative schools, called street academies, led to more permanent structures. Harlem Prep, for example, was initially funded by foundations, businesses, and industry but eventually became one of the public schools of New York City. During the same period, the private sector also responded to the growing aspirations of countercultures with new and different lifestyles, funding schools that were freer in form and substance than the public schools. Some went so far as to allow learners complete control over their own learning.

Before alternative schools, the prevailing belief was that everyone learned in the same way and that one curriculum was sufficient for all. The alternative schools movement has helped us to recognize that different people learn in different ways. Many children learn well in traditional academic public schools. Some children learn better in a differently structured environment such as the "open school." Others learn better in a school that emphasizes the principles of behavior modification. And still others learn better in individualized, continuous-progress schools. The psychology of education—the study of how people learn—is less than a century old, and complete theories of learning and corresponding theories of instruction have been continually developed and examined over the past two decades. What we do know today, as noted earlier, is that some children learn well in one setting while others learn well in a different setting. Alternative schools provide examples of where school reform has worked, where schools are humane, and effective, and where students and their teachers work together in a healthy harmony of learning.

Bear in mind that, although this review of alternative schools places heavy emphasis on their development during the 1960s and 1970s, alternative options were actually available long before then. In many nations, schooling alternatives have existed for centuries. The United States, in particular, has always offered options for both children and parents. Originally, parents with the financial means could send their children to parochial schools, to private tutors, or to private schools. If wealthy enough, they could send their children away to private academies. In the 1800s it was not uncommon for children in the United States to attend church-sponsored schools, boarding schools, or private schools in their community. In the eighteenth and nineteenth centuries, private school outnumbered public schools and a variety of options existed for those able to pay the fees. Dame schools, operated by women out of their homes, offered young boys and girls training in domestic skills and instruction in the three R's. Entrepreneurial schools provided vocational training. Charity schools served the disadvantaged and were supported by church and missionary groups.

During the nineteenth century, enrollment in public education surpassed home and private instruction when the common elementary school became the school of choice. The most famous advocate for the common school was Horace Mann, secretary of the State Board of Education in Massachusetts. The controversy that existed in 1840 between Horace Mann and Ralph Waldo Emerson foreshadowed the current debate in public education.

Mann emphasized the social function of public education and wanted common schools to teach values and skills that would contribute to an orderly, productive society. Emerson, in turn, focused on the needs of the individual. He was more interested in individual freedom than in social order and worried that common schools contributed to needless conformity at the expense of personal growth.

Today, with many more options for schooling, we are witnessing a revolution in public education. Many alternative schools have been organized to defy the concept of "school as a filling station." Early advocates of alternative schools believed that school could be designed to meet ever-changing human and societal needs. It seems that public schools usually mirror the past instead of keeping up with the pace of change. To find support for their position, we need only look at mainstream and, especially, secondary mainstream schools. The way they operate is largely the same as it was forty years ago. The Carnegie unit is still the method used to award course credit, the high school transcript remains the entry pass to higher education, and students are still homogeneously grouped for teacher-directed instruction. In many cases, a look inside the schools might lead one to believe that time has stood still. To this day, students are being placed in the same graded classes and are learning the same subject matter by means of the same teaching techniques. To paraphrase Mary Ann Horenstein (1993), many students continue to learn nineteenth-century answers to twenty-first-century questions. Larry Cuban, former superintendent of schools in Arlington, Virginia, wonders how it is that public schools have remained remarkably the same for the past 100 years while society has changed so much.

Evidence of the public's dissatisfaction with the state of public education can be found in many national reports. The most notable of these is *A Nation at Risk,* issued by the National Commission on Excellence in Education in 1983. Its impact was similar to that of *Sputnik* in 1957. This landmark report warned that "the educational foundations of our society are presently being eroded by a rising tide of mediocrity that threatens our very future as a nation and a people." It also described secondary school curricula as "homogenized, diluted, and diffused to the point that they no longer have a central purpose." Credited with creating a flurry of school improvement initiatives, the commission issued recommendations that became the starting point for a new wave of thinking about education reform in the United States. Those initiatives are now known collectively as the Excellence Movement. Within two years after this report was published, more than 300 national and state task forces investigated the condition of public schooling in the United States.

Another source citing the failings of public schools is the Third International Mathematics and Science Study (TIMSS), published in 1995, which reported disturbing findings about the performance of U.S. secondary school students in science and mathematics, ranking them well below the international average. A third source is the most recent report of the Paris-based Organization for Economic Cooperation and Development (OECD), published in 2000, which singles out U.S. students as having made the least progress in the essential literacy skill of reading as well as in mathematics and science achievement—despite the fact that the United States spends more per elementary and secondary student than any other OECD country except Switzerland. U.S. schools have also been found to lack standards of learning as well as clear lines of responsibility for their attainment.

Since the 1960s, two schools of thought have dominated the controversy over what should be taught and how—that is, over curriculum content and curriculum organization. On one side is the free, open, child-centered, humanistic, and socially oriented movement, based on humanistic-existential theory. On the other side are advocates of standardized subject matter, no-nonsense basic education, high academic standards, and discipline-oriented schools. The philosophical foundation for this latter position traces back to Plato and has been supported by twentieth-century perennialists and essentialists.

Modern spokespeople for the first movement include Edgar Friedenberg, Paul Goodman, John Holt, Herbert Kohl, and Charles Silberman. They oppose the conformity and docility characteristic of the subject-centered school. Accusing traditional schools of indifference to social issues and a meaningless curriculum, these authors demand relevant programs geared to students' actual needs and desires. For them, the content of the curriculum is less important than the process used and the degree to which learners are able to relate to school activities. In other words, curriculum content should be tied to students' actual experiences in life, and the school should deal with social issues, use materials drawn from the mass media, and address problems of the local community. Calling for free and open education, these authors emphasize the development of self-concept, problem solving, the ability to make reasonable choices, and humanistic attitudes. They understand the need for basic skills like reading, but they have no interest in filling students' minds with lots of facts or in urging them to "master specific subjects."

Rather, their emphasis is on fostering a positive attitude toward learning and teaching practical skills for dealing with other people and the outside world. Alternative schools are deeply rooted in this theory—an approach commonly known as the progressive education movement.

Holding the opposite position are such authors as James Koerner, Robert Hutchins, Arthur Bestor, Jacques Barzun, and Mortimer Adler. Similar to the belief expressed by James Conant and Admiral H. G. Rickover after *Sputnik*, their point of view is that schools must concentrate on producing subject-matter experts and superior scholars to lead the technological society. Koerner, as spokesperson for the Council for Basic Education, opposes the "soft" pedagogy of progressive education and demands a return to "solid" academic subjects. Hutchins wants a curriculum composed of those aspects of the culture that reflect the greatest amount of sophistication and refinement (the classics, mathematics, and science). Bestor believes that the function of the school is to teach intellectual disciplines, not to teach about current social problems or different cultural groups. As a general rule, conservatives are more comfortable with time-honored methods such as lectures, textbook assignments, homework, standardized tests, and library reports, whereas liberals tend to promote laboratory methods such as discovery learning, problem solving, and inquiry learning. The activity curriculum and the child-centered approach were not popular with the "back to basics" movement, although both liberals and conservatives support individualized instruction. Computer-assisted instruction is acceptable to the subject-matter curriculum advocates so long as it does not stray from the subject. Team teaching and flexible scheduling are most often found in schools with a progressive orientation. The activity-centered curriculum that began with William H. Kilpatrick in the 1920s centers on life experiences such as field trips, group projects, social enterprises, and local centers of interest. Some modern schools support an activity curriculum by working with community groups, social agencies, and governmental institutions. The activity curriculum requires extensive student and community participation.

Barzun (1945) has said, "Nonsense is at the heart of those proposals that would replace definable subject matter with vague activities copied from life or with courses organized around problems or attitudes" (cited in Pulliam, 1999, p. 223). In the twenty-first century, some advocates of the normal curve of probability based on standardized test scores are supporting school districts in requiring students with low test scores to repeat grade levels. Others are supportive of authentic assessment and a variety of achievement measures, including portfolios and projects chosen by students. The former see high test scores as indicative of success in a competitive environment; the latter see them as culturally biased and as lowering the self-esteem and self-worth of students who are not good test takers.

In the 1970s, the need for alternatives to conventional school was widely recognized. Alternative public schools were developed to complement conventional schools in order to make the school systems within those communities more responsive to the needs of all children and youth. In many communities, students, parents, teachers, and administrators had choices among various optional alternative public schools. Several national reports on education recommended that alternative public schools be offered. For example, the 1973 Report on the National Commission on the Reform of Secondary Education urged that "[e]ach district provide a broad range of alternative schools and programs so that every student would have a meaningful educational option available to him."

During the same decade, school boards and school administrators expressed genuine sympathy for young people who couldn't or wouldn't succeed in the mainstream. School officials also had to contend, however, with a public that was demanding order and tradition in the schools. With the concern generated by depictions of youthful rebellion on TV and in the movies, school boards were more than willing to allocate funds to help alienated youth who didn't fit into the mainstream. Thus, alternative public school programs for disadvantaged and alienated students and those with disabilities expanded and took on varied forms. Unfortunately, what nearly all of these publicly funded programs had in common was a de facto form of segregation.

At that time, alternative schools did not attract, recruit, or enroll students who were on a trajectory for success. This continues to be the case. It is hard to imagine a school counselor ever advising a capable young person, achieving adequate grades in the mainstream, to consider enrolling in an alternative setting. Consequently, our publicly funded alternative schools have become the exclusive preserve of public education's outcasts.

By 1980, the Council for Basic Education and the "back to basics" movement had gained vast public support—partly from parents disappointed with the level of information and skills learned by their children in public schools and partly from members of the "moral majority," who questioned some of the assumptions of an open, humanistic, child-centered, life-adjustment program.

Mortimer Adler, longtime advocate of the Great Books curriculum and philosophical companion to Robert Hutchins, wrote the *Paideia Proposal: An Educational Manifesto* in 1982. His plan advocates giving the same quality of schooling to all; it also requires a program of study that is both liberal and general. Adler believes that the ideal of American education, and of democracy itself, is only half-realized. He states that "providing a quality education for only a few is undermining democratic principles" (cited in Lewis, 1989, p. 50). He further states that "[t]here are no unteachable children. There are only schools and teachers and parents who fail to teach them" (cited in Lewis, 1989, p. 50).

The Paideia proposal gained advocates among those favoring liberal education and thinking skills. It was almost the exact opposite of the models proposed by *A Nation at Risk* and the business sector. The Paideia proposal's principles are as follows:

- All children are educable.
- Therefore, they all deserve the same quality of schooling, not just the same quantity.
- The quality of schooling to which they are entitled is what the wisest parents would wish for their own children, the best education for the best being the best education for all.
- Schooling at its best is preparation for becoming generally educated over the course of a whole lifetime, and schools should be judged on how well they provide such preparation.
- The three callings for which schooling should prepare all Americans are (a) to teach a decent livelihood, (b) to be a good citizen of the Republic, and (c) to make a good life for one's self.
- The primary cause of genuine learning is the activity of the learner's own mind, sometimes with the help of a teacher functioning as secondary and cooperative cause.
- Three kinds of teaching that should occur in our schools are didactic teaching of subject matter, coaching that produces the skills of learning, and Socratic questioning in seminar discussions.
- The results of these three kinds of teaching should be (a) the acquisition of organized knowledge, (b) the formation of habits or skills in the use of language and mathematics, and (c) the growth of the mind's understanding of basic ideas and issues.
- Each student's achievement of these results should be measured against that student's capacity to learn, and should not be related to the achievements of other students.
- The principal of a school should be the principal teacher and educational leader of the school community.

➡ The principal and faculty of a school should themselves be
actively engaged in learning.

➡ The desire to continue their own learning should be the
prime motivation of those who dedicate their lives to the profession of teaching.

Three names that appeared constantly in the reform literature of
the mid-1980s were Ernest Boyer, John Goodlad, and Theodore Sizer.
Boyer's most important contribution was a report for the Carnegie
Foundation for the Advancement of teaching in 1983 entitled *High
School: A Report on Secondary Education in America*, which focuses on
what was happening within classrooms rather than on broad policies.
Goodlad (1984), a recognized expert in curriculum, made a major contribution to the reform literature in *A Place Called School: Prospects for
the Future*. And in *Horace's Hope: The Future of the American High
School*, Sizer (1996) reiterates the continuing need for educational reform and notes the progress that has been made toward an improved
education system for the twenty-first century.

In *The Dictionary of Cultural Literacy*, E. D. Hirsch (1988) suggests
that all educated persons should have knowledge of the best ideals of
humankind. The lack of such knowledge, Hirsch notes, is at the base of
our literacy challenge. Hirsch reiterates this theme in *The Schools We
Need and Why We Don't Have Them* (1996).

According to *Action in the States*, published by the Education
Commission of the States (1984), school reform was a high-priority item
everywhere. As of the 1980s, all but five states had legislatively enacted
initiatives or were awaiting action by the legislature or the state board.
The states have generally followed the public demand to cut down on
curriculum offerings not considered basic—such as art, music, and
physical education—and to require more "solid" courses. Most states
have chosen to mandate the basic curriculum with emphasis given to
courses such as English, mathematics, science, and social studies. In addition to upgrading the curriculum, they wish to strengthen standards
for high school graduation, raise teacher certification requirements, improve salaries for teachers, promote business involvement in education,
and integrate technology into instruction.

State efforts aimed at educational excellence in the mid-1980s
were conservative. Economic and political forces caused the states to
opt for strengthening existing schools rather than designing a new approach to education. State plans tended to call for more testing, more
homework, more hours in the school day and school year, and an emphasis on basics in the curriculum.

The 1980s and 1990s witnessed several state and city school administration reforms and fiscal restructurings. All the changes dealt with what Linda Darling-Hammond, director of the National Center for Restructuring Education at Columbia University, referred to as a new school reform model designed to develop communities of learning, grounded in grassroots democratic discourse. She saw these reforms as a way to bring about empowerment and educational freedom for educators of students as a learning community.

The Chicago School Reform Act of 1988 required basic changes in Chicago public school governance, seeking more involvement and input from local stakeholders in school governance and policy making. The 1990 Kentucky Educational Reform Act, under a state supreme court order, moved the state toward equal opportunity and an efficient system of education for all school districts. To meet this court order, the school districts were reevaluated and reconstructed.

According to Mary Ann Raywid, a leading researcher on alternative education, a number of education reform initiatives of the 1980s have been typical of alternative schools for some time. She lists the following:

> Reduced size of classes and/or schools and increased
>   personalization
> A strong ethos and sense of community
> Greater school-site autonomy and teacher decision making
> Recognition of school as the unit of change
> More parent and community involvement in a wider variety of
>   roles
> More collaboration and collective responsibility among teachers
> Integrated curricula
> Cooperative learning, greater adaptation of content and
>   methods to individual learners, small group and
>   individualized instruction, independent study and learning
>   through school and community service
> Assumption of greater responsibility for learning by students

When Mortimer Adler, Ernest Boyer, Theodore Sizer, John Goodlad, Albert Shanker, Marc Tucker, and others looked at what was happening in classrooms, they often had different views of the problems and came up with different solutions. In an intensive seven-year study, Goodlad completed an analysis of public schools that resulted in the publication of *A Place Called School* in 1983. The study encompassed 13 school districts, 38 schools, intensive classroom observations, central data gathering, and interviews or surveys with 27,000 teachers, parents, and students. The underlying precept of his study is that an understanding of schools must precede attempts to improve them. As Goodlad puts it, "Improvement is essentially a school-by-school process, enlightened by the degree to which those associated with each school and trying to improve it have the data required for building a useful agenda" (p. 196).

David Florio of the National Science Foundation divided these common themes for restructuring of schools into four categories, which in themselves are also applicable to alternative schools:

1. *Content or substance.* The attempt is to begin a fundamental shift away from encyclopedic, surface coverage of content and toward a deeper understanding of substantive knowledge, problem solving, creativity, and analytical thinking. In short, Florio says, "understanding and meaning must replace the 'skimming' that is now the norm in many classes" (p. 48). Not only curricular materials but also the tests used for accountability must change. And as tests change, he adds, teaching will become less reliant upon textbooks and more dependent upon a variety of resources, such as computer databases, original source material, and reference materials.
2. *People.* Personnel structures must be radically changed if schools cannot attract the talent they need, particularly in mathematics and science. Qualified teachers will need to guide and work with a variety of other adults such as instructors, aides, interns, and peer tutors. Technology will need to replace routine tasks, thereby freeing teachers for different roles. And students will need to be "active" learners.
3. *Place.* The physical locations of people, materials, and equipment in schools are based on an antiquated, factory model of efficiency. These arrangements need to be replaced by an array of alternatives ranging from small workstations to large group settings.
4. *Time.* The structure of student learning time needs to accommodate new curricular and learning goals, cooperative learning, and exploration of content in depth. Teachers also need time for their own learning, group interactions, and shared decision making.

It is recommended that these findings be used as a theoretical framework around which school improvement can be developed. During the

1960s and the 1970s, the prevailing attitude within the research community was that schools themselves have little effect on student achievement. The Coleman Report (1966), the landmark study Equality of Educational Opportunity led by James Coleman, maintained that the socioeconomic status of a child's family has a greater influence on student achievement than any other factor. This observation led to the conclusion among some educators that, inasmuch as schools could not do very much to affect student achievement, an excellent school was one that created an atmosphere where kids enjoyed school and learned to feel good about themselves. In 1979 Michael Rutter and his colleagues published results that directly challenged the assumption that schools make very little difference in student achievement. Additional studies by Wilbur Brookover and Larry Lezotte (1979) and Phi Delta Kappa (1980) supported Rutter's findings.

The research of Ron Edmonds (1979) on school effectiveness may have contributed more than any other study to the widespread recognition that schools *do* affect the achievement of students. According to Edmonds, the following seven characteristics are consistently found in effective schools:

1. A safe and orderly environment
2. A clear and focused school mission
3. Instructional leadership
4. High expectations
5. Opportunities to learn and high time on task
6. Frequent monitoring of student progress
7. Positive home-school relations

The Northwest Regional Educational Laboratory (1995) provides a useful synthesis of the research on effective schools. Based on this synthesis, which focuses on studies that have identified schooling practices and characteristics associated with measurable improvements in student achievement and behavior, we can conclude that in an effective school:

1. Everyone emphasizes the importance of learning
2. The curriculum is based on clear goals and objectives
3. Students are grouped to promote effective instruction
4. School time is used for learning
5. Discipline is firm and consistent
6. There are pleasant conditions for teaching and learning

7. Strong leadership guides the instructional program
8. Teachers and administrators continually strive to improve instructional effectiveness
9. Staff engages in ongoing professional development and collegial learning activities
10. There are high expectations for quality instruction
11. Incentives and rewards are used to build strong student and staff motivation
12. Parents and community members are invited to become involved
13. Learning progress is monitored closely
14. Students at risk of school failure are provided programs to help them succeed

Stewart Purkey and Marshall Smith (1983) conducted a review of the research on school effectiveness and identified what they believe are the most important characteristics of effective schools. They then grouped these characteristics into two categories: (1) organizational and structural variables, and (2) process-form variables. The organizational and structural variables are as follows:

- School site management
- Leadership
- Staff stability
- Curriculum articulation and organization
- Staff development
- Parental involvement and support
- School-wide recognition of academic success
- Maximized learning time
- District support

And these are the process-form variables associated with school effectiveness:

- Collaborative planning and collegial relationships
- A sense of community
- Clear goals and high expectations that are commonly shared
- Order and discipline

These research findings provide a clear framework for thinking about and planning for alternative schools and alternative school programs.

In the history of education, the effectiveness of schools has been equated to the degree to which students are prepared to enter the world of work. It follows that, in today's environment, the purpose of schooling is to help students develop the skills needed to succeed in the highly competitive world of work, which requires constant innovation plus the will to use their ability and ingenuity. These skills include the ability to define problems and to work effectively with others to solve those problems. Many advocates of education reform do not believe that our conventional system of schooling teaches students to succeed with integrity in this market-driven economy. Historically, critics have argued that public education in its current form cannot meet that demand. The "No Child Left Behind" legislation is another clear example of the lack of faith in the current system of education in the United States. Schools today face the same transformative challenges they confronted at the turn of the twentieth century: rapidly changing technology, altered lifestyles, and massive waves of immigrants. Alternative schools have provided a viable means for the United States to meet the ever-changing needs of society. They have given us opportunities (in the best interests of children, one hopes) to explore ways to provide an education through a system that perpetuates the American ideal—an education that speaks to the worth and dignity of every human being.

Some communities recognized before others that the single standard school could not meet the needs of all students. They saw the need for starting new schools for talented students, such as the Bronx High School of Science in New York City, founded in 1938. Some communities provided for dropouts and potential dropouts with establishments such as the Metropolitan Youth Education Center, founded in Denver in 1964. Others wanted to change all schools, as in the move toward open elementary education that occurred in North Dakota in 1965. Still others attempted to provide optional schools, such as the Parkway Plan, developed in Philadelphia in 1969. Many educators, particularly those who viewed children not as empty vessels but as "active seeking organisms," wanted different options for teaching and learning. Implicit in the philosophies of these educators was a belief in the whole child and in each child's unique and special needs. Some of these educators—John Dewey, Marietta Johnson, Caroline Pratt, and A. S. Neill, for example—created nontraditional schools to fit learning experiences to their perceptions of children. Contemporary educators, when considering current alternative school options such as those found in the school choice movement and the emergent interest in charter schools, would do well to look back for guidance at some of the original schools representative of the "new education" movement.

In conclusion, choice in public education is a "hot topic" among educational practitioners, theorists, politicians, and the general public. Some see public schools of choice as a solution to the declining educational system in the United States. Dissatisfaction with the public schools in this country has created pressure to experiment with nontraditional approaches to teaching and learning in an attempt to improve their effectiveness. In 1989, president George H. W. Bush, at a White House Workshop on School Choice, labeled choice plans the single most promising reform idea in public education, declaring that "plans like magnet schools, open enrollment programs, and other innovative mechanisms restore opportunities to families to choose the best possible education for their children."

REFERENCES

Adler, M. (1982). *The Paideia Proposal: An Educational Manifesto.* New York: Macmillan.

Barzun, J. (1945). *Teacher in America.* Boston: Little, Brown.

Bereday, G.Z.F., and Volpicelli, L. (Eds.). (1958). *Public Education in America: A New Interpretation of Purpose and Practice.* New York: Harper & Brothers.

Boyer, E. (1983). *High School: A Report on Secondary Education in America.* New York: Harper and Row.

Brookover, W., and Lezotte, L. (1979). *Changes in School Characteristics Coincident with Changes in School Achievement.* East Lansing: Michigan State University, Institute for Research in Teaching.

Carnegie Corporation (1996). "A Nation Prepared: Teachers for the 21st Century." Task Force on Teaching as a Profession, New York.

Carnegie Council on Adolescent Development (1989). "Turning Points: The Education of American Youth for the 21st Century." Washington, DC.

Deal, T. E., and Nolan, R. R. (1978). "An Overview of Alternative Schools." In T. E. Deal and R. R. Nolan (Eds.), *Alternative Schools.* Chicago: Nelson Hall.

DuFour, R., and Eaker, R. (1992). *Creating the New American School: A Principal's Guide to School Improvement.* Bloomington, IN: National Educational Service.

Edmonds, R. (1979). "Effective Schools for the Urban Poor." *Educational Leadership* (October), 15–23.

Education Commission of the States, *Action in the States* (1984). Denver, CO.

Gauld, J. W. (1991). *Character First: The Hyde School Difference.* San Francisco: Institute for Contemporary Studies.

Goodlad, J. (1984). *A Place Called School: Prospects for the Future.* Boston: Houghton Mifflin.

Hirsch, E. D. (1988). *The Dictionary of Cultural Literacy.* Boston: Houghton Mifflin.

_____. (1996). *The Schools We Need and Why We Don't Have Them.* New York: Doubleday.

Horenstein, M. (1993). *Twelve Schools That Succeed.* Bloomington, IN: Phi Delta Kappa Educational Foundation.

Kozol, J. (1982). *Alternative Schools: A Guide for Educators and Parents.* New York: Continuum.

Lewis, A. (1989). *Restructuring America's Schools.* Arlington, VA: American Association of School Administrators.

Miller, R. (1994). *What Are Schools For? Holistic Education in American Culture.* Brandon, VT: Holistic Education Press.

National Alliance of Business. (2000, September/October). *The Changing Face of Public Education, Work America: The Business Voice on Workforce Development.*

National Association of State Boards of Education. (1988). "Rethinking Curriculum: A Call for Fundamental Reform," Alexandria, VA.

National Commission on Excellence in Education. (1983). *A Nation at Risk.* Washington, DC.

National Governors' Association (1986). *Time for Results.* Washington, DC: National Governors' Association, Center for Policy Research and Analysis.

_____. (1991). *Results in Education: 1990.* Washington, DC: National Governors' Association/U.S. Department of Educational Research and Improvement, 1989.

Northwest Regional Educational Laboratory (1995). *Effective Schooling Practices: A Research Synthesis.* 1995 Update. Kathleen Cotton. Portland, OR.

Plank, D. N. (1987). "Why School Reform Doesn't Change Schools: Political and Organizational Perspectives." Unpublished paper for the Department of Administrative and Policy Studies, University of Pittsburgh, Pittsburgh, PA.

Pulliam, J., and Van Patten, J. (1999). *History of Education in America.* Upper Saddle River, NJ: Prentice-Hall.

Purkey, S., and Smith, M. (1983). *School Reform: The Policy Implications of the Effective Schools Literature.* Madison: Wisconsin Center for Education Research, University of Wisconsin–Madison, School of Education.

Raywid, M. A. (1990). "The Mounting Case for Schools of Choice." In Joe Nathan (Ed.), *Public Schools by Choice.* St. Paul, MN: Institute for Learning and Teaching.

Rethinking Schools Online: An Urban Educational Journal. (n.d.) Available online at http://www.rethinkingschools.org.

Rutter, M., et al. (1979). *Fifteen Thousand Hours: Secondary Schools and Their Effects on Children.* Cambridge, MA: Harvard University Press.

Semel, S., and Sadoonick, A. (Eds.) (1999). *Schools of Tomorrow, Schools of Today: What Happened to Progressive Education.* New York: Peter Lang.

Sizer, T. (1985). *Horace's Compromise: The Dilemma of the American High School.* Boston: Houghton Mifflin.

_____. (1996). *Horace's Hope: What Works for the American High School.* Boston: Houghton Mifflin.

Smith, V. (1974a). *Alternative Schools: The Development of Options in Public Education.* Lincoln, NE: Professional Educators Publications.

_____. (1974b). *Optional Alternative Public Schools.* Bloomington, IN: Phi Delta Kappa Educational Foundation.

U.S. Office of Education (1966). "Coleman Report: Equality of Educational Opportunity." James S. Coleman. Washington, DC.

Why Do Some Schools Succeed? (1980). Bloomington, IN: Phi Delta Kappa.

Young, T. (1990). *Public Alternative Education.* New York: Teachers College Press.

Chapter 2
☙ Chronology

1680s

The first Quaker schools are founded.

1751

Benjamin Franklin opens an academy in Philadelphia as an alternative to the classical curriculum of the grammar school.

1753

Benjamin Franklin's academy is chartered, reflecting the transition from Latin schools to a more pragmatic curriculum.

1785

The beginnings of federal support for education take form in the Northwest Ordinances.

1862

The passage of the Morrill Act extends the belief that free public education is not a privilege but a right.

1884

The Catholic Parochial School System is established. The Third Plenary Council of American Catholic Bishops declares that all parishes are to build parochial schools and that all parents are to send their children to them unless exempted by the church.

1894

A limited voucher plan comes into effect in some Vermont districts. The voucher system begins because some small towns in this rural state have formal schools while many others do not. Under the Vermont system, towns without schools are allowed to use state and local funds raised from taxation for education in other towns, at either public or private schools.

1907

Maria Montessori founds Casa dei Bambini (The Children's House) in Rome, where she applies her educational methods.

1925

In *Pierce v. Society of Sisters of the Holy Names of Jesus and Mary*, the U.S. Supreme Court upholds the right of parents to choose their children's education. The ruling overturns an Oregon law that would have required all children to attend public schools.

1947

In *Everson v. Board of Education*, the U.S. Supreme Court upholds a New Jersey program that allows states to use public money to transport students to and from parochial schools.

1952

Many of the Montessori Schools are established in the United States after the death of Maria Montessori.

1955

In his essay "The Role of Government in Education," economist Milton Friedman proposes that parents be provided with government vouchers to pay for tuition at approved private schools. Friedman suggests this voucher program as an approach to increasing educational opportunities for children and encouraging schools to compete for students.

1957

Sputnik, the first space satellite, is launched by Russia, pressing the race for dominance in space. This historic event initiates a wave of reforms in public education, particularly in the areas of mathematics and science. In the period from 1957 to the mid-1960s, emphasis shifts to the pursuit of excellence and curriculum reformers attempt to redesign curricula so as to reemphasize and reassert academic standards. Critics of the progressive movement want to see schools as places that would mass-produce scientists and thereby make the United States "number one" again. This kind of thinking is what fuels the "back to basics" movement.

1960

Alternative public schools first begin to appear in the United States.

MID-1960s

Educational priorities shift back toward the progressive side. Many credit the shift to the Civil Rights movement and to equity-related issues.

1969

The U.S. Office of Economic Opportunity begins planning an experimental voucher program that includes larger vouchers for poor students. However, the OEO cannot find a school district to accept the program in a state that will pass legislation permitting private schools to accept public funds.

1973

Mario Fantini publishes articles calling for choice in public education.

1976

New York City begins its public choice program by allowing teachers in the junior high schools in District 4 to redesign or even create schools, and by empowering parents to choose which schools their children will attend. The East Harlem choice program is credited with raising reading scores and lifting the district from the last of thirty-two New York City school districts. The choice plan also attracts white students to the largely minority school district, creating voluntary desegregation.

LATE 1970s

Voucher proponents begin pushing for state legislation and constitutional initiatives to establish state voucher programs.

Magnet schools are instituted in Kansas City as a way of attracting suburban white children to central city schools, thus promoting voluntary desegregation.

1981

Education Excellence Network is established, demanding competition among schools and among students. This movement, now known as the Excellence Movement, was authored by Chester Finn and Diane Ravitch with a $375,000 grant from the Reagan Department of Education. As assistant secretary of education under William Bennett, Finn organized "education choices," the political jargon for a full voucher program.

1983

Chester Finn creates Tennessee's "Better Schools Program," the first major state reform in the nation. The core of the plan is competition.

In *Mueller v. Allen*, the U.S. Supreme Court upholds a Minnesota statute that provides an income tax deduction for tuition, textbooks, and transportation to parents of children attending public, private, and parochial schools.

1984

Tennessee Governor Lamar Alexander is the first state or national official to call for vouchers, becoming widely touted as the "education reform expert"—a role that is enhanced when he is named chair of the National Governors Conference in 1985.

MID-1980s

Control Data Corporation (CDC), in anticipation of a nationwide voucher plan, significantly upgrades education work. CDC is marketer of the PLATO program, one of the first and most widely used software programs for computer assisted instruction (CAI). Expecting that vouchers will vastly increase the market for alternative schooling, CDC begins research preparing for a core of private schools heavily reliant on CAI.

1985

After realizing that vouchers were still a long way off, CDC sells its research and planning package to corporate trainer John Golle, who created Education Alternatives Inc. (EAI). Golle opens one school in 1987 and another in 1989 under the CDC plan.

Minnesota is the first state to permit high school student enrollment in college for dual credits. This program allows high school juniors and seniors to take courses at local colleges for both high school and future higher-education credit.

1986

The National Governors' Conference Report titled *Time for Results* is published.

In *Witters v. Washington Department of Services for the Blind,* the U.S. Supreme Court upholds a Washington State program that provides a publicly funded tuition grant to a student for use at a religious college.

1988

Former Xerox president David Kearns joins Lamar Alexander's Education Department as deputy secretary and becomes chief fund-raiser for President George Bush's New American Schools Development Corporation (NASDC), a semipublic corporation set up in 1991 to arrange for corporations to help fund new experiments in education that will result in 535 new schools (one for each senator and representative).

1989

An Education Summit is held at University of Virginia, where President Bush and a number of the nation's governors recommend an increase in parental choice and options within public education.

Herbert Christopher ("Chris") Whittle launches Channel One, a plan that offers any secondary school in the country $50,000 worth of television equipment and satellite dishes—free of charge. The schools can use the equipment for any purpose they choose, and at any time, except for two one-hour periods during the week, when Whittle provides "social studies programming."

EARLY 1990s

Public/private partnerships flourish. EAI manages nine Baltimore schools for $27 million annually, holds maintenance and security contracts on two additional schools, and wins a contract to manage fifteen District of Columbia schools. The Minneapolis School Board hands over all of the system's seventy-five schools to Public Strategies Group, Inc., for $220 million annually.

1990

Milwaukee becomes the first school district in the country to provide public tax dollars to families to pay for private and parochial school tuition. The program targets low-income children.

Colorado enacts a seven-year pilot public school choice program that allows parents to select a school outside their own district.

John Golle of EAI puts his private-school plan on hold and sells himself as a private operator of public schools.

Christopher Whittle creates a new division called the Edison Project and announces plans to create 200 new, highly modern K–12 "campuses" by 1996, with 1,000 targeted by the end of the century.

Idaho enacts a statewide, voluntary, open-enrollment plan. Under this law, state funds follow the child to the chosen school.

Iowa enacts a mandatory, statewide interdistrict open-enrollment program.

1991

The Charter School Movement is founded.

EAI wins the contract to run an experimental school in Dade County (Miami), Florida.

Intradistrict school choice becomes mandatory in Washington State for all school districts.

Oregon law creates two provisions for public school choice. The first permits parents of children who have not made progress at any grade level for at least one year to choose another school, provided that the receiving school agrees to accept the student. The second provision creates a tenth-grade Certificate of Initial Mastery, which indicates a certain level of basic skills. When a student earns this certificate, he or she can attend any public school in the state or any state community college to pursue vocational or college preparatory course work.

The Florida Legislature approves the first statewide voucher program, which provides vouchers to students in poorly performing schools. Students who attend failing schools can move to higher performing public schools or receive "opportunity scholarships" to attend secular or religious private schools.

1992

Harold Stevenson, education scholar, publishes the results of a decade's worth of international studies. He looks at hundreds of classrooms and families in the United States, China, Taiwan, and Japan and finds that American parents are by far the most satisfied with their local schools, while their children exhibit the worst performance overall.

1993

Education Options Children, a private fund in Denver, provides partial-tuition scholarships up to $1,250 to thirty-eight children attending twelve private schools.

The Georgia legislature passes a charter school law, but the law provides little governing autonomy, freedom from regulations, or flexibility in staffing, and is available only to existing public schools.

Open enrollment becomes mandatory in Utah public schools.

One hundred percent of state education dollars follow a transferring student to his or her new district.

Puerto Rico passes legislation allowing children to attend the school of their choice, with the allocated money following them to that school.

1994

The Washington (DC) Scholarship Fund provides fifty half-tuition scholarships to low-income children in the District to attend private or parochial school.

The California legislature provides statewide open enrollment to allow some form of choice over public schools, and passes a charter school bill that provides for up to 100 charter schools.

1996

Ohio enacts a pilot voucher program in Cleveland. Students in kindergarten through seventh grade can apply for the program, although the school district gives preference to low-income families. Recipients may use their vouchers at either secular or religious private schools.

1998

The Wisconsin supreme court rules that the Milwaukee Parental Choice Program's practice of giving publicly funded vouchers to parochial schools does not violate the First Amendment. The U.S. Supreme Court refuses to hear an appeal to the decision later in the year.

2000

A Florida appellate court upholds the state's voucher program by ruling that Florida can use public-funded vouchers to send students in poorly performing schools to private schools. The decision reverses an earlier trial court ruling that the program violated the state constitution.

2002

The U.S. Supreme Court hears arguments on the constitutionality of the Cleveland Scholarship and Tutoring Program. The justices agree to decide whether a Cleveland program that uses public money to send thousands of students to private religious schools violates the First Amendment separation of church and state.

REFERENCES

Association for Supervision and Curriculum Development Infobrief. (2001). "Helping Students or Harming Schools?" Issue 24, January.

Banks, S. (1985). *The Education of Black Children and Youths: A Framework for Educational Excellence.* Columbia, MD: C. H. Fairfax Company.

Black Alliance for Educational Options. (2000, December 1). BAEO Manifesto. Available online at http://www.schoolchoiceinfo.org/baeo/index/bsp.

Center for Education Reform. (n.d.). Answers to Frequently Asked Questions About School Choice. Available online at http://www.edreform.com/school_reform_faq/school_choice.htm.

_____. (1994). *School Reform in the United States: State by State Analysis.* Washington, DC.

Florida Department of Education. (2000a, March). *Opportunity Scholarship Program Background Information.* Available online at http://www.opportunityschools.org/osas/osp/background.html.

_____. (2000b, March). *Opportunity Scholarship Program Responsibilities.* Available online at http://www.opportunityschools.org/osas/osp/responsibilities.html.

Walsh, M. (2002, February 13). "High Court, High Noon." *Education Week,* pp. 1, 20.

Chapter 3
⦿ Who's Who in Alternative Education

Jane Addams (1860–1935). In 1889, Jane Addams founded Hull House, the world-famous social settlement in Chicago. She built her reputation as the country's most prominent woman through her writing, her settlement work, and her international efforts for world peace. Along with residents of the settlement, she provided services for the neighborhood, such as kindergarten and daycare facilities for children of working mothers, an employment bureau, an art gallery, libraries, and music and art classes. Addams was a known supporter of the Normal School developed by Colonel Francis Parker.

Mortimer J. Adler (1907–). Mortimer J. Adler has made innumerable contributions to the fields of education and philosophy. Throughout his personal and professional life he has been consumed by the opportunity to learn. He has argued that "no one can be fully educated in school no matter how long the schooling or how good it is." While a student at Columbia University, he was greatly influenced by the work of John Erskine and John Dewey. Along with Max Weismann, he founded the Center for the Study of the Great Ideas, and he is perhaps best known for his work in promoting The Great Books of the Western World, a literary series available in libraries throughout the country. He is a proponent of lifelong learning and believes that no one, no matter how old, should stop learning. He himself has written more than twenty books since he turned seventy. Now, at the age of ninety-five, Adler is working on his sixtieth book—*The New Technology: Servant or Master?*—proving that he does indeed subscribe to the advice he gives to others.

Roland Barth (1937). Roland Barth is a consultant to schools, school systems, state departments of education, universities, foundations, and businesses in the United States and abroad. His particular fields of interest are school leadership, school improvement from within, and the personal and professional development of educators. Central to his thinking is the concept of the school as a community of learners and a community of leaders.

Arthur Bestor (1908–1994). Arthur Bestor, a respected historian, was a critic of progressive education. As a graduate of the Lincoln School, he argued that "regressive education" rather than truly progressive education has eliminated the school's primary role in teaching children to think. He believed that the schools were undermining the democratic goal that all students should receive an education once reserved for the elite. He also thought that the social and vocational emphasis of the schools reflected the belief that not all students are capable of learning academic material. His 1953 publication, *Educational Wastelands,* further voiced arguments against progressive education.

Grace Lee Boggs (1915–). Grace Lee Boggs is a first-generation Chinese American who has been a speaker, writer, and movement activist in the African American community for fifty-five years. She writes a column called "Living for Change" for the Fresh Ideas page of the weekly *Michigan Citizen* and, along with her late husband, James Lee Boggs, co-authored *Revolution and Evolution in the Twentieth Century.* Her autobiography, *Living for Change,* now in its second printing, is an account of the life of an untraditional radical, from the end of the 1930s, through the cold war, the civil rights era, and the rise of Black Power, the Nation of Islam, and the Black Panthers to the present efforts to rebuild crumbling urban communities. Above all, it traces the story of a woman who transcended class and racial boundaries to pursue her passionate belief in a better society. Boggs also founded Detroit Summer, a multicultural youth program and movement.

Mae Carden (1894–1977). Mae Carden was one of the outstanding educators of the twentieth century. She developed an effective method for teaching reading as well as a comprehensive elementary school curriculum that gives children the basis for a broad liberal arts education. In 1934, using her own money, she established "Miss Carden's School for Young Children" in New York City, which she ran as a laboratory school until 1949.

Mabel Chrystie (1932–2001). In 1964, Mabel Chrystie founded the First Street School on New York City's Lower East Side. She conceptualized the school as an antidote to the dehumanization of the public school system. In contrast to the huge, impersonal, and bureaucratic nature of the latter, the First Street School was small and informal and oriented entirely toward the personalities of the students, the teachers, and the parents. The school was radical and experimental. There were no grades, no report cards, and no competitive examinations. The children were not compelled to study or to answer questions when they did not want to. Rather, they were free to consult each other, examine each other's work, leave the room, leave the school building itself, and talk to each other and to the teachers at will. Much of the school's design was based on the writings of A. S. Neill, and Chrystie's philosophy was one of growth and learning in a free environment.

Kenneth Clark (1914–). Kenneth Clark was president of the Metropolitan Applied Research Center and a professor of psychology at the City College of the City University of New York. He authored *Prejudice and Your Child* and *Dark Ghetto: Dilemmas of Social Power,* among other books. He also founded and directed Harlem Youth Opportunities Unlimited. In 1969, Clark stated that alternatives—realistic, aggressive, and viable competitors—to current public school systems must be found. He did not believe that an inefficient system of public schools was in the public interest.

James P. Comer (1934–). In 1968, James Comer was invited by the Yale Child Study Center to collaborate with the New Haven public schools in a school reform effort. Comer used his own life experiences to help develop a program that is now known as the School Development Program (sometimes also referred to as the Comer process). The Comer approach brings school, parents, and community together in the collective enterprise of raising and educating children.

Leonard Covello (1907–1974). An early innovator of community-centered schools, Leonard Covello was principal of East Harlem's Benjamin Franklin High School until 1955. He employed the concept of community-centered schools as a means of helping the area's Italians (1) to acquire coping, educational, social, and other skills to enable them to move into the corporate world and (2) to deepen their understanding of the Italian culture as a tool for contributing effectively to their own private world. Among the unique characteristics of the community-centered school was the fact that it shared power with the community it served: Local organizations joined with parents in "adopting" a piece of the school's program, local community residents were employed and trained as "foster teachers," and parents not only formed informal parents' clubs based on grade levels but also planned class trips in conjunction with the class members and participated in parent training programs.

George Dennison (1925–1987). George Dennison worked with and then eventually married Mabel Chrystie, who, as noted above, founded the First Street School on New York City's Lower East Side. In *The Lives of Children,* he wrote about her successful experiment with the First Street School. This book is considered one of the finest descriptions of the philosophy and practice of alternative education in the entire literature.

John Dewey (1859–1952). John Dewey was an American philosopher whose influence as an educator remains strong today. Although born and raised in Vermont, he became thoroughly enmeshed in the problems of urbanization as a resident of Chicago and chair of the Department of Philosophy, Psychology, and Pedagogy at the University of Chicago. Dewey believed that the goal of education is growth—but within the context of democratic society. He created the Laboratory School as a model for democratic education, whereby children studied basic subjects in an integrated curriculum. Dewey also advocated active learning, starting with the needs and interests of the child; he emphasized the role of experience in education and introduced the notion of teacher as the facilitator of learning rather than the fountain from which all knowledge flows.

Mario Fantini. Mario Fantini served as a program officer in the Division of Public Education at the Ford Foundation and as dean of the School of Education at the University of Massachusetts. In 1974, he said that all meaningful reform of education was tied to the movement toward public schools of choice. He has also written extensively on the subject of magnet schools.

Joseph Featherstone. Joseph Featherstone is a professor of teacher education at Michigan State University. He has written about school reform, has had a long-standing fascination with progressive education and with traditions in the United States and elsewhere that seek to expand democracy, and has extensively studied the work of John Dewey. His other interests include social policy, the history of education, issues of democracy and justice in education, and the humanities curriculum from preschool through graduate school.

George Fox (1624–1691). George Fox is the founder of Quakerism and the organizer of the Religious Society of Friends. He and his followers founded the first Quaker schools in the 1680s.

Paulo Freire (1921–1997). Paulo Freire was an educator and world leader who spent his entire life helping poverty-stricken men and women overcome their sense of powerlessness. His focus was a combination of "grassroots" organizations, college classrooms, and school reform efforts in major urban areas. Freire provided an extensive critique of education in his book *Pedagogy of the Oppressed*. In identifying education as the path to permanent liberation, he focused on two stages: (1) that by which people become aware of their oppression and transform that state and (2) the permanent process of liberating cultural action.

Milton Friedman (1912–). Milton Friedman is an economist who believes that education should be considered a part of the free marketplace.

Freidrich Froebel (1782–1852). Freidrich Froebel is recognized as the father of both the activity movement and the kindergarten. Froebel promoted the basic principles of Pestalozzi's theory: permissive school atmosphere and emphasis on nature. He viewed education as closely related to religion. Froebel's first kindergarten was founded in 1837 in Blakenburg, Germany. It featured games, play, songs, stories, and crafts to stimulate imagination and develop physical and motor skills. He promoted school not just as a place for acquiring knowledge but as a place that facilitates the formation of character. His ideas provided the major direction for kindergarten curricula during the last half of the nineteenth century.

Howard Gardner (1943–). Howard Gardner, like many other educational reformers, calls for the education of the whole child. As a psychologist and former professor at Harvard University's School of Education, Gardner challenged the theory that equates intelligence with a measurable intelligence quotient (IQ) and suggested that there are at least eight different forms of human intelligence. He acknowledges that schools have long offered art, music, and physical education, but he calls for more than just added specialty classes. In particular, he wants to see the use of musical, artistic, kinesthetic, intrapersonal, and interpersonal intelligences integrated into the curriculum and the learning process.

Arnold Gesell (1880–1961). Arnold Gesell, an American psychologist and pediatrician, is well known in the field of developmental education. Filming and observing infants and children, he gathered a tremendous amount of data about how children grow and change. His observations enabled him to formulate broad characterizations of children at different developmental ages, leading to the conclusion that children can be developmentally older or younger than they are chronologically and that rapid or slow maturation does not correlate to either intelligence or academic ability.

Paul Goodman (1911–1972). Paul Goodman held a Ph.D. in Humanities from the University of Chicago. His books include *Communitas, Growing Up Absurd, The Community of Scholars,* and *Compulsory Mis-Education.* He introduced the vision that the whole system of American education can be freed from bureaucratic constraints that stifle real learning and growth, arguing that we should dismantle it completely, from preschool to professional training, and restructure it on the basis of free choice. Goodman believed that youth can be educated entirely in terms of their free choice, stating that nothing can be efficiently learned, or learned at all—other than through parroting or brute training, whereby acquired knowledge is promptly forgotten after the examination—unless it meets need, desire, curiosity, or fantasy. He also stated that it seems stupid to decide a priori what youths ought to know and then try to motivate them, instead of letting the initiative come from them and putting information and relevant equipment at their service. In this connection, he described free choice as responsive, not random.

C. Hanford Henderson (1881–1941). C. Hanford Henderson, a former headmaster of New York City's Pratt Institute, wrote *Education and the Larger Life* in 1902. Over time it became one of the educational bibles. Marietta Johnson borrowed the concept of the "organic school" from Henderson's work.

E. D. Hirsch (1928–). E. D. Hirsch established the Core Knowledge Foundation to promote cultural literacy in schools. He criticizes American education for failing to effectively pass on national literate culture to students. Specifically, he believes that to participate in the economic, political, social, and cultural life of American society, a person must be familiar with the cultural legacy that exists in a shared body of knowledge about the United States. This body of knowledge includes geography, history, literature, science, politics, government, art, and music. Hirsch has produced a series of books containing the essential knowledge appropriate for the various grades.

John Holt (1923–1985). John Holt was the first home-schooling activist. He has stated that "[i]t is essential to realize that children learn independently, not in bunches. They learn out of interest and curiosity, not to please or appease the adults in power. They ought to be in control of their own learning, deciding for themselves what they want to learn and how they want to learn it." He firmly believes that children are better at learning than adults are and that, if left to their own devices, they would learn more than adults could possibly teach them. He has also stated that what goes on in schools is confusing, boring, demeaning, and oppressive, and that "the idea of school as a place separated from the world and reserved for 'learning' is false and ridiculous." Holt has been teaching and observing children for many years. He is the author of *How Children Fail, How Children Learn,* and numerous magazine articles.

Myles Horton (1905–1990). In 1932, Myles Horton founded the Highlander Folk School in Monteagle, Tennessee. Highlander was a controversial school in the South that for years taught leadership skills to both blacks and whites in defiance of segregation laws. Horton worked closely with labor unions, antipoverty organizations, and civil rights leaders and is often credited with being one of the sparks that ignited the Civil Rights Movement in the United States. His Highlander Center developed a literacy program in the 1950s that taught thousands of blacks to read and write in an effort to get them to register to vote. And his Citizenship Schools represent the largest and clearly most effective

mass literacy campaign ever undertaken in the United States. They suc-
ceeded largely because they emphasized not just literacy but the right to
participate in a democratic society.

Ivan Illich (1926–). Ivan Illich, author of *Deschooling Society,* believes that schools are based on a variety of false ideas: that the world
consists of educational and noneducational realms, that learning requires instruction in a school, that grades and certificates attest to
learning and ability, and that the self-taught person is neither compe-
tent nor professional.

Marietta Johnson (1864–1938). In 1907, under the collective influences of Froebel, Dewey, Oppenheim, and Henderson, Marietta
Johnson started the Organic School in Fairhope, Alabama. An experimental, child-centered "school of tomorrow," it began as a kindergarten
in a small cottage in a town established in 1894 by Colonists who sub-
scribed to the economic philosophy of Henry George, an advocate of the
single tax. The Organic School provided an educational-experiment di-
mension to the community; indeed, it was an experiment from its inception. The curriculum of the school derived from ideas developed by
Jean-Jacques Rousseau, who insisted that education must be based on
the needs and innate capacities of children, not on the demands and accomplishments of adults.

Herbert Kohl. Herbert Kohl is best known for his progressive
work in education as well as for his writing—including *The Discipline of
Hope* and *36 Children.* He currently runs a new-teacher preparation
program at the University of San Francisco's School of Education. This
program, known as the Center for Teaching Excellence and Social Justice, is helping inner-city teachers obtain their teaching credentials and
master's degrees. The mission of the Center is to produce progressive,
reform-minded teachers who will be empowered to help schools and
urban centers throughout the nation.

Jonathan Kozol (1936–). Jonathan Kozol, former educational director of the Storefront Learning Center in Boston, received a National
Book Award in 1968 for *Death at an Early Age.* He is a well-known figure
in the alternative schools movement because of the pioneering work he
did in inner-city Roxbury, Massachusetts, starting a school that primarily served African American students at a time when most alternative
schools were in suburban and rural areas.

Grace Llewellyn (1964–). An avid promoter of adolescent self-
schooling, Grace Llewellyn has written two books: *The Teenage Liberation Handbook: How to Quit School and Get a Real Education* and *Real
Lives: Eleven Teenagers Who Don't Go to School.* Llewellyn's approach is
based on her rejection of schools and formal education. She is a propo-

nent of "de-schooling," a tradition founded by John Holt. She attacks high schools for being useless and destructive, arguing that they fail to provide students with opportunities to study English, mathematics, and history and to express themselves in writing and speech. The main point of *The Teenage Liberation Handbook* is that, without going to high school, teenagers can get an education and learn what they need to learn both to pursue a college education and to become happy, mature adults.

Horace Mann (1796–1859). Horace Mann is known as the father of American "common" education—namely, public education. He was a champion of the nonprivileged class and devoted much of his life to overcoming the injustices of the nineteenth-century educational system. In addition, he founded the first state-funded institutions for training teachers in the country. His conviction that appropriate teaching methods were the key to student learning led him to devote many years to the research and study of contemporary theories of psychology and cognition.

Deborah Meier (1931–). In 1985, Deborah Meier established Central Park East Secondary School (CPE) in New York City's District 4 in East Harlem. CPE is guided by the principles of the Coalition of Essential Schools, founded by Theodore Sizer. In her work at this school, Meier demonstrated that progressive pedagogic practices can work with all children, not just children of the affluent.

Ronald Miller. Ronald Miller is a historian of education and founder of the *Holistic Education Review*. A leading advocate of holistic education, he espouses the belief that children's intellectual growth is dependent on their development as physical, emotional, artistic, social, moral, and spiritual beings. Miller promotes the idea that the aim of education is not merely to fill children with information, develop their academic and job skills, and prepare them to fit into the prevailing economic and social system, but also to help them develop into free, creative, compassionate beings who can participate fully in the life of the community.

Maria Montessori (1870–1952). Born near Ancona, Italy, Maria Montessori was the first woman in that country to receive a medical degree. As a physician she became interested in the educational problems of mentally retarded children and designed innovative educational materials and practices for them, which were used in a school in Rome. In 1907, she founded the Casa dei Bambini ("The Children's House") in Rome, where she applied her educational methods with great success with children from the slums of the city. Montessori based her method on the view that young children possess a divine life force.

A. S. Neill (1883–1973). A. S. Neill founded Summerhill, the most famous experimental school, in 1921. Freedom is the main principle upon which the school was run. Children at Summerhill had almost complete freedom in their education and in all aspects of their lives. In 1961, Neill published *Summerhill*, a book describing the experimental primary and secondary boarding school he founded in Leiston, Suffolk, England. His work was based on the philosophy of Jean-Jacques Rousseau.

Nathan Oppenheim (1865–1916). Nathan Oppenheim was a medical author as well as an attending physician in the children's department at New York Red Cross Hospital and New York City Children's Hospital. As a specialist in diseases of children, he wrote *The Development of the Child, Mental Growth and Control,* and other books and essays. Marietta Johnson's work with children at the Organic School is attributed to the influence she received from Nathan Oppenheim's writings.

Francis Parker (1837–1902). The Francis W. Parker School opened in 1901. Influenced by the work of John Dewey, Colonel Parker envisioned a school that held the child at its very center. His fundamental belief was that learning could be fun, and he proved his point not through theories on child psychology but with actual classroom demonstrations. He also believed that education included the complete development of an individual—mental, physical, and moral—and that through the educational journey, students would develop into lifelong learners and active, democratic citizens.

Heinrich Pestalozzi (1746–1827). Heinrich Pestalozzi maintained that human beings are inherently good and capable of taking responsibility for their own intellectual and moral development. He believed that education should include manual labor; physical exercise; the learning of practical skills; drawing, singing, and handicrafts; field trips; and the collecting of natural objects. He rejected coercion, corporal punishment, and rote memorization in education and emphasized the need for a stable nurturing, love-filled, homelike atmosphere and the importance of gentle encouragement of the child's moral intuition.

Jean Piaget (1896–1980). Jean Piaget was a major figure in twentieth-century developmental psychology. His extensive research led him to believe that the mind of the child evolves through a series of clearly defined stages. He asserted that each infant develops, in four main stages, according to an inherent, fixed, genetically determined pattern.

Caroline Pratt (1867–). In 1914, with the goal of fostering rather than drilling children's natural desire to learn, Caroline Pratt began the City and Country School as a play group in a settlement house in New

York City. She tried to interest working-class parents in this school, which aimed to teach children about their world through play, particularly with wooden blocks. In addition, she established what Dewey called an "embryonic community," in which each group had a job or task essential to the maintenance of the school as a whole. This child-centered school continues to use an integrated curriculum that reflects the needs and interests of children at different developmental levels, emphasizing the concept of self-expression and growth through play.

Louise Rosenblatt. Louise Rosenblatt has had a profound influence in the area of literacy. She calls on teachers to develop an awareness of the transaction between the reader and the text. According to her transactional theory of reading, the text is not static but, rather, is interpreted through the lens of experiences that the reader brings to the moment in which words on the page are encountered. Rosenblatt describes this process as a never-ending cycle of reader and text interacting. A graduate of Barnard College and Columbia University, she was elected to the Reading Hall of Fame in 1992 and, more recently, was recognized by the John Dewey Society.

Jean-Jacques Rousseau (1712–1778). Jean-Jacques Rousseau was a philosopher and political theorist who became a seminal figure in the development of humanistic education. He proposed that children, if left to themselves, will grow into loving and free beings of nature and, out of their natural curiosity, will learn what they need to know. He also emphasized that the emotional and artistic dimensions of human nature are as important as the intellectual dimensions. Education, he said, is not just a matter of filling children with information; it also involves drawing out the affective, artistic, moral, and social capabilities latent in the children and helping them develop their innate creativity and goodness.

Sister Clara Mohammad. Sister Clara Mohammad, the wife of Elijah Mohammad, founded the first African American Muslim school in the 1930s. Because she wanted her own children to have a Muslim education, she removed them from the Detroit public schools and educated them at home; eventually, other members of the Muslim community began sending their children to her. In the 1970s, many of the forty Islamic schools founded across the country renamed themselves Sister Clara Schools to honor this Muslim educator.

B. F. Skinner (1904–1990). Burrhus Frederic Skinner is the father of the highly innovative but controversial theory of operant conditioning. His work included the invention of the "Skinner Box," a physical environment designed to shape and reinforce behavior in animals and even humans. Skinner's techniques are still found in areas of curriculum where teachers break down tasks into teachable units. Computer-based self-instruction is also based on his work.

Elliot Wigginton. Elliot Wigginton was a young English teacher at a high school in Rabun County, Georgia, when he founded Foxfire. It began as a project to motivate his students. He had his students create a magazine about the local Appalachian culture and history. The students conducted interviews, did research, wrote and edited articles, and designed, published, and distributed the magazine. A commercial success, the magazine was also called *Foxfire*. Wigginton used his experience to develop an approach to education, called the Foxfire approach, that is based on the progressive ideas of John Dewey.

Preston Wilcox. Preston R. Wilcox taught at the Columbia School of Social Work as a professor and was affiliated with the I.S. 201 in Harlem and the Bedford-Stuyvesant Development and Services Corporation. He was also a major proponent of the community-centered school, which resembled a freedom school. The model for community-centered schools addresses the following community needs: (1) recreation and fun; (2) expression through art, music, drama, and so on; (3) the shaping of community policy as it relates to housing, traffic, health, education, and other social issues; and (4) mutual aid programs designed to assist the less fortunate in dealing with their problems.

REFERENCES

Adams, F. (1975). *Unearthing Seeds of Fire: The Idea of Highlander*. Winston-Salem, NC: John F. Blair.

Collinson, D. (1987). *Fifty Major Philosophers: A Reference Guide*. New York: Routledge.

Glen, J. M. (1996). *Highlander: No Ordinary School*. Knoxville: University of Tennessee Press.

Gross, R., and Gross, B. (1969). *Radical School Reform*. New York: Simon and Schuster.

Koetzsch, R. E. (1997). *Parents' Guide to Alternatives in Education*. Boston: Shambhala Publications.

Maine Indymedia. Available online at http://maine.indymedia.org.

Semel, S., and Sadovnik, A. (1999). *"Schools of Tomorrow," Schools of Today*. New York: Peter Lang.

Chapter 4

⚏ Alternative Learning Options

Emerging public school learning options, created in direct response to public dissatisfaction with the status quo, today include public and private voucher programs, charter schools, magnet programs, for-profit companies running public schools, and, in general, schools in many more varieties than we have seen in the past. Problems associated with public schools that alternative learning options seek to solve include poor achievement, community conflict over the curriculum, ineffective pedagogical methods, financial mismanagement, and the increasing inability to meet the needs of families.

The learning options described in this chapter represent local, state, and national responses to improving the quality of education in public schools and schools funded with public money.

AFTER-SCHOOL PROGRAMS

The After-School Model is very prevalent. To a large extent, it exists because administrators and faculty in traditional schools are unwilling to accept the tension that results from having two sets of rules operating within the same building. The advantages of this model are similar to those associated with the full-time in-house alternative model. The most significant difference is that the alternative model does not have to concern itself with the traditional school and its blanket set of rules and policies. After-school programs are typically offered by commercial firms such as Sylvan Learning Centers, but many schools and community-based organizations such as the Boys and Girls Clubs and the YMCA also offer after-school programs to supplement the regular school day. Programs offered by traditional public schools include Saturday School and evening classes. After-school schools offer a wide range of supplemental educational programs and span from preschool to the college level.

ALTERNATIVE SCHOOLS

Alternative schools were initially developed to reach students with behavior or attendance problems, and many continue to address our "at-risk" learners. These schools have most often been secondary schools, although some districts recognize younger learners' needs and have expanded to middle school populations as well. Alternative schools typically offer a low student-teacher ratio, modified curricula, and flexible scheduling.

Many alternative schools offer additional support services such as childcare, teen-parent education, and individual or small-group counseling. Included in the category of alternative schools are charter schools, private alternative education schools, and alternative programs offered within a traditional public school.

BLUE RIBBON SCHOOLS

Blue Ribbon Schools are not generally described as alternative schools, but they do represent what might be described as a nontraditional orientation. The U.S. Department of Education selects these schools annually. Schools throughout the United States enter into competition each year, with secondary schools and elementary schools being chosen in alternate years. According to M. A. Horenstein (1993), these are functioning schools, not theoretical models. They share many characteristics in common with alternative schools, including a vision, clear goals, and administrators and faculty who work together to meet those goals. Blue Ribbon Schools initiate curriculum changes and their voices are heard. Their teachers and students are empowered. These schools have found ways to break the isolation sometimes associated with traditional schools. In many cases, the community becomes the learning environment.

CHARTER SCHOOLS

Charter schools, which are public schools that operate with public funds but are free from many school regulations, are among the fastest-growing segments of the school choice movement. The charter school movement was founded in 1991 to help students, educators, and families. This movement allows educators, parents, and community groups to create and operate schools, so long as they accept responsibility for meeting academic goals and improving student achievement. Approximately 350,000 students nationwide are now enrolled in this celebrated alternative to public schooling. The first two charter schools opened in Minnesota in 1992. During the 2000–2001 school year more than 2,000 opened across the nation. Thirty-six states and Washington, DC, have adopted charter school laws; 34 states and the nation's capital have charter schools in operation. Charter schools vary from state to state, offering a wide range of educational programs and governance structures. They may receive waivers from state regulations and local contract provisions in exchange for explicit responsibility for improving student achievement. A school becomes a charter school when it enters into a contractual agreement with a district to provide educational services. Charter schools allow more choice for learners and more authentic research for educators who are seeking new ways to educate children. The idea of a competitive public school system is radical and charter schools are just that. They represent a radical approach to improving public schools.

The charter movement can now claim to be considered one of the significant strategies for changing and improving K–12 public education. In contrast to other efforts at systemic change, the charter movement has no organizational structure, no prominent figures to lead it, no big foundation grants, and little support from well-known education and business groups. It offers not a new theory of teaching and learning but simply a new opportunity to try out good ideas.

It is difficult to generalize among charter schools because they vary widely. They do not use a single curricular or pedagogical strategy, either nonprofit or for-profit groups can run them, and they can operate either independently or as part of a local school district.

The number of public charter schools grew from 2 in 1992 to about 2,000 in September 2000. One of the best examples of a charter school is Key Elementary School in Indianapolis, based on Howard Gardner's theory of multiple intelligences. A group of teachers, after visiting Gardner, developed plans for this charter school with multiple intelligences as its theme.

DESIGN-BASED SCHOOLS

The New American Schools Development Corporation (NASDC) is a nonprofit corporate-supported educational design institute. The NASDC sponsors several design teams, which work to create and then market distinctive designs for innovative schools. Two of the school designs that NASDC teams have developed are the Cooperative Networking Educational Community for Tomorrow (Co-nect) and the modern Red Schoolhouse.

ELEMENTARY SCHOOL MODEL

Many programs are being used in elementary schools in an effort to intervene with students who have been identified as potentially at risk. According to Robert Barr and William Parrett (1995), the preventative approach is the best of these in terms of both effectiveness and cost. Their research clearly suggests that prevention of grade retention is the factor most likely to determine school success.

GENERAL EDUCATIONAL DEVELOPMENT CERTIFICATE

The General Educational Development (GED) certificate is rapidly becoming a major educational credential in this country. In 1998, a half-million Americans obtained a GED, more than doubling the number (231,000) who received the credential in 1971. Today, one-seventh of the young Americans who report on government surveys that they are high school graduates are actually GED recipients who obtained the credential after dropping out of school. At least one in every four students quits before receiving a traditional high school diploma. The numbers are even higher in our urban school systems. In Chicago, for example, a third of students do not graduate from regular high schools. Across the country, more and more students are turning to alternative education programs—either those that provide another route to a regular high school diploma or those that offer the chance to earn an equivalency diploma through the GED examinations. The percentage opting for a GED has jumped by more than 5 percent since 1990. The percentage earning a high school diploma in the traditional four years has dropped commensurably.

Changes in the U.S. economy over the last two decades have been extremely unfavorable for school dropouts. Between 1979 and 1996, the real earnings of twenty-five- to thirty-four-year-old male dropouts fell by 28 percent; the comparable figure for female dropouts was 7 percent. The declining economic prospects of school dropouts are especially disturbing given that, according to the National Center for Education Statistics, the percentage of eighteen- to twenty-four-year-old Americans who left school without a high school diploma increased from 21.2 percent in 1994 to 25.3 percent in 1998.

Most state and government programs aimed at improving earnings prospects for school dropouts focus on preparing them to take the GED examinations. These exams cover mathematics, reading, social studies, science, and writing. Since 1988, the GED battery has included a short open-ended writing component, with the remainder consisting of multiple-choice questions.

With support from the National Center for the Study of Adult Learning and Literacy, data from many sources have been used to explore the labor-market value of the GED credential for school dropouts in their mid-twenties and to compare it with the value of the conventional high school diploma. This work focuses exclusively on the value of the GED to those who obtain the credential before age twenty-five—two-thirds of all GED recipients in 1997. The results should play a role in debates about how to improve American education. Increasingly, alternative education programs are feeling the demands of higher standards and greater accountability. Over the past couple of years, more states have begun to require students in alternative education programs to pass the same high-stakes exit exams as those in regular programs. Meanwhile, the GED battery itself is undergoing its first major revision since 1988, with a more demanding math section emphasizing statistics and data analysis being added.

HOME SCHOOLING

Many parents cite dissatisfaction with the public school curriculum or mediocrity in the system as their reason for choosing to home-school their children. Home schooling is legal in every state, and approximately one out of four children in the United States are taught at home. Some states and districts are working with home schoolers, allowing them to attend public school part of the school day so that they can participate in academic and/or other school activities.

John Holt, a longtime supporter of learning and teaching outside the bureaucratic structure of traditional schools, originally referred to his goal as unschooling. This concept accurately reflects the sort of learning and teaching that Holt encouraged—namely, learning that does not in any way resemble learning in school and teaching that does not necessarily have to take place in one's home. By the early 1980s, the term *home schooling* had taken root, and even Holt started using it interchangeably with the word *unschooling*. Holt described the home-schooling movement as a laboratory for the intensive and long-range study of children's learning and of the ways in which friendly and concerned adults can help them learn—a research project, done at no cost, of a kind for which neither the public schools nor the government could afford to pay.

The profile of home-schooling parents identifies them as predominantly white, religious, and members of two-parent households. As a rule, such parents are not wealthier than the norm, but they do tend to have more years of education. Much of the rise in this counterculture movement is credited to Christian home schoolers and to the Home School Legal Defense Association; the latter is responsible for the legal status that it enjoys today. These two groups were not, however, the original home-schooling pioneers.

Critics of formal education such as Ivan Illich, Paul Goodman, A. S. Neill, and John Holt protested tests, grades, curricula, and the whole idea that a specific body of knowledge ought to be transmitted from adults to children. Holt, the first home-schooling activist, espouses the belief that "children learn independently, not in bunches." He regards children as superior to adults in every way and believes that, left to their own devices, they will "learn their hearts out." After the publication of his diary-style books, *How Children Fail* (1964) and *How Children Learn* (1967), he became even more convinced that schools themselves would never allow children to learn what they wanted to learn at their own pace and in their own childish spirit, and began to urge parents to "unschool" their children at home.

When the home-schooling movement started in the 1980s, it seemed that the movement would never last or, if it lasted, would never grow. But in fact it has developed over the past decade or so into a surprisingly vigorous counterculture. In 1985 about 50,000 children nationwide were learning at home. Current estimates range from 1.5 to 1.9 million. By comparison, charter schools—the most celebrated alternative in public schooling—enroll about 350,000 students. The population of kids learning at home is growing by 15 to 20 percent a year. The rise of home schooling is one of the most significant social trends of the past half-century.

In 1983, only four states had laws explicitly permitting home education. By 1993, home education was legal in all fifty states. Not so long ago, home-schooling families were entirely on their own in terms of finding curricula, providing their children opportunities for socializing, and monitoring academic growth, whereas today an increasing number of school districts are offering home-schooling parents a rich array of benefits. In Kansas, California, Colorado, Washington, and other states, school districts that once grudgingly granted permission for home-schooled children to participate in after-school activities now openly court them with virtual curriculum packages, school-based enrichment centers, in-service training sessions, and even, in at least one case, a full-time school designed to satisfy the demands of home-school families.

INTERDISCIPLINARY TEACHING

Interdisciplinary teaching, which takes place in "self-contained class-rooms," eliminates the boundaries between content areas. In such classrooms, content areas are blended, and content-area teachers might team-teach material. Interdisciplinary teaching provides learning opportunities in a complex, interrelated context, similar to real-world issues and problems. It requires learners to engage higher-order thinking skills as they synthesize and analyze information. In short, it allows learners to see the connectedness between things and to discover relationships they might not have seen without the information and varied perspectives gained from blending disciplines. The following teaching strategies support interdisciplinary teaching:

- Thematic instruction, which combines several subject areas in order to focus on a single theme or concept
- Problem-centered learning, which draws learners into several content areas and encourages them to solve complex problems or questions
- Reading, which can be used as the initiating activity to draw students into writing

In interdisciplinary teaching programs, students can also share their writing—a process that activates listening and speaking skills.

MIDDLE SCHOOL MODEL

At the middle school level, at-risk behavior becomes far more apparent than it may have seemed in earlier grades. By an overwhelming majority, the most common middle school alternative is the school-within-a-school model.

Jerry Dawson (1987, p. 85) lists the following ten components of a comprehensive program to help at-risk middle school students:

1. A formalized identification program
2. A schoolwide discipline program
3. A three-year homeroom class
4. A "secret pal" program (in which adult mentors are paired with at-risk youth)
5. A dynamic youth services team (which makes recommendations for intervening with at-risk youth)
6. An early work experience program
7. A "Gram" program (in which handwritten notes are sent home about positive situations involving students)
8. Administrative and counseling duties (assigned specifically to guarantee "shoe-leather" counseling and contact time)
9. A comprehensive retention intervention program (designed to reduce the number of students who must be retained)
10. Firmly established goals for the school

PRIVATELY MANAGED PUBLIC SCHOOLS

In the United States, nearly a dozen private businesses manage public schools via charter of management contracts with a district. The intent of this arrangement is to give sole control of a school to a profit-making business entity, which restructures the school along the lines of a business organization. One example is the Edison Project, which currently operates more than twenty-five schools in eight different states. Early studies of Edison Project schools show positive results in terms of both test score gains and increasing enrollments.

PROGRAMS FOR AT-RISK STUDENTS

As noted earlier, a wide variety of alternative education programs now serve the growing population of at-risk students. Many are run by school districts. These educational institutions have developed and implemented dropout prevention programs in order to make a multidimensional assault on the crisis, but few districts evaluate the success of the programs in serving the clientele. A major component of dropout prevention is having a program that uses active teaching and learning with nontraditional approaches such as cooperative learning, parenting skills, and work-study opportunities in a small, community setting. Some dropout prevention programs address both academic and social skills deficiencies.

PROPRIETARY SCHOOLS

Many of these for-profit entities are chains of schools operated by corporate-style management with shareholders and corporate structure.

REAL CONTEXT FOR LEARNING

Real Context programs give learners a chance to solve real problems and apply specific skills such as reading and writing in an authentic context. Real problems are more meaningful and complex than fabricated ones, and context is more engaging and satisfying when tied to real experiences or issues. Students learn to deal with complexity when given the opportunity to do so.

SCHOOL CHOICE

School choice within the public education system is an innovation that has been gaining strength in the last decade. Choice plans began as a desegregation device but quickly expanded as a means of satisfying parental desires for tailored programs. Such plans were among the recommendations of the 1986 *Time for Results* report from the National Governors' Association and are specifically cited in the 2002 *No Child Left Behind Law*. Advocates of school choice say that the appeal of such programs is that they foster parental involvement and high expectations by giving parents the option to educate their children as they see fit. Advocates also suggest that school choice accommodates a diversity of student interests and needs, and that traditional schools that put forward a "one-size fits all approach" will soon be forced out of business because they fail to meet the needs of students and parents. Critics of the choice movement, on the other hand, have labeled it a controversial public education reform and argue that competition for enrollment destroys cooperation among teachers, schools, and communities. Critics also believe that choice schools exclude difficult-to-teach students and force other public schools to carry an unfair burden. In a case study of school choice, K. Howe et al. (2001) concluded that "given the effort and expense it would take to get school choice right—free transportation and concerted efforts to disseminate accessible information are minimum requirements—we would do well to abandon it as a failed school reform idea." Advocates would counter, however, that they see a direct alignment between schools of choice and restructured schools. Many schools of choice, they say, embody characteristics of school-site management because their curriculum and faculty are oriented around a particular mission. Faculty are selected for their interest in the special offering of the school and frequently have more flexibility in designing the program.

In short, advocates see school choice as a way to improve public schools in the United States, whereas critics fear that "choice" may backfire and take resources away from already-struggling public schools. The argument lies in whether innovations spurred by competition actually improve student achievement. The basic concept behind the movement for "school choice" for low-income families is that innovative alternatives will force public schools to implement positive changes.

Public Schools Versus Private Schools

Another major criticism of school choice is that it increases racial segregation. Many sociologists have voiced the concern that public schools are less well integrated than private schools. Indeed, although public school systems enroll a larger percentage of minority students than private schools, individual public schools are more likely to be virtually all white or all black whereas individual private schools tend to have a more even distribution of racial and economic groups.

Types of School Choice

Public School Choice

Public school choice around the country is one aspect of the overall effort to restructure our education system and create an incentive for schools to improve. In many respects, the concept of choice returns the crucial element of parent and student involvement to the school site.

Public school choice plans are not all alike. They include the following options:

- The intradistrict, districtwide, and postsecondary plans emphasize the rights of families to choose among existing public schools within their home district. This plan is offered in numerous school districts around the country, including Boston, Seattle, Minneapolis/St. Paul, and District 4 in New York City.
- Statewide, or interdistrict, plans allow students to attend public schools outside their home district. Over the past eight years, fourteen states, led by Minnesota, have accepted statewide choice plans, and over twenty states have considered them.

- Second-chance plans extend interdistrict choice and post-secondary options to at-risk youth, offering them alternatives to traditional schooling.
- Controlled-choice plans require all families to choose the school their child attends and are focused on achieving equity.
- Teacher-initiated schools feature restructuring by the faculty of each school.
- Magnet schools set school improvement and family choice within a framework of schools offering special resources.

Private School Choice

More commonly referred to as vouchers, private school choice plans permit parents to use public funds to send their children to private schools. The Center for Education Reform, a national nonprofit education advocacy organization in Washington, D.C., defines choice as follows:

> School choice means better educational opportunity because it uses the dynamics of consumer opportunity and provides competition to drive service quality. This principle is found anywhere you look from cars to colleges and universities, but it's largely absent in our public school system, and the poor results are evident. . . . School choice programs foster parental involvement and high expectations by giving parents the option to educate their children as they see fit.

The Black Alliance for Educational Options (BAEO), a national group of African Americans that supports school choice for minority children, agrees. As one spokesperson put it: "Current systems of K–12 education work well for many of America's children. On the other side of the ledger, for far too many children, the current systems do not work well at all" (2000, p. 2).

SCHOOL-WITHIN-A-SCHOOL

Study after study identifies the many advantages of small schools, ranging from increased student achievement and extracurricular participation to decreased behavior problems and reduced attendance problems and dropout rates. But when small schools aren't possible, school-within-a-school plans can produce similar results. In the school-within-a-school model, large schools are divided into two or more subunits.

There are many variations on this model, with some schools based on particular curricula, special interests, or needs, and others simply smaller versions of regular public schools. Generally, each school-within-a-school is a distinct administrative entity, with significant autonomy and a clear, unified vision.

The school-within-a-school model comes in two varieties: the full-time day model and the after-school model. Because the full-time day model is so easy to establish, it is the most prevalent alternative school model. Because the alternative program is usually located in a wing of a district school, it requires virtually no political effort to establish. There are few additional costs, other than those involving the staffing of the alternative program. Since they're in the same building, students attending the alternative school have access to the same facilities as students who attend the traditional program. The model also facilitates the return of alternative students to the mainstream, should that be the goal of the program or the desire of the students.

SCHOOL WITHOUT WALLS

The school-without-walls model is based on the premise that the entire community can be a classroom. Programs like Philadelphia's Parkway School utilize locations such as businesses, hospitals, museums, zoos, courtrooms, airports, aquariums, theaters, and government offices as learning centers. Founded in Philadelphia in 1968, Parkway was the first school without walls. Such schools attempt to break down physical and education barriers between young people and the community in which they live. Traditional school buildings may be irrelevant to schools without walls. The community and its places of business and institutions become the school. Schools without walls can be extremely effective in providing students with hands-on learning experiences and exposure to real-world activities—outcomes from which all students, whether at risk or not, can benefit.

The planning and coordination required to effectively organize a school without walls can also be extensive.

SCHOOLS ORGANIZED AROUND
A SINGLE UNIFYING THEME (MAGNET SCHOOLS)

This model is most commonly referred to as a magnet school. Like charter schools, magnet schools are public schools with a twist. Sometimes called theme schools or focus schools, they are usually organized around a particular philosophy or focused on a specific academic area, such as science or the arts. The idea of organizing a school around a single unifying theme provides students with opportunities for intensive exploration of that theme. The location, such as a museum, theater, art gallery, or medical or high-tech center, provides students with real-world experiences as they consistently "do" a subject. Many of the students who attend these schools are gifted in one or several areas.

The first magnet schools were mainly intended to integrate schools by attracting students to distant classrooms without compulsory busing. Today, however, magnets serve varied purposes.

Even though the Rand Corporation labeled magnet schools as "high schools with character" because of their special-purpose focus, they first started in the 1970s to help desegregate public schools. In Cincinnati in 1974, for example, magnet and alternative schools were the center of controversy between an extremely conservative school board and the NAACP because the latter viewed the board's magnet school plan as a way to avoid racially and economically integrating schools. Today, they are attractive to parents who want rigorous or specialized academics for their children. Magnet schools compare favorably with private schools as well as comprehensive public high schools in terms of performance. They have been instrumental in providing high-quality public education to minority students.

In 1970, New York City and Berkeley, following a model created in Minnesota, embarked on full-scale alternative school programs, featuring basic skills centers, environmentally oriented programs, and independent contract curricula with businesses. A year later, in 1971, Dallas opened the first "super" high school, designed around the concept of career strands. At about the same time, Houston opened its Performing and Visual Arts School and described it as working like a "magnet" in terms of attracting students of all ethnicities from all over the city. The term appeared to catch on. By 1980, most major cities had a magnet system; yet it was the federal courts that caused the greatest surge in magnet education.

Advocates of magnet education identify the following precepts as central to their belief system:

1. Students vary in terms of the ways they learn.
2. If we take advantage of a student's interest and aptitude, that student will do better in subjects unrelated to his or her reasons for choosing the school.
3. Choice itself will result in improved satisfaction that translates into better achievement.
4. Every child can learn, and it is our job to offer enough

options so that parents will have the opportunity to choose the programs best suited to their children.

VIRTUAL SCHOOLS

Technology has provided an entirely new education delivery system, free from some of the constraints of traditional delivery such as class schedules, transportation, limited curriculum offers, and group pacing demands. Using the Internet and email, students are able to "attend class" twenty-four hours a day from anywhere in the world. Chat rooms and on-line communication provide support for students needing additional help.

In Kansas, for example, Basehor-Linwood teachers have created an on-line compendium of Internet links, teacher web pages, lessons, and assignments for home-schooled children. A second Kansas-based on-line charter, the Wichita e-School, opened in September 2001. A privately managed, publicly funded electronic charter school for home school and at-risk students called e-Cot has opened in Ohio. And former education secretary Willam J. Bennett recently announced that he will serve as chairman of a new cyberschool, named "K12," that is targeted especially to home schoolers.

VOUCHERS

As discussed earlier in the context of private school choice plans, the voucher system is a plan for financing schools with tax money but with parents in control of that money. A voucher is a certificate issued to parents. The parents give the voucher to the school of their choice, and the school exchanges the voucher for payment by the government. The system was studied at Harvard University in the 1960s. Earlier than that, after 1954, voucher plans were tried in the South as a means of supporting segregated schools, but they were found unconstitutional. Some states have attempted to use a voucher system for supporting parochial schools, and cases regarding their legal status are still pending. Modern proposals for voucher plans guard against racial discrimination as well as the use of taxes to supplement tuition at expensive private schools.

Many supporters of vouchers believe that the public schools have failed America's children—and that the schools will not improve unless they feel the pressure of an open market. Some contend that publicly funded school vouchers actually improve the public schools by forcing them to compete with private schools for students and funding. The public schools have to improve, these supporters claim, or they risk losing their students to institutions that better suit their educational needs.

Most Americans believe that improving our system of education should be a top priority for government at the local, state, and federal levels. Legislators, school boards, education professionals, parent groups, and community organizations are attempting to implement innovative ideas to rescue children from failing school systems, particularly in inner-city neighborhoods. Many such groups champion voucher programs, viewing them as a viable public school alternative. The standard program proposed in dozens of states across the country would distribute monetary vouchers (ranging in value from $2,000 to $5,000) to parents of school-aged children, usually in troubled inner-city school districts. Parents could then use the vouchers toward the cost of tuition at private schools. Currently, only three localities—Milwaukee, Cleveland, and Florida—offer vouchers that families can use to send their children to secular or religious private schools.

Florida established the first statewide voucher program, which allows students in failing schools to use state funds to pay tuition at private and parochial schools. President George W. Bush, like many other presidential candidates, has vowed to get tough on public schools, stating that education would be the first major issue he would take to Capitol Hill. In January 2001, he unveiled an education package that included a plan to strip underachieving schools of federal money that parents could use instead to help pay for private schooling. Bush's broad idea that schools should receive federal help up to a point—and that parents should be able to move their children out of schools that continue to fail—enjoys wide support on Capitol Hill. There is disagreement, however, on whether school vouchers can be a solution. The fear is that vouchers would further weaken public education. Many Americans oppose taking money from public schools and sending it to private and religious schools, whereas supporters claim that vouchers even the educational playing field by offering low-income students an alternative to ineffective, unsafe public schools. Supporters also argue that parents should have a choice as to which schools their children attend. They say that the schools would become more competitive and establish many alternatives in curriculum methods; that without the voucher system only those wealthy enough to pay tuition can select schools for their children, while the poor must accept whatever the local public schools offer; and that, properly regulated, a voucher system may bring innovation and reform to schools and give parents much more control over the education of their children. These arguments are especially strong in

California, where a large segment of the population is supporting a law requiring that the state adopt the voucher system. Although the California Voucher System Proposal was defeated in the November 1993 election, efforts to expand school choice continue.

Opponents counter that voucher programs take money, better students, and concerned parents away from already-troubled public school systems without offering any solutions to existing problems. Another criticism is that taxpayer-funded vouchers for tuition at religious schools unconstitutionally breach the separation between church and state. The battle over school vouchers moved to the Supreme Court on February 20, 2002, as the justices heard oral arguments on whether an Ohio program that provides publicly funded scholarships for students to attend private and parochial schools crosses the constitutional line separating church and state. The Ohio program pays about $10 million to send 4,300 Cleveland students to fifty-one private schools—all but five of which are Catholic. The issue of public funding for private school vouchers highlights the historical debate about U.S. democracy. Should society function as a community to provide what is best for the group—or should society provide for the needs of individual citizens?

Many public school organizations such as the American Federation of Teachers (AFT) and the National Education Association (NEA) are opposed to the voucher system. They believe that the schools would become more segregated, with middle-class parents selecting one type of school and the poor and minorities concentrated in others; that competition between schools would foster publicity seeking; and that teachers would opt to be popular rather than professional. Above all, they fear that the system would be unworkable and that it might destroy public education in the United States.

REFERENCES

Aronowitz, S., and Giroux, H. A. (1993). *Education Still Under Siege.* Westport, CT: Bergin & Garvey.

Coulson, A. (1999). *Market Education: The Unknown History.* New Brunswick: Transaction Publishers.

Duke, D. L. (1978). *The Retransformation of the School.* Chicago: Nelson-Hall.

Horenstein, M. A. (1993). *Twelve Schools That Succeed.* Bloomington, IN: Phi Delta Kappa Educational Foundation.

Howe, K., et al. (2001). "Another Look at School Choice." *Phi Delta Kappa,* 83(2), 137–146.

Koetzsch, R. E. (1997). *Parents' Guide to Alternatives in Education.* Boston: Shambhala Publications.

Korn, C. V. (1991). *Alternative American Schools: Ideals in Action.* New York: State University of New York Press.

Kozol, J. (1982). *Alternative Schools: A Guide for Educators and Parents.* New York: Continuum.

Mintz, J. (Ed.). (1994). *The Handbook of Alternative Education.* New York: Macmillan.

Molnar, A. (1992). "What Are Our Choices?" *Educational Leadership, 50*(3), 84–85.

Chapter 5

✎ Curriculum Methods, Innovations, and Alternative Curricular Programs

When the founders and dreamers of alternative schools develop plans and ideas, they generally think of a school so exciting that parents would move thousands of miles so their children can attend, a school where children are the focus of all decisions about programs and resources, a school where children are nurtured in a way that helps them develop into productive, responsible citizens.

Many such models have been developed in response to the expressed need of parents to have options for children within their neighborhood schools. *Alternative*, as defined today, does not always mean an opportunity outside of or away from a child's home neighborhood or community. In the 33rd Annual Gallup Poll of the Public's Attitudes Toward the Public Schools (2001), for the first time in the history of the poll, a majority of respondents assigned either an A or a B to the schools in their communities. The explanation provided is that the closer people are to their public schools, the better they like them. However, when asked to choose between improving schools by reforming the existing system or by finding an alternative to that system, 72 percent of Americans chose reform.

Because education is always on the political agenda, many federal and state legislators have made alternative options a major part of their political platforms. Public opposition to having a school board contract with local businesses or private companies to run the entire school operation also appears to be growing. However, 44 percent of the respondents to the Gallup Poll favored allowing parents to choose a public, private, or church-related school for their children to attend, with the government paying all or part of the tuition. Although this poll suggests that the public is relatively uninformed about charter schools, there is growing public support for home schooling.

The following curriculum methods, innovations, and alternative curricular programs represent some of the current practices in operation in many schools today. Consideration of appropriate alternatives should begin with an examination of the learning environment, scheduling, and/or learning time. A needs assessment of this type can be beneficial to a school, regardless of level.

ALTERNATIVE LEARNING ENVIRONMENTS

Changes in the Classroom Environment

The physical environment and social climate of a classroom can influence how well students learn. Lighting, noise level, visual and auditory stimuli, and the physical arrangement of the room all have powerful effects. Having a variety of environments within the classroom and allowing students to choose according to their own preferences can also accommodate the special needs of many children.

Scheduling Options

A national report on time and learning asserts, "If experience, research, and common sense teach nothing else, they confirm the truism that people learn at different rates, and in different ways with different subjects" (*Prisoners of Time*, 1994, p. 3). The report goes on to recommend that schools be "reinvented around learning, not time" (p. 8).

There are several well-recognized models for alternative scheduling options available. The following is a list of five commonly used models:

1. Alternate Day Block, or A/B Schedule, in which students and teachers meet with their classes every other day for extended time blocks
2. Semester Block, or 4x4 block, in which students take four courses that meet for approximately ninety minutes every other day for a semester (ninety days)
3. Sliding Schedule, in which classes rotate with one class dropped each day
4. Single Periods Daily (traditional schedule)
5. Single Periods Four Days per Week

A sixth option is Parallel Block Scheduling, a scheduling system that is used to create the effect of smaller classes without major funding increases. Teachers work in teams consisting of three base teachers and one enrichment lab teacher. During each time block, one base teacher instructs a whole class, the second teacher sends the highest-achieving half of the class to the enrichment lab, and the third teacher sends the lowest-achieving half of the class to the enrichment lab. The enrichment lab is organized around cooperative learning centers, with an emphasis on hands-on learning. The enrichment lab teacher focuses on teaching students reading and math through science and social studies content. Under this system, teachers find that they have more time to individually assess students and provide appropriate instruction.

Extended Learning Time

The phrase *extended learning time* encompasses the wide range of programs that schools and communities can offer together to make better use of student's nonschool hours. These programs offer safe, stimulating environments that inspire and guide learning beyond the traditional school day, week, or year. They may use volunteers or community-based professionals in addition to teachers, and they may take place either in the school itself or in the community. Some examples follow:

- ➡ Summer Programs
- ➡ Saturday School
- ➡ Year-Round Schooling
- ➡ Before- and After-School Programs

When Grace Boggs developed Detroit Summer, she said that the idea behind it was "education, not incarceration." She believed that what children need most is a sense of themselves as agents of change and decision makers. She advocated for learning beyond academics and suggested that success is based in learning to become resourceful, independent, and critical thinkers. Students, she said, need to see themselves in the context of community and to practice what enhances community life. This alternative model is patterned on the Freedom Schools in the South. In the 1960s, activists had to create Freedom Schools because the existing school system had been organized to produce "subjects, not citizens." These schools initiated a mental revolution by teaching reading, writing, and speaking skills through discussion of black history, the power structure, and building a movement to struggle against the latter. Many children and adults all over Mississippi, taught by volunteer teachers in church basements and parish halls, were empowered through this community curriculum. The beauty of Detroit Summer as a model of Freedom Schools is that it can be organized by all kinds of grassroots community groups in their own neighborhoods.

CURRICULUM METHODS AND INNOVATIONS

Accelerated Learning Techniques

Accelerated learning techniques are strategies that assist learners to better encode memories into long-term storage. These strategies provide learners with strong associations, using sights, sounds, and feelings in order to help them remember and recall information.

Active Learning

Active learning involves the learner in active, physical participation as part of the learning process. Research shows that learning is anchored by one's physical experiences, and that understanding of complex concepts is facilitated through such activities as creating a science project or writing and acting out a play. Active learning is thus a strategy that more fully engages the learner.

Authentic Assessment

Authentic Assessment is a form of student assessment that improves the quality of student projects, enhances communication between teachers and students, encourages students to engage in discovery learning on an individual basis, and brings theory into practice. It is enhanced by a practice known as looping, which involves having the same teacher stay with students for two or more years, and then starting over again with another group.

Career Education

Career education is now a part of general education. At one time there was a clear division between vocational and academic programs, but today the emphasis is on the functional value of career planning for all students. On the theory that almost all students will engage in some sort of work in the future, career education emphasizes occupational training, career information and guidance, and the involvement of business and community groups. (Tech-prep and work-study programs link school and business.) The aim is to make career education available to all students, not just to those in vocational and industrial programs.

Character Education and Conflict Resolution

Character education and conflict resolution programs are being developed through partnerships between schools and universities, public schools and the community, and public schools and businesses. Character education programs are in operation in a growing number of public elementary and secondary schools, and conflict resolution programs designed to deal with student conflicts and preserve a safe school environment are expanding in public schools.

Consumer Education

Consumer education is now part of the social studies curriculum in many schools, reflecting the pressures of inflation and the general need to make wise choices in purchasing. Courses are often included as part of economics or career education classes, but sometimes consumer education is taught as a separate course.

Critical Thinking/Effective Questioning

Critical thinking is an important life skill—one that school experiences should provide learners with opportunities to develop. It is a process in which learners utilize a critically alert mind—one that can weigh multiple perspectives, consider varied alternatives, and discern fact from fiction.

Effective questioning provides information and thus is integral to the critical thinking process. It involves many skills: structuring questions to gain the information one seeks, probing deeper with a well-directed question, knowing when and whom to ask, knowing how long to pause after a query, and knowing how to rephrase a question. Critical thinking allows learners to frame their own questions and to create meaning by delving more deeply into the content. When students generate their own questions and actively participate in discussion, they have more at stake in the learning process.

Drug and Alcohol Abuse Education

Education dealing with drug and alcohol abuse is an expanding program. Because of the widespread problem of abuse and addiction, public demand for such education has been strong, resulting in programs that are coordinated with law enforcement agencies, community health projects, and former drug abusers. The major criticism of these programs comes from those who feel that they are not well taught or effective.

Environmental Education

Environmental education reflects a public concern with energy, pollution, ecology, and depletion of natural resources. Population pressures on the natural environment have created a demand for better understanding of environmental issues. Most schools attempt to build environmental content into standard courses in geography and the sciences. Many of these concerns are multicultural in nature and have created a new demand for global education.

Ethnic and Multicultural Education

Ethnic and multicultural educational offerings have grown rapidly since the "black revolution" and the emergence of interest in ethnic identity. Some states require schools to include courses in ethnic studies or cultural pluralism, and most have policy statements on the subject. The need for identity and for recognition of minorities and ethnic groups is clear. Ethnic education is designed to enhance the self-esteem of culturally different students and to promote understanding by majority students.

Multi-Age Grouping

Multi-age grouping—also referred to as nongraded education, multigrade grouping, and continuous progress—is an alternative to the traditional practice of grouping children by age in classes of twenty-five to thirty students each. By contrast, multi-age grouping involves placing students of varying ages in a single classroom. John Goodlad and Robert Anderson (1963) proposed this model in their book *The Nongraded Elementary School.*

OPEN OR INFORMAL EDUCATION

The primary goal of open or informal education is to respect children as whole, indivisible humans, as people who develop and learn in interaction with their total environment from classroom to community. In this context, teachers are helpers and guides instead of authorities. Parents also have significant roles to play. Learning is experiential and integrated, and the pace and pattern are determined by students in cooperation with their teachers. Time and space are open. Individuals are their own competition and are not compared through letter grades or test scores with others.

School/Family Partnerships

School/family partnerships provide programs for parental involvement at many levels, from decision-making roles to involvement in school and classroom activities to participation in children's educational development.

Sex Education

Sex education was placed in the school curriculum because of high rates of illegitimacy, venereal disease among students, the national increase in divorce, and massive evidence indicating that students are sexually active.

ALTERNATIVE CURRICULAR PROGRAMS

Multiple Subject Areas

The Accelerated Schools Project (K–8)

The accelerated schools approach, developed by Henry Levin of Stanford University, was first implemented in 1986 in two San Francisco Bay Area elementary schools. The Accelerated Schools Project has now reached over 1,300 schools. Unlike many programs for at-risk students, accelerated schools offer enriched curricula and instruction programs, the kind traditionally reserved for gifted-and-talented children. The program is intended to help at-risk students perform at grade level by the end of sixth grade. Members of the school community work together to transform every classroom into a "powerful learning" environment, where teachers are encouraged to think creatively, to explore their interests, and to inspire high levels of achievement. Transformation into an accelerated school begins with the entire school community examining its present situation through a process called Taking Stock. The school community then forges a shared vision of what it wants the school to be. By comparing the vision to its present situation, the school community identifies priority challenge areas. Then it sets about addressing those areas, working through an accelerated school governance structure, and analyzing problems through an Inquiry Process. The Inquiry Process is a systematic method that helps school communities clearly understand problems, find and implement solutions, and assess results.

Levin stressed the importance of socializing teachers from year to year in order to ensure continuity. His model is based on three principles:

1. Unity of purpose
2. Empowerment and responsibility
3. Building on strengths

Contact: Gene Chasin, Director, National Center for Accelerated Schools Project, University of Connecticut, 2131 Hillside Road, Unit 3224, Storrs, CT 06260. Telephone: 860-486-6330. Fax: 860-486-6348. Email: info@acceleratedschools.net. Web site: http://www.accelerated-schools.net.

America's Choice (K–12)

The America's Choice Comprehensive Design Network (begun in 1989 as the National Alliance for Restructuring Education) is a program of the National Center on Education and the Economy (NCEE), in Washington, DC—a leading source for standards-based education in the United States. There are 300 America's Choice schools in fourteen states. The America's Choice School Design is a comprehensive design for schools determined to get their students to high, internationally benchmarked standards in English, mathematics, and science. It is built on the America's Choice Performance Standards and Assessments Program, begun in 1992. America's Choice performance standards complement and extend the content standards that the states and many districts have developed. The America's Choice School Design incorporates a standards-based curriculum focused on the basics, conceptual mastery, and applications. It includes a design for quickly identifying students who are falling behind and bringing them back to standard, as well as a planning and management system for making the most efficient use of available resources to raise student performance quickly. The design focuses in the early years on literacy in reading, writing, and mathematics and at the high school level on a demanding academic core intended to get all students ready for college. Contact: Judith Curtis, National Center on

Education and the Economy, One Thomas Circle, Suite 700, Washington, DC 20005. Telephone: 202-783-3668. Fax: 202-783-3672. Email: jcurtis@ncee.org. Web site: http://www.ncee.org.

ATLAS Communities (PreK–12)

ATLAS Communities was formed in 1992 as a partnership of four leading educational organizations: the Education Development Center, the Coalition of Essential Schools, Project Zero, and the School Development Program. As a design for educational reform, it links elementary, middle, and high schools as partners in creating a pathway of teaching and learning from kindergarten through grade 12. Its goal is to create a coherent educational program for each student and to help all students develop the habits of mind, heart, and work that they will need as informed citizens and productive workers in the twenty-first century. ATLAS addresses dimensions of education that cut across the grade span as well as across the different constituencies involved in education. In ATLAS Communities, educators, students, their families, civic leaders, businesspeople, and cultural institutions all become deeply invested in the learning process. Contact: Sandra J. Wellens, Education Development Center, 55 Chapel Street, Newton, MA 02158. Telephone: 617-969-7100 or 617-618-2401. Fax: 617-969-3440. Email: atlas@ed.org. Web site: http://www.edc.org/ATLAS/.

Audrey Cohen College: Purpose-Centered Education (K–12)

Purpose-Centered Education was invented in 1970 for kindergarten through the bachelor's and master's level by Audrey Cohen College, an accredited, private, nonprofit institution of higher educators based in New York City. It focuses all student learning on the achievement of meaningful purposes that contribute to the larger global society. Twenty-four such purposes are addressed, generally one for each semester at each grade level. Contact: Janith Jorgan, Audrey Cohen College, 75 Varick Street, New York, NY 10013. Telephone: 212-343-1234, ext. 3400. Fax: 212-343-8472. Email: JanithJ@aol.com. Web site: http://www.audrey-cohen.edu.

AVAIL—Anchorage Vocational and Academic Institute of Learning

AVAIL, a four-year business-school partnership, started in 1991 with a grant from the U.S. Departments of Labor and Education in response to the high number of teenage mothers and Alaska native dropouts in Anchorage. AVAIL is located in two storefronts on the first floor of a parking garage in downtown Anchorage's largest shopping mall. The school, which has a GED program, is run as a nonprofit corporation in partnership with the business community. The curriculum emphasizes personality development, parenting skills, life stabilization, and employability skills. Contact: AVAIL—Anchorage Vocational and Academic Institute of Learning, 425 C Street, Anchorage, AK 99501. Telephone: 907-276-2557. Fax: 907-258-0527.

Basic Skill Builders (K–6)

Basic Skill Builders is a K–6 program based on the premise that in order for students to master higher-level skills, they must first have a solid foundation in core skills. It is also important that they be able to demonstrate their comprehension of core skills with both accuracy and speed.

Some students, particularly those considered at risk, do not respond well to approaches such as whole language or the discovery method. The Basic Skills Builders Project can be beneficial for such students, as it provides a set of classroom procedures that includes clear and high expectations, a sequenced curriculum, rapid exercises (designed to promote comprehension of core skills with both accuracy and speed), and direct and daily measurements of student progress. Together these tools help students build and maintain fluency in such basic skills as reading, math, spelling, handwriting, and grammar.

Five steps guide the Basic Skill Builders process: (1) Teachers select the skill and set expectations; (2) students complete Skill Builder Sheets through one-minute timed practices; (3) students score, record, and chart daily progress; (4) teachers review the charts and make instructional/curricular decisions; and (5) teachers, along with students, manage individual as well as group programs.

Basic Skill Builders is not a specific curriculum but, rather, an approach that incorporates accuracy and speed to reinforce a method or approach already being used. Because it is designed to supplement, not supplant, the core curriculum, it can be implemented across content areas to support and reinforce whatever is being taught. Students need twelve to fifteen minutes per day for skill practice. Contact: Ray Beck, Project Director, Basic Skill Builders Project, Sopris West, 4093 Specialty Place, Longmont, CO 80504. Telephone: 800-547-6747. Fax: 303-776-5934. Email: raybeck@sopriswest.com. Web site: http://www.sopriswest .com.

Center for Effective Schools (K–12)

The Effective Schools Model began with research conducted in the 1970s by Ron Edmonds and others on characteristics, or "correlates," that distinguish unusually effective schools from less effective ones. In 1986, Beverly Bancroft, Larry Lezotte, and Barbara Taylor organized the Center for Effective Schools (CES) at Michigan State University to help schools implement the correlates. Then, in 1995, the Center moved to Bloomington, Indiana, where it became the Phi Delta Kappa International Center for Effective Schools. (Lezotte, in the meantime, left to form a private company, Effective Schools Products.) The Effective Schools Model is based on the conviction that all children, regardless of race, socioeconomic status, or gender, can and will learn the required curriculum. The model provides a framework for school reform based on seven correlates, or guiding principles. These correlates, derived from empirical investigations and case studies of schools that have successfully taught the intended curriculum of basic skills to all students, are as follows:

1. A clear and focused mission of learning for all
2. Instructional leadership
3. High expectations for all stakeholders
4. Opportunity to learn and student time on task
5. Frequent monitoring of student progress
6. Safe and orderly environment for learning
7. Positive home/school/community relations

Under the Effective Schools Model, the individual school is viewed as the unit of improvement. Each school, through a faculty administrator-parent-community team-planning approach, uses student achievement data and the seven correlates to develop and implement a long-range improvement plan. In addition, the model promotes districtwide, systemic restructuring for continuous improvement. Contact: Center for Effective Schools, Phi Delta Kappa International, 408 North Union, P.O. Box 789, Bloomington, IN 47402-0789. Telephone: 800-766-1156. Fax: 812-339-0018. Email: effectiveschools@pdkintl.org. Web site: http://www.pdkintl.org.

Child Development Project (K–6)

The Developmental Studies Center of Oakland, California, created the Child Development Project (CDP) in 1981. The Child Development Project is an approach to school restructuring that revamps teaching, learning, school organization, school climate, and teachers' work environments to promote the intellectual, social, and ethical development of students. In particular, the CDP seeks to transform schools into communities where children feel cared for and learn to care in return—communities that help students develop the academic and practical skills needed to function productively in society, and the ethical and intellectual skills needed to function humanely and wisely. The program has five main components:

1. Literature-Based Reading and Language Arts
2. Collaborative Classroom Learning
3. Developmental Discipline
4. Parent Involvement
5. Schoolwide Activities

Contact: Denise Wood, Developmental Studies Center, 2000 Embarcadero, Suite 305, Oakland, CA 94606. Telephone: 510-533-0213. Fax: 510-464-3670. Email: dsc_information@devstu.org. Web site: http://www.devstu.org.

Coalition of Essential Schools (K–12)

Ted Sizer of Brown University founded the Coalition of Essential Schools in 1984. Twelve high schools in seven states joined during the same year. The Coalition of Essential Schools is a national network of schools and centers engaged in restructuring schools to promote better student learning. The schools share a set of ideas known as Common Principles, which guide their whole-school reform efforts. The Coalition was founded in an attempt to address the problems of the American high school as identified in the five-year Study of High Schools (1979–1984), which was chaired by Sizer. Teachers, Sizer concluded, often use practices they know do not support student learning, including fifty-minute periods, lectures, and drills. Partly as a result, students have few opportunities to think deeply about important issues or to produce work that means anything to them. To remedy the situation, Sizer formulated nine Common Principles that he believed would lead to better teaching and more genuine learning in American high schools:

1. The school's focus should be to help students learn to use their minds well.
2. Less is more. Students should achieve a thorough under-

standing of a few essential skills and subjects rather than a casual acquaintance with many.
3. The school's goals should apply to all students.
4. Teaching and learning should be personalized to the greatest possible extent.
5. The school's governing metaphors should be student-as-worker and teacher-as-coach.
6. To graduate, students should demonstrate mastery through public exhibitions rather than through credits, grades, and test scores.
7. The school's climate should be one of "unanxious expectation," trust, and decency.
8. Teachers and administrators should consider themselves generalists first and specialists second, assuming joint responsibility for all students.
9. The school should aim for the following administrative and budgetary targets: eighty students per teacher, adequate time for teachers to plan together, competitive salaries, and per pupil costs not to exceed that of traditional schools by more than 10 percent.

The Coalition recently added a tenth principle encouraging schools to honor diversity, challenge inequity, and model democratic practices. All of these core principles are intended to serve not as a blueprint for education reform but as a set of guidelines to help schools redesign themselves. Accordingly, the coalition imposes no specific curricular innovations or instructional techniques on member schools. Rather, it seeks out exemplars—schools that have done an especially good job of translating some or all of the principles into practice—and shares their approaches with schools. Contact: Hudi Podolsky, Coalition of Essential Schools, 1814 Franklin Street, Suite 700, Oakland, CA 94612. Telephone: 510-433-1451. Fax: 510-433-1455. Email: hpodolsky@ essentialschools.org. Web site: http://www.essentialschools.org/.

The College-Based Model

Many of the successful alternative programs in the United States are located on college campuses. The idea behind college-based programs is as much sociological as pedagogical. The socialization effect that results from integrating disruptive and disaffected high school students into the adult environment of the college campus acts as a "slingshot" for upward social mobility, with many students experiencing an educational and psychological catharsis. Indeed, when the environment in which learning takes place is altered, many chronically disruptive and disaffected high school students, who carry college identification cards and participate in a full range of college activities, begin to think of themselves as college students. Once their mind-set has changed, profound cognitive and affective growth often follows.

One of the largest and best-known alternative high schools is located on the campus of LaGuardia Community College, in the borough of Long Island, New York City. It opened in 1973–1974 as an alternative high school under the joint auspices of LaGuardia Community College and the New York Board of Education. Middle College High School, as the program is known, has achieved great success in helping disruptive, disaffected students turn their lives around. Despite the high-risk nature of the student body, nearly 75 percent of each graduating class enrolls in college. In its more than twenty-five-year history, Middle College High School has earned numerous citations and awards, and its excellence has been recognized by the Carnegie Foundation for the Advancement of Teaching, the National Commission on Excellence in Education, and the Rockefeller Foundation.

Despite the difficulties associated with establishing a college-based alternative program for at-risk students on a college campus, Middle College High School has enjoyed tremendous success. It has even been able to break down the political opposition that, in many cases, interferes with bringing such a program to fruition.

Community for Learning (K–12)

The Community for Learning (CFL) program was developed in 1990 by Margaret C. Wang, executive director of the Temple University Center for Research in Human Development and Education (CRHDE). It has been implemented in 188 urban and rural schools in the mid-Atlantic region and across the country. The classroom instruction component, Adaptive Learning Environments Model, was developed under the aegis of the National Follow Through Project.

The CFL program promotes the belief that school is not the only place where students learn. They learn in a variety of environments, including libraries, museums, workplaces, and their own homes. CFL links the school to these and other institutions, including health, social services, and law enforcement agencies. The idea is to provide a range of learning opportunities for students, to coordinate service delivery across organizations, and to foster a communitywide commitment to student success. The emphasis on collaboration extends into the class-

room itself, where regular teachers and specialists (e.g., special education teachers, Title I teachers, and school psychologists) work in teams
to meet the children's diverse academic and social needs. The instructional component of Community for Learning, known as the Adaptive
Learning Environments Model (ALEM), is an inclusive approach to
meeting the learning needs of individual students in regular classes, including students with special needs. As the name suggests, ALEM teachers adapt instruction for each student, using a variety of instructional
strategies and grouping patterns (e.g., whole class, small groups, individuals). Students are taught to take responsibility for planning and
monitoring their own progress. Learning tasks are divided into small
units and evaluated frequently by the teacher, who modifies learning
plans and instructional strategies on an ongoing basis. Students
progress at their own pace, advancing when ready and taking extra time
when necessary. Individualized attention is provided for those who are
not progressing as well as for those who are exceptionally talented and
ready for advanced lessons in given subjects. Each CFL school has a full-
time facilitator who oversees implementation and assists with training,
and districts with clusters of CFL schools generally appoint a project coordinator, who serves as the liaison between schools, the district office,
and the CRHDE. The project coordinator, the facilitator, and the principal work together to develop a site-specific plan that mobilizes the
school's resources in support of classroom and communitywide implementation. Contact: Frederick McCoy, Laboratory for Student Success,
Temple University Center for Research in Human Development and Education, 1301 Cecil B. Moore Avenue, Philadelphia, PA 19122-8091. Telephone: 800-892-5550. Fax: 215-204-5130. Email: lss@vm.temple.edu.
Web site: http://www.temple.edu.LSS.

Community Learning Centers (PreK–Adult)

Minnesota educator Wayne B. Jennings created Community Learning
Centers (CLC) in 1992 as one of the original New American Schools designs. The Community Learning Centers program is a comprehensive
school design that aims to dramatically increase the achievement of all
learners, preK–adult. The curriculum, based on achieving standards and
outcomes through powerful learning experiences, is defined as all the
experiences of the learner irrespective of place, time, or persons. The
school acts as the broker in arranging learning experiences within and
beyond its walls for real-world application. Learning experiences feature
modern learning principles and are child-centered, life-centered, and
brain-based (i.e., compatible with the power of the brain to assimilate

and organize learning). Community Learning Centers emphasize active learning environments such as media centers, production studios, discovery centers, theaters of learning, labs, community-based learning, and work stations for various computer applications. Each learner has a personal learning plan (PLP) for recording goals, attempts to reach goals, and progress toward goals. The PLP also defines each student's schedule of learning activities. Each learner has an advisor who meets periodically with the learner and parent(s) to review the goals. Students participate in decisions about the school program. Social services are integrated with education through agreements for collaborative services and shared costs, revenues, and location. Community Learning Centers, as headquarters for learning in the community, are open year round and for extended hours during each day. Adults are served through community education and other means, while parents and preschool children are served through early childhood and other family education programs. Contact: David Alley, Designs for Learning, 1745 University Avenue West, St. Paul, MN 55104. Telephone: 651-645-0200. Fax: 651-645-0240. Email: david@designlearn.com. Web site: http://www.designlearn.net.

Co-nect (K–12)

Members of the Educational Technologies Group at BBN Corporation founded Co-nect in 1992. Co-nect helps schools work through a structured process of comprehensive school reform. Its primary purpose is to boost academic achievement for all students in core subject areas, including mathematics, reading, writing, science, and the social sciences. The design is based on a set of five benchmarks derived from best practices in some of the most effective schools in the United States. These benchmarks are as follows:

1. High expectations for all students and schoolwide accountability for results
2. Schoolwide emphasis on practical application of academic knowledge to authentic problems
3. Use of assessments that measure actual student and school performance
4. Organization of the school into small learning communities (known as clusters)
5. Sensible use of the best available technology for everyone

Co-nect provides a combination of on-site and on-line assistance aimed at helping each participating school implement these design benchmarks within a period of three years. However, in order to make the most of the products and services available on-line, schools that work with Co-nect need to have computers in every classroom and on every teacher's desk as well as Internet access for every teacher.

The Co-nect Exchange, the organization's web site, delivers specialized professional training for teachers and leaders and supports the growth of a collaborative professional community among participating schools. The exchange offers a rich and growing array of tools, tele-collaborative projects and other curriculum resources, discussion areas, on-line training modules, and membership utilities. The site has been field-tested over a period of three years with thousands of teachers around the United States and is undergoing continuous development.

Other offerings include Co-nect Critical Friends (a national school visitation and quality review program), Co-nect Tech (a new program that helps school leaders design procedures for integrating technology into the curriculum), and an annual technology conference. Contact: Heather Corbitt, Co-nect, 1770 Massachusetts Avenue, Suite 301, Cambridge, MA 02140. Telephone: 877-726-6328. Fax: 617-955-3103. Email: info@co-nect.net. Web site: http://www.co-nect.net

Core Knowledge (K–8)

The Core Knowledge Foundation is an independent, nonprofit, nonpartisan organization founded in 1986 by E. D. Hirsch, Jr. The foundation's essential program, a core curriculum called the Core Knowledge Sequence, was first implemented in 1990. By September 2000, it was being used in 1,020 schools. Core Knowledge is an approach to curriculum based on Hirsch's work and described in his books *Cultural Literacy* and *The Schools We Need and Why We Don't Have Them.* The focus of the approach is on teaching a common core of concepts, skills, and knowledge that characterize a "culturally literate" and educated individual. The purposes of the approach are to increase academic performance as demonstrated on national and state norm- and criterion-referenced tests, to help narrow the gap between academic "haves" and "have-nots," and to build consensus among teachers, parents, and administrators. Core Knowledge is based on the principle that the grasp of a specific and shared body of knowledge will help students establish strong foundations for higher levels of learning. Developed through research examining successful national and local core curricula and through consultation with education experts in each subject area, the Core Knowledge sequence provides a consensus-based model of specific content guidelines for students in the elementary grades. It offers a progression of detailed grade-by-grade topics of knowledge in history, geography, mathematics, science, language arts, and fine arts, so that students build on knowledge from year to year in grades K–8. Instructional strategies are left to the discretion of teachers.

The Core Knowledge sequence typically comprises 50 percent of a school's curriculum; the other 50 percent allows schools to meet state and local requirements and teachers to contribute personal strengths. Teachers are also expected to provide effective instruction in reading and mathematics. The Core Knowledge curriculum is detailed in the Core Knowledge Sequence Content Guidelines for Preschool through Grade Eight and illustrated in a series of books entitled *What Your First-Grader Needs to Know, What Your Second-Grader Needs to Know* (etc.).

Parent involvement and consensus building contribute to the success of the Core Knowledge Sequence. Parents and community members are invited to become involved in terms of obtaining resources, planning activities, and developing a schoolwide plan that integrates the Core Knowledge content with district and state requirements and assessment instruments. Additionally, parents and teachers are encouraged to cooperate in planning learning goals and lesson plans. Contact: Constance Jones, Core Knowledge Foundation, 801 East High Street, Charlottesville, VA 22902. Telephone: 804-977-7550. Fax: 804-977-0021. Email: jonescore@aol.com. Web site: http://www.core knowledge.org.

Different Ways of Knowing (K–7)

Different Ways of Knowing (DwoK) is a multiyear professional development program for teachers, administrators, and other stakeholders that provides an integrated approach to curriculum instruction, assessment, and reporting. Recognizing that every child has talent and that children learn by doing, the DwoK curriculum provides clear and flexible guidelines for learner-centered classroom practice as well as interdisciplinary, nongraded modules that integrate social studies and history themes with mathematics, science, and the visual, performing, and media arts.

As a research-based and tested school reform initiative, DwoK attempts to engage and strengthen the linguistic, mathematical, artistic, and intuitive abilities of students in grades K–7. Specifically, it

- ⟶ Regards students as creative, capable learners and builds on their strengths
- ⟶ Provides a framework for hands-on, student-centered learning that guides classroom teaching as well as continuous professional development

- •• Uses compelling themes to develop the multiple intelligences of children
- •• Provides the best in children's literature, reference materials, study prints, transparencies, audio- and videotapes, and software from various publishers
- •• Adapts instruction to include various symbol systems as learning tools—not only language and numbers but also the visual, performing, and media arts
- •• Builds a classroom community, encourages shared responsibility for classroom management and learning, and promotes an understanding of democratic ideals
- •• Offers guidelines and resources to assess students' learning
- •• Invites active, collaborative reflection by both teachers and students
- •• Provides a common language for educators to use in creating an educational partnership among parents, school, district, and community

Contact: Sue Beauregard or Amy Berfield, The Galef Institute, 11050 Santa Monica Blvd., Third Floor, Los Angeles, CA 90025-3594. Telephone: 301-479-8883. Fax: 310-473-9720. Email: sue@galef.org or amy@galef.org.

Direct Instruction Model (K–6)

Zig Englemann's theory of instruction is that learning can be greatly accelerated in any endeavor if instructional presentations are clear, rule out likely misinterpretations, and facilitate generalizations. He and his associates have developed over fifty instructional programs based on this theory. Each program is shaped through field tryouts; student errors are carefully evaluated and lessons revised prior to publication. The lessons themselves are carefully scripted and tightly sequenced.

The comprehensive Direct Instruction Model incorporates teacher development and organizational components needed to optimize use of these programs. Through substantial training and in-class coaching, teachers in the lower grades learn to present highly interactive lessons to small groups. Students make frequent oral responses, and teachers monitor and correct errors immediately. Students are placed at appropriate instructional levels based on performance, so that those who learn rapidly are not held back and those who need additional assistance receive it. The model calls for inclusion of students with special needs except in the most extreme cases.

Although the Direct Instruction Model incorporates curricula for all areas, its reading, language arts, and math curricula can be implemented separately. Contact: Bob Fox, National Institute for Direct Instruction, 805 Lincoln Street, Eugene, OR 97401. Telephone: 541-485-1973. Fax: 541-683-7543. Or Bryan Wickman, Association for Direct Instruction, P.O. Box 10252, Eugene, OR 97440. Telephone: 541-485-1293. Fax: 541-683-7543.

Expeditionary Learning Outward Bound (K–12)

Expeditionary Learning Outward Bound (ELOB) focuses teaching and learning toward enabling all students to meet rigorous academic standards and character goals. Curriculum, instruction, assessment, school culture, and school structures are organized around producing high-quality student work in learning expeditions, in long-term, in-depth investigations of themes or topics that engage students in the classroom, and in the wider world through authentic projects, fieldwork, and service.

Learning expeditions are designed with clear learning goals that are aligned with district and state standards. Ongoing assessment is woven throughout each learning expedition, pushing students to increasingly higher levels of performance.

In Expeditionary Learning schools, teachers, students, and school leadership build a culture of high expectations for all students. Teachers work collaboratively in teams, with regular common-planning time to plan interdisciplinary expeditions, critique each others' expedition plans, and reflect on student work and teacher practices to improve curriculum and instruction. To strengthen relationships in the classroom, students stay with the same teacher or team of teachers for more than one year. Teachers and school leadership participate in a sequence of professional development activities. Schools assess the progress each year and use ELOB benchmarks to drive improvement. Contact: Jane Heidt, Expeditionary Learning Outward Bound, 122 Mt. Auburn Street, Cambridge, MA 02138. Telephone: 617-576-1260. Fax: 617-576-1340. Email: janeheidt@worldnet.att.net. Web site: http://hugse1.harvard.edu/~elob.

Foxfire (Foxfire Fund, Inc.)

The Foxfire approach to teaching and learning is implemented through teacher networks that promote active learner-centered approaches to education and foster frequent interaction between students and their local community. Teachers use the Foxfire approach to bring new excitement and meaning to the work they and their students do together. Guided by eleven Core Practices and supported through formal and informal connections to Foxfire, these teachers create classrooms with strong community connections where learning grows out of student interest and where high standards for achievement are both set and met. In the Foxfire approach, learning environments are characterized by student involvement and action, thoughtful reflection and rigorous assessment, imagination and problem solving, applications beyond the classroom for what is learned, and meaningful connections to the community. The Core Practices were tested and refined by hundreds of teachers working mostly in isolated and diverse classrooms around the country. When implemented, they define an active, learner-centered, community-focused approach to teaching. They also serve as highly effective, lifelong tools for self-reflection, assessment, and ongoing professional development. These Core Practices are as follows:

1. The work that teachers and learners do together is infused from the beginning with learner choice, design, and revision.
2. The academic integrity of the work that teachers and learners do together is clear.
3. The role of the teacher is that of facilitator and collaborator.
4. The work is characterized by active learning.
5. Peer teaching, small-group work, and teamwork are all consistent features of classroom activities.
6. There is an audience beyond the teacher for learner work.
7. New activities spiral gracefully out of the old, incorporating lessons learned from past experiences and building on skills and understandings that can now be amplified.
8. Reflection is an essential activity that takes place at key points throughout the work.
9. Connections between the classroom work, the surrounding communities, and the world beyond the community are clear.
10. Imagination and creativity are encouraged in the completion of learning activities.
11. The work that teachers and learners do together includes rigorous, ongoing assessment and evaluation.

Contact: The Foxfire Fund, Inc., P.O. Box 541, Mountain City, GA 30562. Telephone: 706-746-5828. Fax: 706-746-5829. Email: foxfire@foxfire.org. Web site: http://www.foxfire.org.

Higher Order Thinking Skills (HOTS)

HOTS is a pullout program that develops students' higher-order thinking skills, using technology and Socratic methods to replace the drill and practice approach employed in many Title I programs (grades 4–6). This program removes children from regular classrooms for needed instruction. Contact: HOTS, P.O. Box 42620, Tucson, AZ 85733. Telephone: 800-999-0153. Fax: 520-795-8837. Email: info@HOTS.org. Web site: http://www.HOTS.org.

International Baccalaureate Organization

The International Baccalaureate is a broad liberal arts program that challenges high school students to work at the college level in every academic subject. Many program advocates claim that it has been tremendously successful at raising the academic standards and level of achievement in both private and public schools. The idea for International Baccalaureate began in international schools, where students, from many countries, typically attend through the twelfth or thirteenth grade. These international schools had the awesome task of preparing students to return to colleges and universities in their native countries. The problem was addressed through development of a standardized two-year curriculum and a set of examinations that would lead to accreditation acceptable to any college or university in any country. The curriculum was first used at international schools in Copenhagen, Frankfurt, New York, Barcelona, and a few other cities. Contact: George Walker, Director General, International Baccalaureate Organization, Route des Morillons 15, Grand-Saconnex, Geneva, CH-1218 Switzerland. Telephone: +41 22 791 7740. Fax: +41 22 791 0277. Email: ibhq@ibo.org. Web site: http://www.ibo.org.

Liberty School

Liberty School is a learning community in Blue Hill, Maine, that combines academic skills with artistic work and other educational opportunities that enable young people to meet the demands of the twenty-first century. The curriculum is based on the belief that students learn best in cooperative rather than competitive environments and that education must be seen as a part of life and not preparation for life. Contact: Liberty School, P.O. Box 857, South Street, Blue Hill, ME 04614. Telephone: 207-374-2886. Fax: 207-374-5918.

Modern Red Schoolhouse (K–12)

The Modern Red Schoolhouse (MRSh) works in partnership with schools throughout the country to reinvent the virtues of the little red schoolhouse in a modern context. At an MRSh school, students master a rigorous curriculum, develop character, and promote the principles of democratic government. These elements of the traditional red school-house are then combined with innovative teaching methodologies and student groupings, flexibility in organizing instruction and deploying resources, and advanced technology as a learning and instructional management tool.

The core principle of MRSh is that all students can and will reach high academic standards. Mastery of subject matter is the only accept-able goal, regardless of a child's background, learning style, and pace. Because students learn at different rates and in different ways, instruc-tional methodologies and time spent on lessons vary. Thus, students progress through the curriculum in the ways that are best suited to their individual strengths and abilities.

The MRSh strives to help all students achieve high standards through the construction of a standards-driven curriculum, traditional and performance-based assessments, effective organizational patterns, professional-development programs, and effective community-involve-ment strategies.

The primary tool for monitoring continuing progress is the Indi-vidual Education compact, an agreement negotiated by the students, parents, and teacher. This "educational road map" establishes measura-ble goals, details parents' and teachers' responsibility for helping stu-dents achieve, and lists services that the school, parents, or community should provide. Contact: Karen White, Production Manager, Modern Red Schoolhouse, 208 23rd Avenue North, Nashville, TN 37203. Tele-phone: 651-320-8804. Fax: 615-320-5366.

National Writing Project

The National Writing Project is a program designed to improve student writing by providing professional development opportunities to teachers and stressing the role of the teacher as expert. It can be utilized in several departments at high schools and as part of language arts instruction in elementary schools. Contact: National Writing Project–University of California, 2105 Bancroft, #1042, Berkeley, CA 94720. Telephone: 510-642-0963. Fax: 510-642-4545. Email: nwp@writingproject.org. Web site: http://www.writingproject.org.

Paideia (K–12)

Paideia's purpose is to prepare each student for earning a living, being a citizen of this country and the world, and pursuing life-long learning. Paideia educators believe that high academic achievement should be expected of all students, that it is society's duty to provide this opportunity, and that universal, high-quality education is essential to democracy.

Instructional goals are based on acquisition of knowledge, development of intellectual skills, and enlarged understanding of ideas and fvalues. These are addressed through three instructional approaches:

1. *Didactic instruction,* which involves teacher lecturing that provides opportunities for "acquisition of knowledge"
2. *Coaching,* or one-on-one instruction from the teacher, which takes place while students work independently at their own level and pace
3. *Small-group seminars,* which generally use the Socratic method of questioning to explore issues in greater depth

Schoolwide restructuring is necessary to fully implement all three instructional pieces, as Socratic seminars often require longer class periods (up to two hours each) and coaching may call for smaller classes enabling teachers to spend more time with individuals. The National Paideia Center helps partner schools align their program goals and instructional practices to achieve local standards for students. Contact: Terry Roberts, National Paideia Center, School of Education CB#8045, University of North Carolina, Chapel Hill, NC 27599-8045. Telephone: 919-962-7379. Fax: 919-962-7381. Email: npc@unc.edu. Web site: http:// www.unc.edu/paideia/.

Roots and Wings (PreK–6)

The purpose of Roots and Wings is to create well-structured curricular and instructional approaches for all elementary subjects, pre-kindergarten through grade 6, based on well-evaluated components and well-researched principles of instruction, assessment, classroom management, motivation, and professional development.

Roots and Wings builds on the Success for All program, initiated in 1987, which provides research-based curricula for students in pre-kindergarten through grade 6 in reading, writing, and language arts, one-on-one tutoring for primary-grade students struggling in reading, and extensive family support services. To these, Roots and Wings adds Math Wings, a practical, constructivist approach to mathematics for grades 1–5, and WorldLab, an integrated approach to social studies and science emphasizing simulations and group investigations for grades 1–5.

Roots refers to the strategies that every child needs in order to meet world-class standards in language skills, reading skills, and health. It involves early intervention for at-risk children, research-based curricula with extensive training support, one-on-one tutoring, integrated health and social services, and family support. *Wings* refers to a curriculum and instruction strategy designed to let children soar. Each school has a full-time facilitator to help implement the program, a Family Support Team to foster community and parent involvement, and a Building Advisory Team to evaluate the entire school climate and advise the principal on general direction and goals. Contact: Roots and Wings, Johns Hopkins University, 3505 North Charles Street, Baltimore, MD 21218. Telephone: 800-548-4998. Fax: 410-516-0543. Email: info@ successforall.com. Web site: http://www.successfulforall.com.

Reading/Language Arts

Breakthrough to Literacy (K–2)

Breakthrough to Literacy focuses on teaching pre-kindergarten through second-grade students to relate oral language and pictures to print. Stories are provided at each child's level of language/literacy development, along with access to direct and explicit instruction for phonemic awareness. The latter is achieved through the use of "big books," pupil books, and computer modules.

The typical Breakthrough classroom focuses on one "big book" per week. The book is read for ten to fifteen minutes per day, and during each session a different objective is covered. On Monday, for example, the objective is introduction. The teacher introduces the author and illustrator, reads a passage in the book to the students, asks them what they liked or disliked about it, and then reads it again. On Tuesday, the objective is review. The teacher asks the children to recall what they learned the previous day and to role-play based on the story's characters. On Wednesday, when integration is the focus, the children are asked to relate what they've learned to something in their own lives. And so on through Friday.

Children also spend fifteen to twenty minutes per day at the computer making connections between what they have "read" and what they see on the computer screen, and vice versa. When the teacher chooses a new "big book," the children will already have seen many of its words on the computer several times. This combination of literature-based instruction and instructional technology is intended to help children develop better phonemic awareness, enhance their vocabulary development, and promote an understanding of sound-symbol relationships. Children progress through the program at their own pace as a result of daily one-on-one sessions with teachers and computers. The program does not end in the classroom, however, as parents are urged to read stories to their children every night. Contact: Henry Layne, The Wright Group, 19201 120th Avenue NE, Bothell, WA 98011. Telephone: 800-523-2371, ext. 3433. Fax: 425-486-7704.

Carbo Reading Styles Program (K–8)

The philosophy behind the Carbo Reading Styles Program (RSP) is to increase student literacy by making the process of learning to read so easy and enjoyable that students become motivated, confident, fluent readers in a short period of time. Research conducted by Marie Carbo and her colleagues indicates that students have different learning styles for reading, or "reading styles," that predispose them to learn far more easily with particular reading techniques. In other words, since children's individual strengths and interests vary widely, no single reading method is best for all children. Teachers must therefore master a wide range of reading strategies so that their reading program can accommodate the diversity of their students' reading styles. For example, many poor readers are global, tactile, kinesthetic learners. An ideal reading program for these youngsters would include large amounts of activity and holistic reading methods, such as choral reading, echo reading, and recorded books.

Implementation of RSP requires that schools use several key materials and strategies, including the Reading Style Inventory (RSI) and the Carbo Recorded-Book Methods. The RSI provides teachers with a compact profile of each student's key strengths and weaknesses, listing the top reading methods, materials, and strategies that will best meet his or her instructional needs. The RSI also includes a three-page, in-depth profile of each student.

The Carbo Recorded-Book Method is another integral part of RSP. After identifying books and other reading materials of high interest to students, the teacher divides these materials into small segments and records them onto a tape in short phrases at a slightly slower speed than normal. The students then listen repeatedly to the recordings, later reading the passages aloud to the teacher. Carbo believes that such recordings enable "any student to read immediately" and help to build children's confidence. Also, students are reading something they find genuinely interesting. Contact: Marian S. Gordon, National Reading Styles Institute, P.O. Box 737, Syosset, NY 11791. Telephone: 800-331-3117. Fax: 516-921-5591. Email: nrsi@mindspring.com. Web site: http://www.nrsi.com.

Reading Recovery (Grade 1)

Reading Recovery is an intensive early-intervention program designed by Marie M. Clay to assist children who are having difficulty learning to read and write. Their regular classroom instruction is supplemented with daily one-on-one, thirty-minute lessons for twelve to twenty weeks with a specially trained teacher. As part of this tutorial, students develop self-monitoring strategies. On average, Reading Recovery students make enough progress within twelve to fourteen weeks to be discontinued from the tutorial. The majority of the children who participate in this program also progress satisfactorily without further assistance.

First-grade children who score in the lowest 20 percent of their class (based on individual measures of assessment and teacher judgment) are eligible to participate. Reading Recovery lessons provide such children with individualized instruction that focuses on their strengths, using experiences with books and stories, accelerated learning expectations, and strategies that help them become independent learners. Each day, Reading Recovery teachers record the details of every lesson they provide. Instruction continues until participants can read at or above the class average and demonstrate the use of independent reading and writing strategies. These students are then "discontinued," providing the opportunity for other children to enter Reading Recovery.

Typically, Reading Recovery teachers spend a half-day teaching Reading Recovery lessons and a half-day in other instructional activities. Each teacher is expected to serve at least eight children over the course of one academic year. Contact: Jean F. Bussell, Executive Director, Reading Recovery Council of North America, 1929 Kenny Road, Suite 100, Columbus, OH 43210-1069. Telephone: 614-292-1795. Fax: 614-292-4404. Email: bussell.4@osu.edu.

Success for All (PreK–6)

The Success for All Foundation (SFAF) is a not-for-profit organization dedicated to the development, evaluation, and dissemination of proven reform models for preschool, elementary, and middle schools, especially those serving at-risk children. Instead of being age-grouped, students are grouped by reading level and experience a core reading and language arts curriculum. School personnel are also reorganized to allow for special reading tutors who work with individual children experiencing difficulty. Cooperative learning is emphasized, as is at-home reading every night. Family support teams that include teachers, social workers, and parent liaisons help to facilitate closer cooperation between home and school. As of spring 2000, the Success for All Foundation was serving about 1,550 elementary schools in forty-eight states and assisting related projects in five other countries.

The SFAF restructures elementary schools, usually high-poverty Title I schools, to ensure that every child learns to read in the early grades.

The idea is to prevent reading problems from appearing in the first place and to intervene swiftly and intensively if such problems do appear.

As noted, students are grouped according to reading level, and they read for one ninety-minute period per day. The rest of the day they are assigned to regular age-grouped grades. Every eight weeks, teachers assess the students' progress using formal measures of reading comprehension as well as observation and judgment. The assessments determine change in the composition of the reading groups and help identify students in need of extra assistance. These students receive one-on-one tutoring for twenty minutes per day at times other than regular reading or math periods. First-graders get priority for tutoring. Tutors are generally certified teachers, although well-qualified paraprofessionals may tutor children with less severe reading problems.

Because parental involvement is considered essential to student success, each Success for All school forms a Family Support Team that encourages parents to read to their children, involves parents in school activities, and intervenes when problems at home interfere with a child's progress in school. The operation of Success for All is coordinated at each school by a full-time facilitator who helps plan the program and coach teachers. In addition, an advisory committee composed of the principal, facilitator, teacher and parent representatives, and family support staff meets regularly to review the progress of the program. Contact: Success for All, Johns Hopkins University, 3505 North Charles Street, Baltimore, MD 21218. Telephone: 800-548-4998. Fax: 410-516-0543. Email: infor@successforall.com. Web site: http://successforall.com.

Mathematics

Comprehensive School Mathematics Program (K–6)

The Comprehensive School Mathematics Program (CSMP/21) is a K–6 elementary mathematics program that focuses on problem solving and concept development. It is designed to help even very young children grasp mathematical concepts and ideas through the use of varied situational teaching methods. These include graphic, nonverbal "languages," colorful and unusual manipulatives, and even fantasy stories to activate the imagination of young children and engage them in an exploration of mathematics.

CSMP emphasizes a three-pronged approach to learning that involves (1) understanding content and applications, (2) developing techniques and processes for learning content, and (3) applying the appropriate means to solve problems. The idea is that mathematics is best learned through applications that are appropriate to students' levels of understanding and natural interests. Contact: Claire Heidema, McRel-CSMP, 2550 South Parker Road, Suite 500, Aurora, Colorado 80014. Telephone: 303-632-5520. Fax: 303-337-3005. Email: cheidema@mcrel.org. Web site: http://www.mcrel.org/products/csmp.

Connected Mathematics Project (6–8)

Connected Mathematics Project (CMP) is a mathematics curriculum for middle school students that is designed to foster knowledge of and skill in using the vocabulary, forms of representation, materials, tools, techniques, and intellectual methods of the discipline of mathematics. CMP is intended to enable students to define and solve math problems with reason, insight, inventiveness, and technical proficiency. Its overall project goal is to enable all students to reason and communicate proficiently in mathematics.

CMP's development, which has focused on the tight alignment of curriculum, instruction, and assessment, is guided by five instructional themes:

1. *Mathematical Investigations.* The curriculum is organized around "big ideas" in mathematics—namely, clusters of important, related mathematical concepts, processes, ways of thinking, skills, and problem-solving strategies that are studied in depth with the development of deep understanding as a goal.
2. *Reasoning.* Students grow in their ability to reason effectively with information represented in pictorial, graphic, numeric, symbolic, and verbal forms, and learn to move flexibly among these representations.
3. *Teaching for Understanding.* Instruction emphasizes inquiry and discovery of mathematical ideas through investigation of rich problem situations.
4. *Connections.* The curriculum not only emphasizes significant connections among various mathematical topics and problems in other school subjects but also offers an opportunity to revisit and deepen understanding of ideas over time.
5. *Technology.* Selection of mathematical goals and teaching approaches reflects the information-processing capabilities of calculators and computers and the fundamental changes these tools are making in the way people learn and apply their knowledge.

During grades 6 through 8, CMP students develop knowledge and skill within five mathematical strands: number, geometry and measurement, probability, statistics, and algebra. Outcomes are specified for each of these areas by the end of grade 8.

CMP is a problem-centered curriculum. It is organized into units that address mathematical ideas through a series of "investigations," each of which contains problems for teachers and students to explore. As students solve a series of connected problems, they develop deep understandings of important mathematical concepts embedded within the problems. Contact: Elizabeth Phillips, Connected Mathematics Project, A715 Wells Hall, Michigan State University, East Lansing, MI 48824. Telephone: 517-432-2870. Fax: 517-432-2872. Email: cmp@math.msu.edu. Web site: www.mth.msu.edu/cmp.

MATH Connections (9–12)

MATH Connections was created by a diverse team of curriculum developers comprising mathematicians; scientists; educators in the fields of math, science, and technology; and businesspeople. Its overall mission is to develop a core curriculum for grades 9–12 that opens the concepts of higher mathematics to all students and inspires new interest and excitement in mathematics for both students and faculty.

MATH Connections is a three-year core curriculum usually used in grades 9–11 or 10–12. It integrates the concepts of higher mathematics—such as algebra, geometry, probability, statistics, and trigonometry—into a package that is interesting for all students. The project uses the National Council of Teachers of Mathematics (NCTM) standards as a guide for student performance, teacher professional development, and alternative student assessment. Technology is integrated into the curriculum with graphic calculators and computers, which students use to investigate concepts in greater depth and breadth, make conjectures, and validate findings.

Math Connections uses a common thematic thread, blending many mathematical topics that traditionally have been taught separately to emphasize the interconnectedness among mathematical ideas. The project is built around connections, including those between mathematics and the real world of people, business, and everyday life; between mathematics and science; and between mathematics and other subjects such as history, geography, and language arts. The project focuses on four aspects of mathematics: (1) mathematics as problem solving, (2) mathematics as communication, (3) mathematics as reasoning, and (4) mathematics as making connections.

Each of the three years of the program is built around a general theme that links the topics covered. The three themes are (1) Data, Numbers, and Patterns, (2) Shapes in Space, and (3) Mathematical Models, and six textbooks are used, each for a half-year. The 100-plus assessments built into the curriculum include written, oral, and demonstration formats. In addition to assessing students' ability to perform standard procedures, such as solving equations, the assessments measure students' approaches to nonroutine problems taken from the real world as well as their understanding of mathematical concepts and how they relate to each other. Contact: June G. Ellis, Math Connections: A Secondary Mathematics Core Curriculum, 31 Woodland Street, Suite 9R, Hartford, CT 06105. Telephone: 860-244-1900. Email: mathconx@aol.com. Web site: www.mathconnections.com.

Project SEED (Elementary)

Project SEED is a nonprofit national mathematics program that uses a unique Socratic group discovery teaching methodology to show elementary school students the joy and fascination involved in learning advanced conceptual mathematics. Programs are currently operating in Camden (Philadelphia), Dallas, Detroit, Indianapolis, Milwaukee, and the San Francisco Bay Area. In its forty-year history of success and consistent quality, the project has introduced many higher-mathematics topics to students who traditionally would not have opportunities to experience such content. The outreach occurs through local school districts to communities where too many children drop out of school or end up without academic skills that would otherwise carry them successfully into careers in twenty-first-century science, computers, and technology. Project SEED's goal for all students is to ensure success both in academics and in an increasingly technological future. Contact: Howard Baker, 2961 Yorkship Square (2nd floor), Camden, NJ 08104. Telephone: 214-954-4432 or (toll free) 888-628-SEED. Fax: 214-954-0507. Email: pseed2e3@airmail.net.

University of Chicago School Mathematics Project (K–12)

The University of Chicago School Mathematics Project (UCSMP) seeks to improve mathematics education for the vast majority of students in grades K–12. The project began with research on the teaching of mathematics through real-life applications, including the examination of mathematics curricula taught in other countries. UCSMP has gone on to develop innovative materials for the teaching of mathematics as well as for teacher training programs. It continues to engage in extensive evaluations of its own work.

UCSMP develops its materials with three key goals in mind: to update mathematics curricula, to upgrade student achievement, and to increase the number of students continuing their mathematics education beyond algebra and geometry. The project also has three major components: elementary, secondary, and resource development. USCMP materials, including textbooks, teacher resource kits, and workbooks, are published by Everyday Learning Corporation and Scott, Foresman/Addison-Wesley. Translations of foreign textbooks and evaluation reports are published by the project itself as well as by the National Council of Teachers of Mathematics (NCTM) and the American Mathematical Society.

UCSMP's K–6 curriculum helps children make the transition from intuition and concrete operations to abstractions and symbol-processing skills. In the early stages of this curriculum, the program emphasizes playful verbal interactions and manipulative activities, helping to create a mathematics-rich atmosphere in the classroom and to lay the groundwork for a greater breadth and depth of mathematical understanding. The curriculum in UCSMP's secondary texts, for grades 7–12, stresses the use of applications, readings, problem solving, and technology. Both the elementary and secondary components of UCSMP actively involve teachers in the writing of the materials. Contact: Carol Siegel, UCSMP, University of Chicago, 5835 South Kimbark, Chicago, IL 60637. Telephone: 773-702-1130. Fax: 773-702-0248. Email: ucsmp@ cicero.uchicago,edu.

Science

Developmental Approaches in Science, Health and Technology (DASH) (K–6)

DASH provides a comprehensive, integrated, inquiry-based program in science, health, and technology for grades K–6. Students with a wide range of backgrounds, learning styles, and abilities learn concepts and skills through authentic technological and scientific exploration, investigation, and explanation. The sequential, spiral curriculum reflects both children's acquisition of concepts about how the world operates and the historical development of the sciences. DASH also connects school studies to the world of daily living, reinforcing lessons and allowing students to apply what they learn.

DASH students are technologists and scientists working with and making sense out of natural and, eventually, experimental phenomena. Seventy-five to 80 percent of student time is involved in hands-on activity, with the remainder spent reflecting, recording, and reporting. Over 650 interconnected activities progressively support students' construction of the basic concepts and skills of science, health, and technology. For instance, studies in the science component for grades K–3 engage students in observing, categorizing, and generalizing about the natural world (weather, plants, animals, and astronomy). And from grade 4 on, students meet anomalies that stimulate them to experiment, create research designs, and test their own hypotheses.

The program is organized thematically at each grade level into ten clusters, including Food and Nutrition, Energy and Communication, and Matter, Space, and Construction. Assessment is built into each lesson, is shared between teacher and student to develop self-assessment capacity, and includes student-generated products that go into student portfolios. The use of student research teams fosters collaborative learning. Science kits are not used; instead, students make much of their own equipment through readily available and recyclable materials, thereby reducing costs and increasing students' sense that science learning is accessible.

DASH addresses the standards and goals for science education set by the National Research Council, the American Association for the Advancement of Science, and the National Center for Improving Science Education. Contact: Donald B. Young, Associate Director, Curriculum Research and Development Group, University of Hawaii at Manoa, 1776 University Avenue, Honolulu, HI 96822. Telephone: 800-799-8111. Email: young@hawaii.edu. Web site: www2.hawaii.edu/crdg/science/dash/dash.html.

Foundational Approaches in Science Teaching (FAST) (Middle School)

The Foundational Approaches in Science Teaching (FAST) program is a sequence of three inquiry science courses especially designed for middle school students. These courses emphasize the foundational concepts and methods of the physical, biological, and earth sciences. Student investigations are organized into three strands: (1) physical science, (2) ecology, and (3) "relational study," which integrates the study of science, technology, and society. The goal of FAST is to develop scientifically literate students who have the background necessary for understanding environmental concerns in our technological society as well as the basic tools for further study in science. Its main objectives are to develop relevant thinking skills, laboratory skills, and knowledge of core science concepts.

FAST students develop a scientific worldview by doing science—generating questions, designing and carrying out experiments, collecting and analyzing data, researching, drawing conclusions based on evidence, writing reports, and communicating findings. They work in small collaborative groups that function as research teams, becoming producers rather than just receivers of information. The teacher is the research director and coordinator, a colleague who stimulates and facilitates ever-deeper probing into problems. Through the process of inquiry and research, student teams generate the theoretical content of the program.

As scientists-to-be, students design many of their own experiments. In a physics unit, for example, students formulate theoretical models of heat and light and test their models; for other investigations, they invent and build tools and instruments. As technologists-to-be, students apply recently mastered scientific principles, such as the concepts of buoyancy and density in designing and constructing a working model of a submarine. By experiencing multiple roles (scientists, engineer, technologist, politician, and citizen), students practice and reinforce skills from many areas, including math, written and oral communications, and social studies.

FAST meets the standards and goals for science education set by the National Research Council, the American Association for the Advancement of Science, and the National Center for Improving Science Education. Contact: Donald B. Young, Associate Director, Curriculum Research and Development Group, University of Hawaii at Manoa, 1776 University Avenue, Honolulu, HI 96822. Telephone: 800-799-8111. Email: young@hawaii.edu. Web site: http://www2.hawaii.edu/crdg/science/fast/FAST.html.

GALAXY Classroom Science (K–5)

GALAXY Classroom Science is an inquiry-based, student-centered curriculum and instructional approach supported by a global interactive network of elementary schools, which are linked by satellite and computer technologies. Curricula consist of three one-year units: (1) Fixer Upper for grades 1 or 2, (2) S.N.O.O.P.S. for grades 4 or 5, and (3) Finders, Seekers, Science Keepers for kindergarten or grade 1. There is also a one-year language arts unit called The House for grades 3, 4, or 5.

GALAXY Classroom Science seeks to improve science learning for all students by giving teachers tools to create learning environments that stimulate and nourish inquiry-based learning. Through the "hands-on/minds-on" curriculum, students learn specified core science concepts and practice using scientific thinking processes (e.g., observing, communicating, organizing, and comparing). The science units are organized around themes that follow the National Science Education Standards on science concepts and processes appropriate for students at each level. Additional underlying principles include constructivist thinking, cultural diversity, authentic inquiry, relevance for all students, and connection to state and national standards to improve student performance.

The themes of this program, such as "Science Is Doing" and "What-Ifs to Use and Compare Materials," are developed through television broadcasts and classroom hands-on activities. In each fifteen-minute video episode, a diverse group of children model for students how curiosity, observation, comparing, and problem solving can help them construct knowledge about science from the content and context of their lives. Students in the classroom investigate questions posed by the episode and attempt to answer them through a variety of activities. Teachers facilitate and encourage student collaboration, open-ended exploration, testing of ideas, and active involvement in the process of discovery. Students then use fax or email technology to communicate their findings to the television show and to the recipients of student bulletins sent to all GALAXY classrooms. Contact: Marci Schwenn, EMG GALAXY Classroom, 6710 East Camelback Road, Scottsdale, AZ 852251. Telephone: 800-303-9070, ext. 1. Fax: 602-481-6484. Email: Marci. Schwenn@emg.com.

REFERENCES

Adler, M. (1983). *Paideia: Problems and Possibilities.* New York: Macmillan.

Association for Supervision and Curriculum Development (ASCD) Student Achievement Research Panel (1995). *Educating Everybody's Children: Diverse Teaching Strategies for Diverse Learners,* edited by R. W. Cole. Alexandria, VA.

Black Alliance for Educational Options (2000, December 1). BAEO Manifesto. Available online at http://www.schoolchoiceinfo.org/baeo/index.gsp.

Blair, L. (1998). *Transforming Learning with Block Scheduling: A Guide for Principals.* Thousand Oaks, CA: Corwin Press.

Bransford, J. D., et al. (1986). "Teaching Thinking and Problem Solving: Research Foundations." *American Psychologist, 41*(10), 1078–1089.

Brookfield, S. D. (1987). *Developing Critical Thinkers: Challenging Adults to Explore Alternative Ways of Thinking and Acting.* San Francisco: Jossey-Bass.

Butler, K. A. (1984). *Learning and Teaching Styles: In Theory and Practice.* Maynard, MA: Gabriel Systems.

Canady, R. L., and Rettig, M. D. (1995). "The Power of Innovative Scheduling." *Educational Leadership, 53*(3), 4–10.

Carbo, M., and Hodges, H. (1988). "Learning Styles Strategies Can Help Students at Risk." *Teaching Exceptional Children, 20*(4), 55–58.

Cotton, K. (1996). *School Size, School Climate, and Student Performance.* Close-up #20. Portland, OR: Northwest Regional Educational Laboratory.

Catterall, J. (1995). *Different Ways of Knowing 1991–1994: National Longitudinal Study, Final Report, Program Effect on Students and Teachers.* Executive Summary. Los Angeles: Galef Institute.

Comer, J. (1996). *Rallying the Whole Village: The Comer Process for Reforming Education.* New York: Teachers College Press.

Dawson, J. (1987). "Helping At-Risk Students in Middle School." *NASSP Bulletin,* pp. 84–88.

Dezmon, B. (Ed.) (1999). *Toward Achievement: Programs and Practices.* Baltimore: Maryland State Department of Education.

Dooley, C. (1997). "Problem-Centered Learning Experiences: Exploring Past, Present, and Future Perspectives." *Roper Review, 19*(4), 192–195.

Farber, P. J. (2001). The New Face of Home schooling. Available online at http://www.edletter.org/past/issues/2001-ma/homeschool.shtml.

Fowlery, W. J., Jr. (1995). "School Size and Student Outcomes." In H. J. Walberg (Series Ed.) and B. Levin, W. J. Fowler, Jr., and H. J. Walberg (Vol. Eds.), *Advances in Educational Productivity: Vol. 5. Organizational Influences on Educational Productivity,* pp. 3–25. Greenwich, CT: JAI Press.

Foxfire Fund, Inc. (1992). "The Foxfire Approach: Perspective and Core Practices." In Foxfire Fund, Inc., *Hands On.* Mountain City, GA: Author.

Gardner, H. (1983). *Frames of Mind: The Theory of Multiple Intelligences.* New York: Basic Books.

Gilligan, C., Lyons, N. P., and Hanmer, T. J. (1990). *Making Connections.* Cambridge, MA: Harvard University Press.

Good, T., and Brophy, J. (1994). *Looking in Classrooms,* 6th ed. New York: Basic Books.

Goodlad, J., and Anderson, R. (1963). *The Nongraded Elementary School.* New York: Harcourt, Brace and World.

Hirsch, Jr., E. D. (1993). "The Core Knowledge Curriculum: What's Behind Its Success." *Educational Leadership, 50*(8), 23–35.

Hodges, H. (1994). "A Consumer's Guide to Learning Styles Programs: An Expert's Advice on Selecting and Implementing Various Models in the Classroom." *The School Administrator, 51*(1), 14–18.

Holt, J. (1964). *How Children Fail.* London: Putnam.

_____. (1967). *How Children Learn.* London: Putnam.

Hopfenberg, W. S., Levin, H. H., and Associates (1993). *The Accelerated Schools Resource Guide.* San Francisco: Jossey-Bass.

Jacobs, H. H. (1991). "Planning for Curriculum Integration." *Educational Leadership, 49*(2), 27–28.

Koetzsch, R. E. (1997). *Parents' Guide to Alternatives in Education.* Boston: Shambhala Publications.

Levin, H. M. (1988a). "Structuring Schools for Greater Effectiveness with Educationally Disadvantaged or At-Risk Students." Paper presented at the annual meeting of the American Educational Research Association, New Orleans, LA.

_____. (1988b). *Accelerated Schools for At-Risk Students.* CPRE Research Report Series RR–010. New Brunswick, NJ: Center for Policy Research in Education, Eagleton Institute of Politics, Rutgers, State University of New Jersey.

Lewis, A., and Steinberger, E. (1991). *Learning Styles: Putting Research and Common Sense into Practice.* Arlington, VA: American Association of School Administrators.

MacMullen, M. M. (1996). *Taking Stock of a School Reform Effort: A Research Collection and Analysis.* Providence, RI: Annenberg Institute for School Reform.

Marzano, R. J., Brandt, R. S., Hughes, C. S., Jones, B. F., Presseisen, B. Z., Rankin, S. D., and Suhor, C. (1988). *Dimensions of Thinking.* Alexandria, VA: Association for Supervision and Curriculum Development.

National Education Commission on Time and Learning (1994, April). *Prisoners of Time: Report of the National Education Commission on Time and Learning.* Washington, DC: U.S. Government Printing Office.

Pinnell, G. S. (1995). "Reading Recovery: A Review of Research." *Educational Report #23, Special Topics Issue.* Columbus, OH: Martha L. King Language and Literacy Center.

Pogrow, S. (1995). "Making Reform Work for the Educationally Disadvantaged." *Educational Leadership, 52*(5).

Pritchard, A., and Taylor, J. (1980). *Accelerated Learning: The Use of Suggestion in the Classroom.* Novato, CA: Academic Therapy.

Raywid, M. A. (1982). *The Current Status of Schools of Choice in Public Secondary Education.* Hempstead, NY: Project on Alternatives in Education, Hofstra University.

_____. (1993). "Community: Alternative School Accomplishment." In Gregory A. Smith (Ed.), *Public Schools That Work: Creating Community*, pp. 23–44. New York: Routledge.

Resnick, L. B. (1987). "Learning in School and Out." *Educational Researcher,* *16*(9), 13–20.

Rutter, R. A. (1988). *Effects of School as a Community.* Madison, WI: National Center on Effective Secondary Schools.

Slavin, R. (1986). *Using Student Team Learning,* 3rd ed. Baltimore, MD: Johns Hopkins University Press.

Slavin, R. E., Madden, N. A., Dolan, L. J., and Wasik, B. A. (1966). "Success for All: A Summary of Research. *Journal of Education for Students Placed at Risk, 1*(1), 41–76.

Smith, M. (1996). "The National Writing Project After 22 Years." *Phi Delta Kappan, 77*(10), 688–692.

Strickland, D. S. (1985). *Integrating the Basic Skills Through the Content Areas.* Workshop Materials. New York: Teachers College, Columbia University.

Talbot, M. (2001). The New Counterculture. Available online at http://www.theatlantic.com/issues/2001/11/talbot.htm.

Wang, M. C. (1992). *Adaptive Education Strategies: Building on Diversity.* Baltimore, MD: Paul H. Brookes.

_____. (1997). *Community for Learning Implementation Manual.* Philadelphia: Temple University Center for Research in Human Development and Education.

Wang, M. C., Haertel, G. D., and Walberg, H. J. (1993). "What Helps Students Learn?" *Educational Leadership, 51*(4), 74–79.

_____. (1997). *What Do We Know? Widely Implemented School Improvement Programs.* A special report issued by the Laboratory for Student Success at Temple University Center for Research in Human Development and Education.

_____. (1998). *Achieving Student Success: A Handbook of Widely Implemented Research-Based Educational Reform Models.* Philadelphia: Temple University Center for Research in Human Development and Education.

Wehlage, G. G., Rutter, R. A., Smith, G. A., Lesko, N., and Fernandez, R. R. (1989). *Reducing the Risk: Schools as Communities of Support.* London: Palmer Press.

Chapter 6
🔗 Public Alternative Schools and Alternative School Programs

Although there are thousands of alternative programs located across the United States, all are based on just a few models. Originally, these models operated only at the secondary level, but today we are seeing an increase in the number of innovative alternative models at the elementary level. (Middle school–level alternative programs are still the exception rather than the rule.) Characterized by broad goals, these programs change the conventional school's management and organization. They employ flexible scheduling and small learning communities that work together to create interdisciplinary curricula. They also bring together parents, educators, students, and community members to define a coherent vision of the school. In some cases, these stakeholders are free to define their own vision and to promote schoolwide reconceptions of where learning takes place and how to measure it.

Attempts to reduce racial isolation in public schools are one reason for the evolution of alternative public schools. The McCarver Elementary School in Tacoma, Washington, offered choice to parents in 1968. A year later, in 1969, Trotter Elementary School in Boston opened for the same reason. Both were referred to as "alternatives." In Minneapolis, an alternative experiment created four elementary schools and one high school with different organizational designs. The year was 1970. One of these schools was referred to as "free"; the second, as "open"; the third, as "continuous progress"; and the fourth, as "contemporary," which reflected a traditional approach. New York City and Berkeley soon followed the Minnesota model. Many school districts across the country have received local as well as national acclaim for successful alternative programs. Examples of these programs include the following.

Adlai Stevenson High School (Lincolnshire, IL)

Adlai Stevenson High School District is a large 4,000-student single-building high school district in Illinois. It is touted as a model of how alignment, efficiency, and human leadership, combined with simple structures and practices, can produce astounding results. And, based on student success on Advance Placement exams, it is ranked by the College Board as the top high school in the Midwest and the sixth in the world. The key features that support Adlai Stevenson's success are

1. Frequent, focused, data-driven teamwork
2. High-quality, carefully aligned lessons, instructional units, and end-of-course assessments—all the product of teamwork
3. Recognition and praise for the individuals and teams whose contributions have helped them achieve the school's vision

Contact: Rick DuFour, Adlai Stevenson High School, One Stevenson Drive, Lincolnshire, IL 60069. Telephone: 847-634-4000. Email: rdufour @district125.k12.il.us. Web site: http://www.district125.k12.il.us.

The Alpha Program, Shelburne Community School (Shelburne, VT)

The Shelburne Community School is a public school that opened in the 1960s when the open-school concept was among the variety of options available for school reform. As part of the Alpha Program, the "Alpha Team" consists of about seventy-five children in grades 6, 7, and 8, three full-time teachers, and several assistants. All of the project work of the Alpha Team is integrated and interdisciplinary; there are no discrete subjects. The children use community resources for much of their work. They go on field trips related to the projects they are working on but also do ongoing work in basic reading, writing, and mathematical skills. Contact: Walter Nardelli, Shelburne Community School, 345 Harbor Road, Shelburne, VT 05482. Telephone: 802-985-3331. Fax: 802-985-8951. Email: wnardell@shelburne.k12.vt.us. Web site: http://www.shelburne.k12.vt.us.

Alternative High School (Cape May, NJ)

The Alternative High School is the secondary component of the Cape May County Special Services School District. It serves students whose home schools are unable to provide the services they need. The program is highly individualized. The goal is to equip students with the skills they need to be employable. There are prevocational offerings and school-to-careers initiatives. This unique institution provides a wide range of programs for its students and takes into consideration the special needs each pupil brings to the school. Contact: Alternative Transitional Schools, Office of Education. Telephone: 609-588-3157. Fax: 609-588-7237. Web site: http://www.state.nj.us.

The Atrium School (Watertown, MA)

The Atrium School, a culturally diverse learning community, focuses on teaching students how to get along with people who are different from themselves. Students study minority cultures in North America as well as cultures in other parts of the world. Contact: Elise LaTorre, Director. Telephone: 561-496-3044. Email: info@atriumschool.org. Web site: http://www.atriumschool.org.

Baltimore Orioles Academy (Baltimore, MD)

The Orioles Academy (housed in a wing at Harlem Park Middle School) was organized by the nonprofit organization known as Communities in Schools, Inc. It takes a different approach to helping children with problems in school, focusing on influences in pupil's homes and neighborhoods that make them less likely to succeed academically and more likely to drop out of school. The Academy gets it name from a partnership with the Baltimore Orioles, which pledged $50,000 a year to the school for its first three years. This is the first such school associated with a Major League baseball team. Since 1997, Communities in Schools has helped start four academies across the country, each of them in partnership with a National Football League team. The private resources this organization provides are aimed at the fifty seventh- and eighth-graders in the Academy's first class. Orioles Academy pupils are in classes of only twelve or thirteen students each. They have teacher's aides in every room, and counselors are on hand at all times to deal with problems. In the character education class, the pupils talk about what has kept them from succeeding. Teaching takes place on an individual basis, focusing on each child one at a time. Contact: Harlem Park Middle School, 1500 Harlem Avenue, Baltimore, MD 21217. Telephone: 410-396-0612.

The Bank Street College of Education (New York, NY)

The Bank Street College of Education is a teacher education and staff development center. It is organized as a laboratory school where teachers are constantly engaged in research—observing the children, testing their theories against the realities of the classroom, and refining theory and practice. Contact: The Bank Street College of Education, 610 West 12th Street, New York NY 10025. Telephone: 212-875-4400.

Beauclerc Elementary School (Jacksonville, FL)

Beauclerc Elementary School is a Communications Magnet School based on the goal of parents, professionals, and the community to create an atmosphere that fosters the individual child's growth. The Written, Oral, and Visual Communication Theme at Beauclerc provides students with an instructional program that is both academically challenging and meaningful as preparation for the future. The students use computers, videos, and broadcasting equipment to participate in hands-on experiences in communications and technology. Contact: Monica Trammell, Principal, 4555 Craven Road, W. Jacksonville, FL 32257. Telephone: 904-739-5226. Fax: 904-739-5317. Web site: http://www.educationcentral.org/beauclerc.

The Bellwether School (Willston, VT)

The Bellwether School, founded by Ronald Miller, opened in 1995. Miller's vision for the school, based on a holistic understanding of human development and learning, is that children should not be isolated in self-contained school buildings and that the entire community should be involved in their education. Contact: P.O. Box 8345, Burlington, VT 05402. Telephone: 802-862-0292. Fax: 802-862-3549. Email: info@vanpo.org. Web site: http://www.vanpo.org.

Blue Mountain School (Cottage Grove, OR)

The Blue Mountain School is a democratic learning community. Its innovative environment is designed to foster the education and development of responsible citizens. As a publicly funded, nonprofit learning community open to students between the ages of five and nineteen, it has adopted a mode of operation known formally as noncoercive, nonauthoritarian problem solving. Conflicts between members of the community are resolved in problem-solving sessions where community members are invited to examine the root causes of the disagreement or complaint. Contact: Blue Mountain School, 76132 Blue Mountain Road, Cottage Grove, OR 97424. Telephone: 541-942-7764. Web site: www.bluemountain-school.org.

Central Park East Secondary School (New York, NY)

Central Park East Secondary School, founded by Deborah Meir in the 1980s, is one of the Coalition of Essential Schools flagship schools. Its organization reflects an effort to create a sense of community. Classes are arranged in two-hour blocks, and students do research projects in each subject. Art and music are woven into the academic subjects. The principles and practices of the Coalition of Essential Schools are based on classical Deweyan progressive education. Contact: Ann Purdy, Community Services Coordinator, 1573 Madison Avenue, New York, NY 10029. Telephone: 212-860-8935. Fax: 212-876-3494. Web site: http://www.nycenet.edu.

City-As-School (New York, NY)

City-As-School (CAS) is an alternative program that combines academic learning with the world of work for high school students, including at-risk individuals. Its features include the following:

- Students spend up to forty hours per week in learning experiences utilizing community resources of a business, civic, cultural, social, and political nature.
- Academic credit is granted for each learning experience that is successfully completed.
- Specialized, small classes support activities at community resources.
- Weekly seminar groups serve as a forum for discussions of guidance, academic, and social issues.

The City-As-School can operate either as a stand-alone school or as a program within an existing school. Contact: William Weinstein, City-As-School, 16 Clarkson Street, New York, NY 10014. Telephone: 212-645-6121 or 212-691-7801. Fax: 212-675-2858. Email: Bill.Weinstein@nycenet.nycps.edu.

The Coca-Cola Valued Youth Program (San Antonio, TX)

The Coca-Cola Valued Youth Program is a cross-age tutoring program for grades 7–8, designed to reduce dropout rates among middle school children who are limited in English-language proficiency and at risk of leaving school. It is unique in that the tutors themselves are limited-English-proficient students at risk of dropping out of school. When placed in a responsible tutoring role and supported in their efforts, these tutors gain significant social and economic benefits.

The program has three levels that incorporate all the major features of the model: philosophy, instruction, and support. The philosophical base consists of such tenets as (1) all students can learn; (2) all students, parents, and teachers have a right to participate fully in creating and maintaining excellent schools; (3) excellence in schools contributes to individual and collective economic growth, stability, and advancement; and (4) commitment to educational excellence is created by including students, parents, and teachers in setting goals, making decisions, monitoring progress, and evaluating outcomes. The instructional strategy incorporates five major components: classes for tutors, tutoring sessions, field trips, role modeling, and student recognition. Contact: Josie D. Supik, Intercultural Development Research Association, 5835 Callaghan Road, Suite 350, San Antonio, TX 78228. Telephone: 210-684-8180. Fax: 210-684-5389.

Cooperative Federation for Educational Experiences (Oxford, MA)

The Cooperative Federation for Educational Experiences (COFFEE) is a comprehensive dropout prevention/reclamation program that offers regional, instructional, and occupational training as well as counseling for adolescents with histories of academic failure, truancy, poor self-concept, family problems, and social misconduct. Its student population comprises at-risk youth from seventeen school districts. The program integrates the following five components:

1. *An academic component,* which provides relevant basic skills instruction based on individualized education plan
2. *An occupational component,* which provides hands-on educational experiences in an adult-like work environment, preparing students for high-demand jobs
3. *A counseling component,* which provides character building, occupational, and emotional support, utilizing existing state, regional, and local service organizations
4. *A pre-employment education component,* designed to enhance the employability of at-risk students through classroom instruction and student internships
5. *A physical education component,* which offers a program of recreational activities adapted to enable students to develop a sense of self-accomplishment and group cooperation

Contact: Edward Sikonski, Executive Director, Oxford High School Annex, Main Street, Oxford, MA 05140. Telephone: 508-987-6090.

CyberSchool (Eugene, OR)

Eugene's CyberSchool program offers interactive, credit-bearing high school courses developed and taught by Oregon-licensed teachers. Students who have an email account and Internet access can participate in the courses from either home or school. This extremely innovative approach permits small schools with limited resources to provide broader curriculum opportunities. The school now offers forty-two online courses, all of them fully accredited and asynchronous. Contact: Tom Layton at Layton@4j.lane.edu or http://www.cyberschool.k12.or.us.

The Dalton School (New York, NY)

The Dalton School is a K–12, urban independent school founded by Helen Parkhurst. Although large and very successful, it has deemphasized its progressive roots since the 1960s. In addition, while it does not showcase Parkhurst's practices, her influence is evident in descriptions of the program. Dalton has survived as a market-sensitive institution that delivers a first-rate education. It is located amid some of the most expensive real estate in the world; from its inception, the student population has reflected its location. The school seeks to mirror life through its students, whose parents reflect different occupations—including a large percentage of creative types and highly successful businessmen. Contact: Ellen C. Stein, 108 East 89th Street, New York, NY 10128. Telephone: 212-423-5200. Fax: 212-423-5259. Email: http://www.dalton.org/directories/contacts.ctm. Web site: http://www.dalton.org.

DeLaSalle Model (Kansas City, MO)

The DeLaSalle Education Center is a private not-for-profit agency. It includes individualized programs of special services coupled with a core academic curriculum for students who have dropped out of grades 9–12 to help them improve their academic skills and complete their high school education. Students for whom the DeLaSalle Model is appropriate are those who have typically had sporadic school attendance and low academic performance in their previous schooling. Contact: Regina Hansen, DeLaSalle Education Center, 3740 Forest, Kansas City, MO 64109-3200. Telephone: 816-561-3312. Fax: 816-561-6106.

Diversified Educational Experiences Program (Wichita, KS)

The Diversified Educational Experiences Program (DEEP), for grades 9–12, is a new method of organizing and managing an academic classroom. The major goal of DEEP is to develop an instructional process for secondary school classrooms that allows instructors to create an academic environment emphasizing success for every learner while decreasing learner hostility to educational institutions. DEEP offers learners in academic subjects alternative ways to create, gather, develop, and display information. Extensive use is made of both electronic and nonelectronic media. The role of the teacher is that of advisor, consultant, and learning-systems manager. The classroom is a workshop where students work cooperatively to complete tasks. Community resources are also utilized. Contact: J. Connett, Director, DEEP, KEDDS/Link, 412-18 South Main, Wichita, KS 67202. Telephone: 316-833-5100. Fax: 316-833-5103.

Focus Dissemination Project (St. Paul, MN)

The Focus Dissemination Project is a "school within a school" that provides an alternative education plan for secondary students who have been identified as disaffected, showing a lack of motivation, a lack of confidence, and low self-esteem. The program effects responsible institutional change and positive student attitude and performance by helping students learn responsibility to self, school, and society. Courses in English, social studies, and mathematics are also offered.

In addition to reducing student disaffection with school and learning, Focus seeks to improve each student's ability to relate effectively with peers and adults, and to give each student a reason to be optimistic about the future. All Focus students are involved in a group counseling experience called Family. Each Family consists of eight to ten students and one teacher who meet together for one hour daily throughout the year. Family attempts to help the students develop feelings of caring, self-worth, and concern for others. It includes examination of their own behavior in relation to the reactions of others within an atmosphere of positive support from the group. Contact: Don May, Focus Dissemination Project, Human Resource Associations, Inc., Suite 200, 201 North Concord Exchange, South Saint Paul, MN 55075. 612-451-6840 or 800-345-5285.

The Fratney School (Milwaukee, WI)

The Fratney School, founded by Escuela Fratney, is a thoroughly multicultural establishment. Located in an integrated, poor, working-class neighborhood in Milwaukee, it is a site-based school run by a management council consisting of the principal, nine teachers, five parents, one community representative, and one school staff representative. Fratney is funded by the city of Milwaukee as a public school but is virtually autonomous. Contact: Escuela Fratney, 3255 North Fratney Street, Milwaukee, WI 53212. Telephone: 414-264-4840.

Graduation, Reality, Dual-Role Skills (Columbus, OH)

Graduation, Reality, Dual-Role Skills (GRADS) is a family and consumer-sciences instructional and intervention program for grades 7–12, designed to keep pregnant and parenting teens in school. Additional goals include encouraging good health-care practices and helping young parents set occupational goals. Regular GRADS classes are supplemented with seminars and individual projects. Teachers trained in the program serve one school or travel among three or four. The instructional component focuses on the teacher-written *Adolescent Parent Resource Guide,* which, at 1,300-plus pages in length, comprehensively covers the practical concepts and strategies needed to guide the development of skills in teenage parents. Contact: Sharon G. Enright, Ohio Department of Education, Division of Vocational and Adult Education, Room 909, 65 South Front Street, Columbus, OH 43215-4183. Telephone: 614-466-3046. Fax: 614-644-5702. Email: ve_enright@odevax.ode.ohio.gov.

The Greenfield Center School (Greenfield, MA)

As the National Foundation for Children's laboratory/demonstration school, The Greenfield Center School is a leading example of a school based on developmental understanding of the child. Started in 1982 by a small group of public school teachers, the school and its curriculum were organized around the ideas of Arnold Gesell, Jean Piaget, and other developmental thinkers. The Responsive Classroom social curriculum is used to accomplish the goal of creating an orderly classroom climate that is conducive to learning and teaches children attitudes, social skills, and habits that will serve them well throughout their lives. Contact: Northeast Foundation for Children, 71 Montague City Road, Greenfield, MA 01301. Telephone: 800-360-6332.

The Hoboken Charter School (Hoboken, NJ)

The Hoboken Charter School is a preK–12 school committed to community building and democratic citizenship through its program of service learning. Its purpose is to develop the academic, artistic, personal, and civic growth of all its members through its commitment to service learning and learner-centered education. The school opened in September 1998, and it is the 2000/2001 National Service Learning Leader School and Learn and Serve grantee. Admission to the school is by lottery. Contact: Hoboken Charter School, 4th and Garden Street, 3rd floor, Hoboken, NJ 07030.

Jeffersontown High School Magnet Career Academy (Jeffersontown, KY)

Jeffersontown High School Magnet Career Academy offers beginning and advanced courses in engineering and the liberal arts. In addition to integrating college-preparatory programs with state-of-the-art technical applications, it engages in numerous business partnerships with the city of Jeffersontown and the surrounding Jeffersontown Bluegrass Industrial Park community. The program features a full range of academic, athletic, co-curricular, and extracurricular activities, including a variety of foreign language courses and a Marine Corps JROTC Program. Contact: Marsha Dohn, 9600 Old Six Mile Lane, Louisville, KY 40299. Telephone: 502-485-8275. Fax: 502-485-8832. Web site: http://www.jefferson.k12.ky.us.

The Learning Center (North Platte, NE)

The Learning Center is an alternative school that develops programs and procedures for at-risk students. The students who attend this school have not been successful in the traditional school setting and, in many respects, find it to be a very different experience. For example, classes are attended for one-half day in three-hour sessions on only four days a week; the curriculum is individualized and self-paced, emphasizing social skills and character development; and the student-teacher ratio is lower than in the regular school. Contact: The Learning Center, 1511 West 14th Street, North Platte, NE 69101. Telephone: 308-535-5311.

The Lincoln-Bassett Elementary School (New Haven, CT)

In New Haven, Connecticut, virtually all public schools use the Comer approach to some extent. The Lincoln-Bassett Elementary School is one of these. Lincoln-Bassett is located in a neighborhood of modest two-story frame homes. Members of the school community manage it. Decisions affecting the life of the school are made not by state, city, or district administrators but by people in the school itself. The main governing body of Lincoln-Bassett is the School Planning and Management Team. It includes the principal, representatives of the faculty, parents, the school support staff, and the members of the mental Health Team—altogether about twenty persons. Contact: Ramona Gatison, 130 Bassett Street, New Haven, CT 06571. Telephone: 203-946-8839. Fax: 203-946-8840. Email: ramona.gatison@new-haven.k12.ct.us. Web site: http://www.nhps.net/schools.

Lincoln Park High School (Chicago, IL)

Lincoln Park was one of the first schools in the country to adopt the International Baccalaureate program. Teachers in this program believe that it is the most rigorous and challenging pre-university program available. Students focus on a few topics that are important to helping them understand the discipline they are working in, whether literature, history, or biology. The skills they acquire enable them to continue their studies in that discipline at the undergraduate level. Contact: 2001 Orchard Street, Chicago, IL 60614. Telephone: 773-534-8130.

The Little Red Schoolhouse (New York, NY)

The Little Red Schoolhouse, founded by Elizabeth Irwin in Greenwich Village, originally operated as a public school. When its progressive philosophy was challenged, it was converted into a private school to save its integrity as a progressive experimental school. Contact: 196 Bleecker Street, New York, NY 10012. Telephone: 212-477-5316. Fax: 212-675-3595.

Miami-Dade Parks After-School Programs

These after-school programs provide a secure place in which Miami schoolchildren can play, do homework, practice sports, and participate in arts programs. A sports development program, an arts academy, and holiday camps are among its offerings.

The Marion Cross School (Norwich, VT)

The Marion Cross School is a K–6 elementary school that has been using the whole-language approach for years. It is known as a successful school with an experienced, dedicated faculty.

Middle Years Alternative (Philadelphia, PA)

The Middle Years Alternative School is a public school that serves grades 7 and 8. An outgrowth of the open classroom program, it was established in 1976 with ninety-four students as the direct result of persistent parent pressure.

The Milton L. Fuller School (Gloucester, MA)

The Milton L. Fuller School is a preK–5 school that received a three-year grant in 1992 from the U.S. Department of Education to further develop a Multiple Intelligences (MI) program. The school-within-a-school model for this MI program accommodates 325 to 800 students enrolled at the school. Although the theory of multiple intelligences is used as the basis for curriculum development, the school displays all of the characteristics of progressive education. The whole-language approach is used to teach reading and writing. Theme projects, cooperative learning, and multifaceted assessment also support the curriculum.

The Monhegan School (Bronx, NY)

The Monhegan School is a public elementary school located in a disadvantaged, minority area in the South Bronx. All of its students are poor; 99 percent are African American. Monhegan is one of the growing number of public schools using the Core Knowledge Curriculum.

Open Classroom Program

The Open Classroom Program opened in 1982 as a public school serving grades 1–6. It is now known as the Bach Open School. Under pressure, supposedly as an experiment, the Ann Arbor School Board allowed 260 children, chosen by lottery, to experience this environment in which students are taught to value themselves, not their production.

Paxon School for Advanced Studies (Jacksonville, FL)

The Paxon School for Advanced Studies is a college preparatory school whose mission is to prepare students for a life of excellence, success, joy, and self-fulfillment. As an advanced magnet academy, it limits its enrollment to no more than 1,400 students. At present, approximately 850 students are enrolled in grades 9–12. Contact: Paxon School for Advanced Studies, 3239 W. 5th Street, Jacksonville, FL 32254. Telephone: 904-693-7583.

Project Intercept

Project Intercept is a positive program for intervention and remedy of students at risk for suspension, truancy, dropout, academic failure, and behavior problems. The basic premise of Project Intercept training is to restructure a school's teaching philosophies so as to provide more effective techniques to deal with at-risk students. The Intercept program is highly individualized; goals for each individual school are developed in concert with the participants of the project. Teachers, counselors, and administrators are trained as a team to approach all problems that affect at-risk students. Contact: James E. Loan, M.A., Project Intercept, 1101 South Race Street, Denver, CO 80219. Telephone: 303-777-5870.

Public and Private School Collaboration

The Public and Private School Collaboration is a Connective Scholars Program designed to provide an opportunity for advanced residential study for academically promising urban school students. Whereas public and private schools have not traditionally joined forces, they can do so within a collaborative framework. This framework allows them to apply their finest resources to meet significant needs. It also permits them to gain the support of leading corporations and foundations as well as research institutions and museums as they seek to respond to those needs. The Connective Scholars Program requires full participation of public and private school partners, definition of genuine need, and the commitment to work together to find and apply resources to meet that need. Contact: Howard Hand, Director, Summer Programs, Office of Public and Private School Collaboration, Choate Rosemary Hall, Box 788, 333 Christian Street, Wallingford, CT 06492. Telephone: 203-284-5364.

The Ralph B. O'Maley Middle School

The Ralph B. O'Maley Middle School is one of eleven schools in Massachusetts constituting the Coalition of Essential Schools. Its membership in this coalition has enabled it to implement site-based management, establish a student-centered curriculum, and eliminate student tracking. In addition, it uses the latest in education research to promote hands-on experiential learning for the students.

Richard Montgomery High School (Rockville, MD)

The International Baccalaureate (IB) program at Richard Montgomery High School has helped to boost enrollment (at present, more than 500 students are participants); however, only one-eighth of the students who apply for admission to the program can be accepted. The IB is intended for academically oriented students who are willing to work hard, to be self-disciplined, to learn and practice time management, to study in an interdisciplinary way, and to be measured against demanding, international standards.

The Robert Muller School (Arlington, TX)

Robert Muller, founder of the Robert Muller School, is a former assistant secretary general of the United Nations and author of *New Genesis: Shaping a Global Spirituality*. His belief in the holistic approach to life and to education led him to develop a curriculum called the "World Core," designed to develop the child physically, emotionally, mentally, and spiritually, from birth through adolescence. The Robert Muller School publishes a resource catalog that contains materials about this curriculum. Contact: Robert Muller School, 6005 Royal Oak Drive, Arlington, TX 76016. Telephone: 818-654-1018. Fax: 817-654-1028.

SAIL High School (Tallahassee, FL)

SAIL High School is recognized as one of the top twenty alternative schools in the nation by Phi Delta Kappa. Founded in 1975 as a public alternative school of choice, SAIL now serves about 250 students. Its curriculum emphasizes individualization, democratic decision making, and application of academics in a humanistic atmosphere. Contact: SAIL High School, 725 N. Macomb Street, Tallahassee, FL 32303. Telephone: 850-488-2468. Fax: 850-922-8483. Email: sail@mail.sail.leon.k12.fl.us.

School Without Walls (Rochester, NY)

Teachers, students, and parents created the School Without Walls, which opened in 1971. Consistent with the school's original mission, the entire school community is involved in any changes that are made at the school. Contact: School Without Walls, 480 Broadway, Rochester, NY 14607. Telephone: 585-546-6732. Fax: 585-262-8947.

Score for College

Score for College (SCORE) is a comprehensive co-curricular support program that brings together administrators, counselors, teachers, parents, and students to increase student performance and eligibility. SCORE provides a comprehensive, holistic approach, training schools to institute a program incorporating appropriate placement, study skills, academic support, multiple-modality teaching techniques, counseling, and mentoring. SCORE trainers work with schools to design a customized program for accelerating the achievement of high-risk youth, train staff, and provide follow-through support with a set of materials, workbooks, videotapes, and consultation. Contact: Sharon Johnson, Director, Orange County Department of Education, 200 Kalmus, P.O. Box 9050, Costa Mesa, CA 92628-9050. Telephone: 714-966-4394. Fax: 714-662-3148.

Student Assistance to Further Education Alternative School

Student Assistance to Further Education Alternative School (SAFE) was designed to provide academic and support services to eligible Houston Independent School District (HISD) elementary students who are at risk for expulsion. The school focuses on assisting such students to excel in academics while also helping them to learn the skills necessary to improve and control their behavior. Program components include counseling, case management, and parental involvement activities.

Synergy Alternative High School (Hartford, CT)

Synergy Alternative High School, founded in 1973, serves high-risk, unmotivated, dissatisfied high school students. The program, which is designed to keep these students in school until they earn their high school diploma, provides personalized service and a curriculum that supports the development of life-long learners and responsible citizens. Contact: Synergy Alternative High School, 40 Butternut Drive, East Hartford, CT 06118. Telephone: 860-622-5999. Email: synergy_school@ hotmail.com.

Urban Academy (New York, NY)

Urban Academy is a progressive public/private alternative secondary school whose population consists of poor, urban, minority students.

Urban Little Schools

Urban Little Schools (ULS), modeled after their forerunner, the experimental Syracuse Institute for Enabling Education (SIEE) elementary school, can best be described as a parent-choice alternative within public school districts striving to meet the challenge of education in U.S. cities. The development of ULS represents a change from the conventional education being practiced in failing urban schools—that is, at schools where most children leave unprepared to hold their own in a highly competitive modern economy and, hence, are unable to make it out of the poverty cycle. The ULS rejects the factory-like institutions that instill uniformity among teachers and children and instead creates an environment where teachers work sensitively with each student on an individualized basis. Students are guided, one-on-one, by teachers who help them take responsibility for their own learning.

W. Haywood Burns School (New York, NY)

The W. Haywood Burns School is a product of the New Vision Schools Program, a New York City Board of Education initiative that supports new schools founded upon the principle of faculty autonomy.

REFERENCES

Hirsch, E. D. (1988). *Cultural Literacy.* Boston: Houghton Mifflin Co.

_____. (1996). *The Schools We Need and Why We Don't Have Them.* New York: Doubleday.

Koetzsch, R. E. (1997). *Parents' Guide to Alternatives in Education.* Boston: Shambhala Publications.

Lessons About Learning. (2001, March 26). *The Sun* (Baltimore), p. 1B.

Myers, C., and Simpson, D. (1998). *Re-creating Schools: Places Where Everyone Learns and Likes It.* Thousand Oaks, CA: Corwin Press.

National Association of Secondary School Principals (1973). *More Options: Alternatives to Conventional School.* ERIC Document, Reproduction Service No. ED099995.

Newman, R. (2000). *Building Urban Little Schools: Where Every Child Succeeds with Dignity.* Cambridge, MA: Brookline Books.

Northwest Regional Educational Laboratory, *Catalog of School Reform Models* (2001). Portland, OR/Washington, DC: National Clearinghouse for Comprehensive School Reform.

Chapter 7
Private and Independent School Options

Private education in the United States represents another alternative that has not lost its popularity. Schools not funded exclusively by federal or state dollars come in many different varieties. Many private and parochial schools are very traditional. They often see high achievement levels because of a select student body, rigorous discipline and conduct standards, strong parental support, high-quality teachers, and a demanding curriculum. Private schools are not subject to the same state regulations and controls as public schools (unless they request state accreditation). They are therefore free to pursue innovative programs and alternative learning techniques. Very few private schools adopted radical or innovative programs before 1986.

The growth in private education has been most dramatic among religious fundamentalists and others dissatisfied with the quality of public education. Evangelical fundamentalists such as Jerry Falwell and other conservative groups gave considerable support to private religious schools in the 1980s. Some parents in cities such as Seattle choose to send their students to private schools deemed to be of high quality. Both evangelical fundamentalists and conservative religious groups supported the Reagan administration's plan to provide vouchers for schools. Both political parties during the Clinton administration supported privatization programs, charter schools, parental choice, and involvement in education. And as of this writing, in 2002, George Bush has boasted of bipartisan support for legislation that gives more opportunities to private/independent school programs.

This chapter provides a broad sampling of private, religious, and independent schools.

Al-Nur Home Education Center (Springfield, MA)

The Al-Nur ("The Light") Home Education Center is a tiny school affiliated with the Sister Clara Mohammed school movement. It is located in the home of teacher Katara Aleem on a quiet residential street. The school has six students, all of them girls. They range in age from seven to twelve. The curriculum is both academic and moral, covering the same subjects as the public schools. The teaching strategies support both whole-group and small-group instruction.

Albany Free School (Albany, NY)

Albany Free School, also known as The Free School, is a private school where the kids themselves make the choice to join after a week's visit. Because the founders and operators of the school believe that the changes students want to make occur over time and that they need space to discover for themselves who they really are, parents are asked for a commitment to allow their children to stay in the school for at least a year. Founded in 1970, the Free School has stood the test of time. It has forty-five students, ranging in age from two to fourteen, and it offers multi-age classes as well as a preschool group. Tuition is based on income. The Free School is run and supported by a core community of about twenty people. Some school parents are members of this core community, but parents are not required to join.

Alpine Valley School (Wheat Ridge, CO)

Alpine Valley School, based on the Sudbury Valley School, is a school dedicated to freedom, respect, and the joy of learning. Students are encouraged to fully engage and freely explore their interests, gifts, and talents. All students take part in school decisions and stand on an equal footing with the staff and each other.

Amherst Montessori School (Amherst, MA)

The Amherst Montessori School was founded in 1969 by a group of parents who wanted to make the Montessori method available in their community. Each classroom is equipped with a one-way window, as the Montessori method encourages teachers and parents to observe children in their activities to help them understand what and how the children are ready to learn.

Carden Memorial School (Salt Lake City, UT)

The Carden Memorial School, which describes itself as a "nondenominational Christian school," was founded in 1969 by Anna Lou Jeffs. Cur-

rently it has an enrollment of approximately 400 children from preschool to grade 8. It uses the Carden reading method and the comprehensive Carden curriculum. The school is organized in "forms" rather
than classes. The forms are based on level of academic skill rather than
on age. The curriculum is comprehensive and sequential. Throughout
the grades, the children study history, geography, math, science, physical education, and art, as well as language and literature. They begin
learning French in the first grade and Latin in the sixth. Contact: Carden
Memorial School, 1452 East 2700 South, Salt Lake City, UT 84106. Telephone: 801-486-4895.

Cathedral High School (Springfield, MA)

Cathedral High School is typical of the Catholic high schools found in
many suburban areas of the country. It was founded in 1883 to educate
the children of the Irish laborers who came to work in the armories and
factories of Springfield. Cathedral High School prides itself on the well-
rounded general education it offers, including a focus on basic skills and
on knowledge of the world and how it works. The school does not have
many of the elective programs that one might find in public schools in
the area, but it reports that 93 percent of its seniors go on to college.

The Circle School (Harrisburg, PA)

The Circle School philosophy is based on the belief that each person has
the wisdom to know what is best for him or her. The teachers at Circle
believe in the fullest expression of that wisdom in the lives of students.
They work to serve students' needs by modeling the highest values and
offering exposure, resources, and guidance in the exercise of body,
mind, and spirit.

Christa McAulliffe Academy (Yakima, WA)

Christa McAulliffe Academy is an accredited global private school, dedicated to bringing first-class learning experiences to learners of all ages,
backgrounds, abilities, and circumstances through the innovative use of
technology.

City & Country School (New York, NY)

City & Country School is an urban independent school and one of the
oldest progressive elementary schools in the United States. It opened in

1914 in a three-room apartment in New York City's Greenwich Village. The school's founder, Caroline Pratt, believed in child-centered practices. She opened the school after becoming frustrated with what she called "the repression of formal education." As a small K–8 school, City & Country School attracts parents who consciously favor progressive schools. It selects faculty members who are interested in or are graduates of progressive institutions.

Clearwater School (Seattle, WA)

The Clearwater School is open to students between the ages of four and nineteen. It is a school where, according to its founders, children direct their own learning and in the process become creative, confident, capable people. There is no set curriculum or constant evaluation, but abundant resources, time, and space are made available to students so that they can discover for themselves their place in the world. As a participatory democracy, Clearwater allows all students and staff equal votes in all matters pertaining to the school.

Clonlara School (Ann Arbor, MI)

Clonlara School, an independent, private, innovative, free school based on A. S. Neill's philosophy, was founded by Pat and Jim Montgomery in 1967. It serves students ranging in age from two and a half to sixteen. The school reinforces learning to live with other people and to take responsibility for one's own actions. Children neither follow adult-made rules nor study only that which adults say they must. The actual style of teaching is often traditional. Each student is valued as a unique individual; the school's goal is to encourage the child to grow as a whole person, undivided, much more complex and complete than just a head stuffed with learning. An extension of Clonlara School is the Home-Based Education Program, which serves families in ten countries.

The Common School (Amherst, MA)

The Common School, founded in 1967, is a small independent school established and still run on the basis of progressive principles. The aim of the school is to realize the full human potential of each child, not just intellectually but also artistically, socially, creatively, and physically. The learning environment is rich with opportunities for discovery, experimentation, and self-directed learning.

Community School (Camden, MA)

The Department of Educational and Cultural Services has approved the Community School as a private secondary school since 1974. Located in the small town of Camden, it offers two main programs: the Residential Program, which focuses on high school dropouts between the ages of sixteen and twenty, and the Passages Program, which focuses on parents between the ages of fifteen and twenty who have not yet completed their high school education. The Community School teaches using one-on-one tutoring, small seminars, vocational training, guided life-experiences, and experiential courses. Each student follows an Individual Graduation Plan, which includes course requirements as well as special courses to meet his or her own specific needs.

Crossroads Academy (Lyme, NH)

Crossroads Academy, founded in 1990, is an independent school that uses the Core Knowledge curriculum and is strongly committed to character education. It now has more than 100 students who adhere to a strict dress code and a moral education program. The Core Knowledge curriculum is identified as a major force shaping the school. Contact: Crossroads Academy, 13 Dartmouth College Highway, Lyme, NH 03766. Telephone: 603-795-3111.

The Diamond Road School (Brownstown, PA)

The Diamond Road School is an elementary school founded and supported by a group of Old Order Mennonite and Old Order Amish families. Like other Mennonite and Amish schools, this one tries to insulate and protect the children from the outside world and to preserve the distinct and sectarian life of the community.

Eagle Rock School and Professional Development Center (Estes Park, CO)

Eagle Rock School is a residential, independent secondary school for students "not experiencing success" in mainstream school situations. It uses a student-centered curriculum and pedagogy and has a strong character education program similar to that used at the Hyde School. Contact: Eagle Rock School and Professional Development Center, P.O. Box 1770, 2750 Notaiah Road, Estes Park, CO 80517. Telephone: 970-586-0600. Fax: 970-586-4805.

Francis W. Parker School (Chicago, IL)

The Francis W. Parker School was founded by Colonel Francis W. Parker in 1901. A highly successful college preparatory school as well as a progressive school, it illustrates the importance of leadership as a primary factor in determining the direction of a school. The school is also highly sensitive to the needs of the marketplace. It reminds us that teachers as curriculum makers have had a long history.

Harmony School Education Center (Bloomington, IN)

The Harmony School, founded in 1974, is a place where teachers, students, administrators, researchers, parents, and community members come together to create learning experiences that will help students participate in a democratic society. The school services all levels: elementary, middle school, high school, and community youth programs. This collaborative environment brings together community resources, outreach services, research agencies, state officials, business leaders, and professional associations. In addition to creating the elements necessary for life in a democratic society, the school "fosters creative, working solutions to complex challenges of educating today's young people." Contact: Harmony School Education Center, P.O. Box 1787, Bloomington, IN 47402. Telephone: 812-334-8349. Fax: 812-333-3435.

Highlander Folk School (Monteagle, TN)

Frank Adams, author of a book on the idea of the Highlander Folk School, acknowledges that Highlander exemplifies his philosophy that education should foster individual growth and social change and nourish the fundamental value of complete personal liberty while encouraging thoughtful citizenship in community.

    Although Highlander was part of a larger campaign against segregation and racial discrimination, there is much to be learned about this alternative school from the work of Myles Horton and staff members at the Highlander School. The Highlander Folk School opened in 1932 in Monteagle, Tennessee, and during its first thirty years served as a community folk school, a training center for southern industrial labor and farmers' unions, and a major meeting place for black and white civil rights activists. By all accounts, Highlander served the purpose that many believe schools should serve today. At the very heart of Highlander's program was a belief in the power of education to change society.

    Highlander's historical roots trace back to the Danish folk schools of the nineteenth century. Today there are about 100 folk high schools in Denmark, where the 50,000 students enrolled spend time developing their personal and professional lives. These high schools combine vocational education with personal and social experiences. Several attempts were made to apply the folk school approach to the South, particularly southern Appalachia, but these met with limited success.

The Hyde School (Bath, ME)

The Hyde School is an independent, coeducational high school that serves students in grades 8 through 12. Founded in 1966 by Joseph Gauld, it has "education for character" as its main focus. Gauld established the school with the belief that character is the most important element in education and in life—that if good character is developed, everything else will follow from it. Almost all of the school's 230 students are boarding students, but parent participation is absolutely necessary: Parents must come to the school at least three times a year. The Hyde approach is based on the following five principles:

1. *Destiny.* Each of us is gifted with a unique potential.
2. *Humility.* We believe in a power and a purpose beyond ourselves.
3. *Conscience.* We attain our best through character and conscience.
4. *Truth.* Truth is our primary guide.
5. *Brother's Keeper.* We help others achieve their best.

While the Hyde approach is radical, it seems to work for most of the students who come to the school. The school also has a campus in Woodstock, Connecticut. Contact: The Hyde School, 66 High Street, Bath, ME 04530. Telephone: 207-443-5584.

Keystone National High School (Bloomsburg, PA)

Keystone National High School is an independent, innovative, fully accredited, and privately licensed online and correspondence high school. It blends correspondence-based independent study with Internet-based instruction.

Kraybill Mennonite School (Mount Joy, PA)

In 1949, progressive Mennonites from the Brethren in Christ and Church of the Brethren founded the Kraybill Mennonite School. They wanted to have a school that provides a sound education and supports and nurtures Christian values and a Christian way of living. Because of its progressive nature, Kraybill Mennonite has more in common with mainstream Episcopal or Lutheran day schools than with other Mennonite schools.

Laurel Springs School (Ojai, CA)

The Laurel Springs School is a private, international K–12 school offering independent study and distance learning. From elementary to high school, it provides computerized instruction through its online learning program and curriculum, in which home schooling is achieved via the Internet.

Lincoln School (Miami, FL)

The Lincoln School was founded in 1917 by the General Education Board, a Rockefeller philanthropy originally established to aid southern education. It served as a laboratory school for Teachers College, providing clinical placement for Columbia students participating in curriculum design and development as well as observation and demonstration sites. The Lincoln School locates its curriculum in the world in which its students live. It emphasizes "real-life experience" and develops its curricula around the life of the school and the local community.

The Meeting School (Rindge, NH)

The Meeting School is an alternative boarding school for high school–aged students with a Quaker philosophy. Today this school has about thirty students and twelve faculty. Students and teachers live, family-style, in five residences, cooking, eating, studying, and working together.

The Modes Maimonides School (Brookline, MA)

The Modes Maimonides School is an Orthodox Jewish school that serves about 600 students in kindergarten through twelfth grade. It uses some elements of progressive education, such as whole language supplemented by phonics, cooperative learning, and the social curriculum.

The Moses Brown School (Providence, RI)

The Moses Brown School serves about 800 students from kindergarten through high school. It was founded in 1784 in Portsmouth, Rhode Island, as a Quaker school and moved to Providence in 1819.

The New School of Northern Virginia

The New School of Northern Virginia is a small, holistic school that seeks to educate the whole child for the twenty-first century. Its student body is inclusive, co-educational, and reflective of the diversity and richness of the Northern Virginia community. The New School seeks families who believe that it can make a significant contribution to their children's growth, and who can contribute to the life of the school.

In *Culture of Education*, Jerome S. Bruner (1996) states that reform begins when we focus on how learning takes place and how children are acculturated into society. He believes that we need to move toward an understanding of how we interpret the ambiguities we face in life, and that we should utilize a collaborative school culture. In particular, Bruner stresses holistic learning as a way of more effectively relating school to community. The New School of Northern Virginia school is representative of Bruner's philosophy.

Oak Meadow School (Putney, VT)

Oak Meadow School provides distance learning opportunities for students in grades K–12 around the world. Educational programs and learning materials are provided for home schoolers, traveling families, and gifted and special-needs students. Oak Meadow also serves English-speaking students living in foreign countries.

Play Mountain Place (Los Angeles, CA)

Founded in 1949 by child development specialist Phyllis Fleishman, Play Mountain Place is often referred to as the "Summerhill of the West." Fleishman was influenced by the work of humanistic psychologist Carl Rogers and that of A. S. Neill, founder of Great Britain's famous Summerhill school. She encouraged self-motivation, expression of feelings, strong bonds of friendship, cooperation, and development of self-confidence. Play Mountain enrolls children between the ages of two and thirteen. The environment of the school is primarily outdoors, and students are encouraged to express thoughts and feelings freely and without judgment.

Puget Sound Community School

According to Puget Sound Community School (PSCS), the best education is that which ensures the freedom of students of all ages to think for themselves and to control their own destinies, structuring their time and activities as they see fit. The school's web page includes links to other educational resources as well as to student and staff home pages.

St. Matthew's Lutheran School (New Britain, CT)

In the 1960s, the congregation of St. Matthew's founded this school to give the children of the church a strong Christian education. Even though the majority of the children currently enrolled at St. Matthew's are not Lutheran, the curriculum includes a daily religion class. The children study the Bible, Christian beliefs, and the church and have to memorize Bible verses as part of their normal schoolwork.

The School Around Us (Arundel, MA)

The School Around Us was founded in 1970 by parents interested in creating a new type of education for their children. Two of the founding parents donated the land for the school, and they and other parents and community members built the structure. There is no established curriculum here; students decide what they want to study, and the teachers teach it or help the children conduct their own research and do their own projects.

The Sister Clara Mohammed School (Atlanta, GA)

The Sister Clara Mohammed School, originally named the University of Islam, opened its doors in 1977. The high school branch—W. Deen Mohammed School—is located in the same facility. The curriculum includes elements that are distinctly Islamic: a daily ten-minute presentation about Muslim etiquette; the application of Islam to daily life; Islamic history, culture, philosophy, and literature; and weekly Friday trips to the mosque for congregational prayers. Contact: Sister Clara Mohammed/W. Deen Mohammed School, 735 Fayetteville Road, Atlanta, GA 30316. Telephone: 404-378-4219. Fax: 404-378-4600.

The Solomon Schechter School (Newton, MA)

There are sixty-five Solomon Schechter day schools around the country. All share a common educational philosophy as Conservative Jewish day schools, and all have a Lower School (grades K–4) and a Middle School (grades 5–8) on separate campuses.

Sudbury Valley School (Framingham, MA)

The Sudbury Valley School is a private school where students from age four on up are free to do as they wish during the day, as long as they follow the school rules. The campus is "open," and people may come and go as they please. No one is required to attend classes, which, in any case, are rare and bear little resemblance to the usual notion of a "class." There are no tests or grades of any kind, and students and teachers are equal in every regard.

Summerhill (Great Britain)

A. S. Neill founded Summerhill, probably the best known of all private residential schools, in 1921. Neill described this progressive, co-educational school as a "free school." The freedom he was referring to was the personal freedom of the children in his charge.

The Valley Christian School (Northhampton, MA)

The Valley Christian School, founded in 1974, is housed in a building owned by College Church, an evangelical church. Virtually all of the students' families belong to a fundamentalist or evangelical church themselves. The school serves children from kindergarten through the eighth grade.

Walden School (San Francisco, CA)

The Walden School, founded in 1972, is dedicated to creative instruction. As a five-week summer music camp, it provides theoretical music training for students between the ages of nine and eighteen. Students study music in a holistic manner through a process that begins in discovery and exploration, continues through mastery, and culminates in creative application.

Waldorf Schools

Rudolf Steiner conceived of Waldorf education. He believed that modern Western society had placed too much emphasis on external, materialistic values at the expense of the imaginative, creative innermost spirit of the human being.

REFERENCES

Bruner, J. (1996). *Culture of Education*. Cambridge, MA: Harvard University Press.

Glen, J. M. (1996). *Highlander: No Ordinary School*. Knoxville: University of Tennessee Press.

Harmony School Education Center. Available online at http://www.harmony.pvt.k12.in.us/.

Horenstein, M. A. 1993). *Twelve Schools That Succeed*. Bloomington, IN: Phi Delta Kappa Educational Foundation.

Koetzsch, R. E. (1997). *Parents' Guide to Alternatives in Education*. Boston: Shambhala Publications.

Levine, D., Lowe, R., Peterson, B., and Tenorio, R. (Eds.). (1995). *Rethinking Schools: An Agenda for Change*. New York: The New Press.

National Association of Independent Schools (1999). *Choice in Education*. Washington, DC.

National Catholic Educational Association (1992). *Parental Choice in Education*. Washington, DC.

Northwest Regional Educational Laboratory (1997). Alternative Schools: Approaches for Students at Risk. Available online at http://www.nwrel.org.

Chapter 8

✏ Organizing and Administering Alternative Schools and Programs

Alternative schools represent what has been described as a truly grassroots movement. The trend toward alternative schools is based in the civil rights movement, the counterculture movement, and theories of progressive education. Alternative schools offer choices of learning and teaching styles. Research on alternative schools had provided more realistic insight into the concept of lasting education reform.

Alternatives have been started by parents, teachers, school administrators, school boards, philanthropic foundations, and even courts and federal agencies. There is no single best way to initiate the development of an alternative school or an alternative program. There are, however, issues, decisions, and financial challenges that must be considered before one ventures into such development. A basic knowledge of business practices—including strategic thinking, strategic planning, and program development and implementation—is necessary for this kind of work.

This chapter provides insight into the strategies that can be used to establish and implement alternative programs. It addresses the components needed to ensure successful development, including processes, structures, and funding considerations. It also discusses how to set up an alternative program with attention to planning population, student selection process, district support, and resources, site, staffing, and curriculum.

Since education touches the lives of all people, there is seldom universal agreement about the administering and organizing of alternative education programs. As a result, many different models are used to develop successful programs.

Ideas, strategies, and a systematic framework for administering effective alternative school programs can be found in the literature on school improvement and total quality management. After collecting findings from diverse sources such as research on effective schools, studies of outstanding businesses, analysis of leadership, and specific practices and procedures from a number of fine schools, Rick DuFour (1992, pp. 5–8) concluded that excellent schools share the following characteristics:

1. The key to school improvement is a commitment to people improvement.
2. Excellent schools have a clear vision of what they are attempting to accomplish, what they are trying to become.
3. The day-to-day operation of an excellent school is guided by a few shared central values.
4. Excellent schools have principals who are effective leaders.
5. The shaping of organizational culture and climate is critical to the creation of an excellent school.
6. The curriculum of an excellent school reflects the values of the school and provides a focus that helps teachers and students "stick to the knitting."
7. Excellent schools monitor what is important.
8. In an excellent school, teachers are expected to act as leaders within their classrooms.
9. Excellent schools celebrate progress toward their vision and the presence of their core values with ceremonies and rituals.
10. An excellent school is committed to continual renewal.

The recommendations and ideas presented here merge the work from the education profession and the business community in order to answer critical questions related to the best possible way to provide education for today's youth. Schools where children "learn without compulsion" are, for some, a utopia. The learning in such environments is continually re-created in a flexible response to the ever-changing needs of children. Many believe that alternative schools enable children to learn to live together and to assume responsibility for themselves and their society. Many call alternative schools a mirror image of the "free schools" movement that exist outside of public education.

Many think that open education disappeared in the 1970s. But in actuality, alternative, free, open education remains alive and well. The term *free school*, once identified more with political ideology than with educational philosophy, is seldom used today. The free schools of the 1960s and the open schools of the 1960s and 1970s are now considered focus schools with worldview as their theme. These focus schools take a particular approach to instruction, but they also recommend a fairly distinct set of educational goals and projects and a clear character ideal or model, as well as a recognizable outlook on life and its purpose.

Developers and implementers of alternative programs wish to create, within and outside of the public school environment, programs modeled after the "free schools" movement. The models and programs discussed in previous chapters present evidence of the wide range of possibilities available for such purposes. Before the journey can begin, however, several words of caution should be considered.

Despite the thousands of alternative programs throughout the United States, a significant percentage of "alternative" schools are alternative in name only. Given the existence of so many "bad" alternative programs, the public often perceives all alternative programs as second-rate—rather than innovative. Guarding against the view of alternative schools as havens for "misfits" and dumping grounds where difficult children are warehoused can be a major challenge.

The basic idea underlying alternatives, as described in extensive reviews of literature on schools and schooling, is to educate youth to become productive, functioning members of society, both now and in the future. Because the development of alternative schools and alternative programs to prepare children to cope successfully with future conditions is always uncertain, you should preview and review this chapter with the idea that it can be used to plant a seed for development. The suggestions herein are presented with the thought that they can be used to tailor programs that meet the specific needs of the audience being served. But successful implementation of these recommendations requires clear thought and a great deal of planning, as well as a consensus among developers and implementers. There are no quick fixes or one-size-fits-all models for alternative education. On the contrary, many researchers would suggest that you use the "SMART" process for development of your program. SMART goals are goals that are specific and/or strategic, measurable, attainable, results-oriented, and timebound. When program developers use SMART goals, they

- •• Set specific, measurable goals
- •• Plan how to accomplish these goals
- •• Gather evidence of individual and group progress toward the goal
- •• Share the results
- •• Adjust strategies based on what they've learned
- •• Develop new plans for meeting the goals.

Once you have determined the SMART goals for your program, you are ready to begin the development process. Suggestions for strategic planning and program development are shown in Appendices A, B, C, D, and E.

The first step in the process is to gather information. And the best way to collect information is through research. The listings of organizations and agencies in Chapter 10 and of print and nonprint resources in Chapter 11 are a good resource in this respect. Many researchers say that American school reformers suffer from "historical amnesia" and tend to be future oriented, spending an inordinate amount of time reinventing the wheel. Indeed, many creators of alternative schools have failed to examine past models, to plan carefully, and to learn from the mistakes and triumphs of former educators. Accordingly, you could begin your research by studying the child-centered progressive schools for models of what worked, what failed, and why. Past experience, including knowledge of history, can provide clues to the probability of success or failure of alternatives. Sample data collection formats, including the interview protocol developed by Daniel Duke (1978), can be found in Appendices F and G.

Second, organize your thoughts and ideas. Alternative programs involve the examination of values, norms, and attitudes. What is important to you? What are your specific aims, goals, and purposes? How will you promote interest in your ideas? A list of guiding principles for program development is provided in Appendix H.

Third, learn the language of the alternative school environment. What is the difference between an alternative school and an independent school? How do both compare with "free schools"? What are vouchers, and how are they used? What is open education? What are nonprofit or not-for-profit schools? These are only a few of the questions that should be asked when attempting to determine the type of alternative school or program you wish to develop.

Fourth, review the characteristics of alternative schools. The following is a representative list of such characteristics:

- The students are active participants in decision making.
- Their parents are expected to be active partners in education.
- Teachers and students trust and respect one another.
- Creativity and curiosity are valued and encouraged.
- Learning how to learn is more important than specific content.
- Educational goals include self-responsibility and independent learning.
- Students and/or their parents choose to attend the school.

Fifth, determine whether the characteristics of alternative schools match the ideas you've presented. Can your objectives for a different type of educational environment or a different learning experience be satisfied through an alternative program?

Committed individuals dedicated to educational choices and improving schools have developed thousands of alternative schools and programs over the past thirty years, but the long-time survival of these alternatives is inextricably linked to good, sound development and implementation practices.

The following sections summarize the initial steps to consider when planning a program, a problem-solving model, and an action plan for an alternative initiative. This information represents the merging of several ideas from various sources: The overall concept is based on the business practice of strategic thinking, the problem-solving model is borrowed from curriculum development, and the action plan is an aspect of professional development.

In 1984, John Bransford and Barry Stein presented the IDEAL model for problem solving and decision making, which consists of the following elements: *I*dentifying the challenge, *D*efining the challenge, *E*xploring alternatives, *A*cting on the plan, and *L*ooking at and reflecting on results. I recommend this model as a useful approach for individuals and groups interested in developing an alternative school.

In this chapter and the next one, I take up the topics of planning and organizing alternatives, but I do so within the framework of the IDEAL model. The present chapter examines the *I, D, E,* and *A* components of the model, whereas Chapter 9 examines the *L* component. Keep in mind that the elements of decision making are not always sequentially followed; developing any new initiative is a complex process. In general, however, a good decision-making strategy will help you plan, deliver, and evaluate a successful program.

What is strategy? It is hard to imagine any group or organization's conversation about a new venture that does not include the word *strategy.* Yet, in the context of strategic thinking, the term is ambiguous. Some would have you believe that it is well understood, but unfortunately it is not. Nevertheless, a simple one-sentence definition, for our purposes, can be stated as follows: *Strategy is about positioning an organization for long-term survival and existence.* In particular, it involves making choices about which programs to participate in, what services to offer, and how to allocate resources to achieve the group's stated purpose. Crafting an effective strategy is hard work and requires considerable analysis, assessment, and appraisal. The broadest level of strategic thinking involves determining the answers to three basic questions:

1. Analysis: *Where are you now?*

2. Assessment: *Where do you want to go?*
3. Appraisal: *How do you get there?*

IDENTIFYING THE CHALLENGE

Where are you now? Alternative schools often emerge as a rational response to a variety of community problems. Some alternatives deal with crime, truancy, dropouts, changing demographics, redevelopment, and the like. Most school districts in the nation operate at least one alternative program, but few acknowledge having developed a sufficient number of programs to meet the challenge of successfully educating the community's youth. Assessing need and gaining public support are thus imperative. Numerous methods can be used to collect accurate information. These include observations, interviews, focus groups, outside consultants, organizations, and print media. Strategies for assessing the current status of the school district and obtaining information about its readiness for alternative options are as follows.

1. Professional organizations that support alternative public schools are a great resource, as are networks of parents, educators, and concerned citizens. Allies can be recruited through parents' groups, bulletin boards (both manual and electronic), the media, church organizations, social service providers, and so on. A word of caution, however: Be aware of what motivates group members to participate in such an initiative. Be very discriminating in selecting options to embrace. Those who promise support may be motivated by reasons very different from yours. They may simply want alternatives that remove disruptive students from their home schools and be not at all interested in developing a quality program as an alternative. Many organizers of alternative programs, particularly those who initiate charter schools, are overwhelmed with support from "private schoolers" or "home schoolers" who are simply seeking federal and/or state financial support for their own children. Some politicians, too, should be avoided—especially those who are promoting charter schools only to advance an agenda of giving tax credit to private school parents. In short, some individuals' motives may have little to do with establishing effective schools for children.

2. Community surveys are excellent for assessing interest and support in starting alternative schools or programs. The surveys can range from multipage to a single question, and they can describe a range of alternatives as a way of obtaining demographic data on areas of strongest support.

3. School community forums—which should include teachers, administrators, parents, business leaders, politicians, newspaper editors, police, and other interested parties—are an excellent way to promote discussion for alternatives focused on future growth and quality of community life. Several organizations have long, impressive histories in designing and implementing community forums that achieve the identified purpose; these can be located through the Kellogg Foundation Community Forum and the United States Extension Service Action Forum. Also available through these two sources are handbooks and guides that provide information on comprehensive community involvement and interaction that result in the development of action plans. Regardless of how a forum is organized, the idea is to bring together school, community, and government leaders to solve problems and provide enhanced opportunities for all youth.

4. Check out the relevant law and state regulations. Request information regarding policies that relate to alternative schools and the types of alternatives currently available or mandated in your school district or state. It is important that you learn about state legislation affecting alternatives and understand the specifics of the policy and legislation involved.

DEFINING THE CHALLENGE

Where do you want to go? When defining the challenge, you need to examine what it is you want to do and where it is you want to go with the development of your program or project. Some organizers find it helpful to begin with a mission statement; others prefer to use a vision statement or some combination of both. But whatever you decide to call it, the most important aspect of this process is its completion. The mission/vision statement will provide a framework and, ideally, serve as a roadmap for the work you are about to do. It will also define your purpose, enabling each person in the group to share in the overall goal; thus, developing a mission/vision statement is valuable as a product in itself. It represents an opportunity for people to explore, discuss, debate, and ultimately share understanding of the purpose of the work they are about to do.

Appendix H in this chapter outlines the process for developing the three major components necessary for effective group work: a mission, a vision, and guiding principles. Appendix I provides guidelines for evaluating the mission/vision statement itself.

After completing that very important process, you should begin to collect information about the program or project you are interested in. There are numerous methods that can be used to collect accurate information. They include observations, interviews, outside consultants, print media, and reports from other organizations. The needs assessment method you use will depend upon the criteria involved. Here are a few examples of the questions you may want to consider:

- ⤳ How much time and money is involved? How much do you have?
- ⤳ How many people are involved, and who are they?
- ⤳ To what extent is the information already known? Can the sources be validated?

The data collection strategies that have been found most effective for this type of development process are described below.

Observations: Observations are often used to validate other data collection methods such as interviews or questionnaires. They can also be used to obtain information that may be difficult to acquire through other methods.

Interviews: Interviews can be used to obtain information that might be difficult to access using conventional instruments. The interview protocol in Appendix F, developed by Daniel Duke (1978), provides a series of questions that can be used to organize thoughts and ideas during the planning and development process. These questions pertain to five broad categories of areas that should be considered: educational goals, pedagogical dimensions, administrative organizations, composition, and impetuses to the development of alternative schools. Regardless of the size of your program, the questions listed in this interview design are worthy of consideration.

Focus Groups: Focus groups combine elements of both interviewing and observation. The focus group session involves an interview (Patton, 1990), not a discussion, problem-solving, or decision-making session. The hallmark of focus groups is the use of group interaction to generate data and insights that would be unlikely to emerge without the interaction found in a group. Focus groups are gatherings of eight to twelve people who share some characteristics relevant to the information being sought. These groups were originally used as a market research tool to investigate the appeal of various products, but the technique has since been adopted in other fields, such as education, as a tool for data gathering on a given topic.

The data gathering strategy should include an investigation of what already exists. The difference between a successful and an unsuccessful initiative sometimes lies in the degree to which an existing need is met. If you are attempting to develop an alternative in an area where a need is already being fulfilled, you may run into roadblocks. Be aware that many school districts have structures in place that determine the procedures to be used to consider alternative school options. Two of these procedures are identified as follows:

1. *School district planning teams.* School district planning teams, composed of teachers, administrators, and parents from every school in the district, are sometimes already established and in operation. Such large planning efforts budget for planning and development. They use consultants, travel to other cities to visit alternative schools, conduct exhaustive literature reviews for information, and research different types of alternatives. Ad hoc teams may also be developed when there is a specific initiative under development.
2. *School district decision-making processes.* You should know the process by which school districts make decisions about alternative schools. Some school districts, such as those in San Antonio and Corpus Christi (Texas), use the "decide and announce" approach. They simply state that one or more public schools in the community will be replaced by new alternative schools. When this happens, all students, parents, and teachers must choose a new program that they wish to attend. The Vancover School District in Washington uses the "evolution" approach, which supports and nurtures a menu of offerings and allow the district to evolve. A five-year planning and development strategy was used to create clusters of alternatives in each of this district's four high schools. The

clusters include such alternatives as the International Baccalaureate Degree program; Eagle's Wing, an interdisciplinary self-directed study option; Pan Terra, a dropout prevention program; extended class periods for greater in-depth study; and a variety of career academies. Vancover's approach has required a considerable amount of time and expense, but school leaders believe it will yield long-term, positive change.

Starting an alternative school has become easier in recent years, but you should be prepared for problems. Although alternatives are almost universally accepted as an essential part of any school district's efforts to educate all students, they are often viewed with suspicion and distrust. Determining the extent of a problem or issue often involves both communication and clarification. School officials may be unaware of the problem or may misunderstand its exact nature. In a hallmark study of fourteen alternative schools and programs for at-risk youth conducted at the University of Wisconsin–Madison, Gary Wehlage (1989) reported the following findings:

- In some communities, alternative schools are considered illegitimate by teachers and the public.
- Effective alternative schools almost always attract attention.
- Some see alternatives as an opportunity to purge schools of disruptive, difficult, and emotionally disturbed students.
- Innovative, creative, and novel learning experiences typify alternative schools.
- Some seek alternative schools as a new sophisticated tracking system.

The Concerns-Based Adoption Model (CBAM), developed by Shirley Hord and her colleagues (1987), was originally designed as a staff development model to help teachers identify the stages of concern that they are likely to experience as they learn about, prepare for, and use a new practice. Today, the CBAM can also be used as a strategy to unearth existing problems and issues in a community. The stages of concern typically flow from a focus on self, to managerial issues associated with the task, to the impact of the program. (A summary of these stages of concern is provided in Appendix L.) In the ASCD publication *Taking Charge of Change,* Hord and her colleagues (1987) introduce the CBAM in its most comprehensive form. National certified trainers also provide workshop sessions to help prospective users better understand this model.

Robert Eaker and Jim Huffman (1980) have developed a consumer-validated approach to assisting teachers with change that is based on the assumption that before teachers can become willing "consumers" of research, they must first act as "testers" to determine the effects of implementing the findings in their classroom. This consumer validation process involves three steps:

1. *Research reporting seminars.* The primary purpose of these seminars is to provide teachers with a clear understanding of research findings on a particular topic such as time on task, questioning strategies, and classroom management. The findings are synthesized and presented as clearly and concisely as possible. Teachers are then invited to brainstorm specific activities or strategies for implementing the research findings in their classrooms.

2. *Classroom implementation.* During the next three to four weeks, teachers apply these research findings by initiating some of the strategies or activities that were identified in the brainstorming sessions. Teachers are then asked to reflect on and evaluate the results of their efforts. Forms are provided to enable teachers to briefly describe the activities and strategies they attempted as well as their reactions to what occurred.

3. *Sharing sessions.* In this final stage, the seminar groups reconvene and teachers share their findings. These sessions serve two important purposes. First, the pooling of information gives teachers new ideas to try in their own classrooms. The "testimonial" of a colleague is of tremendous value in motivating teachers to pursue an idea, as they tend to hold the experiences of a colleague in much higher regard than the findings of a researcher. Second, the sessions give teachers an opportunity to interact with each other about teaching.

EXPLORING ALTERNATIVES

How will you get there? Once you have collected the data you need, you should begin to analyze them in an organized, effective way. If this is not your area of expertise, seek help from a person with professional knowledge and experience in this area. You will enjoy a higher degree of respect for your ideas if you are able to present information with good sound data to support your proposal. Knowledge of statistics is helpful in this regard. Statistics provide a means of reporting findings from your data collection activities. The difference between what you think is going on as a result of your needs assessment and what is really happening can often be discovered only by using statistics. It would be helpful for the planning team to learn to do a few basic statistical procedures. A good introductory statistics textbook or a team member with knowledge of statistics would be quite helpful toward this end. Knowing the value of descriptive statistics—in terms of calculating and analyzing data by way of means, medians, modes, percentiles, and standard deviations—is an extremely useful way of presenting information to justify the development or implementation of a project or program. You needn't be a statistics expert, but you should know what the data mean when they are presented.

In many instances, organizers of alternative school programs discover school environments to be much more receptive than early adopters of such programs had found. It is still a good idea, however, to thoroughly research the environment within which you intend to present your plan for an alternative program. Determining what the protocol is in your district or area will decrease the level of frustration among innovators and increase the level of communication among initiators and receivers of the information.

Originally, many alternative schools were started by small groups of activists who organized political campaigns to force school boards to allow them to create new schools that reflected their particular interest or philosophy. Today, by contrast, school districts are increasingly being required by states to develop alternative schools and programs as a safety net for dropouts, and many states provide special funding formulas to support the development and maintenance of alternative schools. In addition, many districts now provide policies that enable groups to propose new alternative public schools so that, over time, these communities will offer an increased variety of learning opportunities to parents and students. Yet despite these more user-friendly approaches to developing alternative options, school districts sometimes have difficulty accommodating highly innovative alternative schools within existing state and local regulations and policies. Often their greatest problem is trying to relate interdisciplinary and nontraditional study to typical high school graduate requirements. Mediating between state and district policies, on the one hand, and effective practice in alternative programs, on the other, will always be a challenge to school and district educators and developers of alternative programs. Those who develop alternative schools that focus on approaches to learning rather than on certain types of students, and who work to attract a heterogeneous cross-section of students, tend to be the most successful in their efforts.

When trying to gain support for initiatives such as an alternative school program or project, you will often be called upon to present information relative to the project. Regardless of whether you are creating a new project or seeking continued funding for an existing one, it is helpful to know and use strategies for making effective presentations. It often helps to put your findings in summary form, using simple charts or overheads to illustrate your main points and discussing just the high- lights of the proposal. The people who need more detailed information will often request that it be presented in a less formal venue.

Before you make a presentation, it is important to consider the objectives you wish to accomplish. This six-step model can be used as an organizer:

1. Summarize major findings
2. Present preliminary conclusions
3. Make recommendations
4. Obtain reactions
5. Solicit ideas
6. Plan strategies to provide feedback of needs assessment findings

Turning Ideas into Action

At this stage it is time to move from thinking about the alternative to developing a plan and implementing a design process. You and the other members of your group should be prepared to work hard and work together, to recognize that you do not need to be an expert in all areas, and to seek out resources both inside and outside of the school districts.

Developing a Plan

You are now down to the very basic level of planning. Some of this planning can be done at an individual level, while other aspects of plan development should be done by a group. Build consensus. The task of developing the preliminary proposal is in itself part of the consensus-building process, for it requires a group to assemble ideas and beliefs into a written plan. Having all committed partners at the table during the initial stages of development is an excellent way to build commitment and long-term involvement in the process. The design process described below is taken from *Learning from the Best: A Toolkit for Schools and Districts Based on Model Professional Development Award Winners*, published by North Central Regional Laboratory (NCREL). This process is an excellent tool for organizing and providing direction and clarity for your group:

1. Decide who should be involved in the initial design working team.
2. Decide what role other stakeholders will have in the design, both initially and ongoing.
3. Invite/notify stakeholders to participate.
4. Determine leadership roles for the design working team.
5. Determine the process for the design working team. Some questions to consider during this phase are: When should you meet? Who will schedule meetings? What do you need in advance, and who will provide it? Who will facilitate the meetings? How will you make decisions?

When implementing your plan, keep these considerations in mind:

1. Develop a strong rationale. Address a specific problem (start with a real community concern such as crime, gangs, dropouts, students who will not go on to four-year colleges). Meet the needs and interests of students in terms of the talents they have and the instructional approaches they need. Take advantage of unusual opportunities. Build on unique characteristics of the community. Provide special services such as year-round schools, extended day schools, evening or GED programs, educational reforms or restructuring, non-graded or multi-age classrooms, major enhancements of technology, interdisciplinary studies academies, or tech-prep programs. For example, Philadelphia's "school without walls" capitalizes on the city's cultural and business resources, and a Los Angeles magnet school uses resources provided by the television and motion picture industry. Successful alternative schools are grounded in well-defined philosophies and clear goals.
2. Develop a preliminary proposal consisting of rationale, philosophy, description of problems, overall school goals and objectives, general statement regarding your teaching and learning approach, the curriculum to be emphasized, the

types of students to be served, timeline, budget, and recommendations for evaluation.

3. Seek authorization and approval. The appropriate decision-making body, such as the school board, should be approached on at least two or three different occasions. At these meetings, be sure to (a) present your group's rationale and purpose, (b) present your preliminary proposal or concept paper, and (c) seek approval for an official planning process to study the issue and make recommendations.

ACTING ON THE PLAN

A careful process of marketing, recruitment, selection, and enrollment is a must at this stage.

1. Select teachers. Your preliminary planning team must include teachers and administrators. Choosing a leader is perhaps the most critical element in the staffing process.
2. Approve a process for planning and development. Successful alternative schools should not take more than a year to plan. Shorter planning and implementation schedules lead to maximum participation, enthusiasm, and commitment. Continued planning and staff development should include visits to other schools.
3. Select a facility.
4. Market the program. Inform the community of the new educational option. Newspaper articles, media announcements, information and orientation sessions for all building principals and counselors, open community meetings, help sessions for students and parents, and multiple information contacts are all great ways to get the word out.
5. Enroll students. Approval criteria/procedures should be a part of your recruitment package. The admission procedures and policies should be clearly identified in terms of whether they involve personal interviews with students and parents, auditions, portfolios, or demonstration of minimal skills. Many alternative programs use a written commitment or contract from parents as well as students, acknowledging their expectations and understanding of the program.
6. Institute shared decision making, which is as essential to effective alternative programs as is school choice. The decision-

making process should grow out of the planning process and include a carefully planned school management team consisting of parents, students, and teachers. Successful alternative schools provide a range of models of governance and decision making.

REFERENCES

Bransford, J., and Stein, B. (1984). *The Ideal Problem Solver*. New York: W. H. Freeman.

Conley, B. (1993). "Framework for the Strategic Plan." Baltimore, MD: Baltimore City Public School System.

Conzemius, A., and O'Neill, J. (2001). *Building Shared Responsibility for Student Learning*. Alexandria, VA: Association for Supervision and Curriculum Development.

DuFour, R. (1992). *Creating the New American School*. Bloomington, IN: National Educational Service.

Duke, D. (1978). *The Retransformation of the School*. Chicago: Nelson-Hall.

Eaker, R., and Huffman, J. (1980). *Helping Teachers Use Research Findings: The Consumer Validation Process*. East Lansing: Michigan State University, Institute for Research on Teaching.

Hassel, E. (1999). *Professional Development: Learning from the Best*. Oak Brook, IL: North Central Regional Educational Laboratory.

Hord, S., et al. (1987). *Taking Charge of Change*. Alexandria, VA: Association for Supervision and Curriculum Development.

Kellmayer, J. (1995). *How to Establish an Alternative School*. Thousand Oaks, CA: Corwin Press.

Krallingher, J. (1989). *Strategic Planning Workbook*. New York: John Wiley & Sons.

"Leadership Guide to Initial Planning for Improvement" (1992). University of Wisconsin–Madison, Office of Quality Improvement.

Leatherman, D. (1990a). *The Training Trilogy: Assessing Needs*. Amherst, MA: Human Resource Development Press, Inc.

_____. (1990b). *The Training Trilogy: Designing Programs*. Amherst, MA: Human Resource Development Press, Inc.

Lewis, A. (1989). *Restructuring America's Schools*. Arlington, VA: American Association of School Administrators.

Patton, M. Q. (1990). *Qualitative Evaluation and Research Methods*. Newbury Park, CA: Sage Publications.

Schmoker, M. (1996). *Results*. Alexandria, VA: Association for Supervision and Curriculum Development.

Six Sigma. Affinity Diagram. Available online at http://www.sytsma.com/tqmtools/affin.html.

Thompson, S. (2001). *Decision-Making in Planning and Teaching.* New York: Longman.

Wehlage, Gary. (1989). "Empowering Communities for School Reform [Microform]: The Annie E. Casey Foundation's New Futures Initiative." Madison: University of Wisconsin Center for Education Research, National Center on Effective Secondary Schools.

APPENDIX A:
DESIGN PRINCIPLES FOR
AN EFFECTIVE ALTERNATIVE PROGRAM

An effective alternative program

1. Is based on an assessment of needs
2. Provides students with a variety of learning experiences
3. Involves students in the learning
4. Reduces classroom management and behavior problems
5. Is relevant to the students' "real world"
6. Results in teaching that relates to students' experiences
7. Takes into account that students tend to remember what they see and hear, versus what they are told
8. Provides students with an opportunity to do what it is they are being taught
9. Uses repetition to help students learn
10. Focuses on quality, not quantity
11. Provides for follow-up on what has been taught
12. Includes evaluation as part of the original planning process

APPENDIX B:
PROGRAM PLANNING PROCESS

The NCREL design principles listed earlier can be used to make good decisions about the content of your alternative program. Each of the following program-planning steps should be approached with these design principles in mind:

1. Identify a list of outcomes to be achieved.
2. Identify undesirable outcomes, and rewrite them in positive form.
3. Order the final list of all outcomes.
4. Conduct verification interviews with selected members of the community or the planning group to determine which outcomes are being achieved, and which are not.
5. Write objectives.
6. Determine milestones for each objective.
7. Identify reasons for which the objectives are important.
8. Identify evidence for each of the reasons listed in step 7.
9. Determine strategies and methods to accomplish objectives.
10. Design the program's evaluation.

APPENDIX C:
INITIAL PLANNING PROCESS

Population to be served
    Who is impacted by our work?
    What are their needs?
    ↓

Mission
    Why do we exist?
    ↓

Vision
    Where are we going?
    ↓

Critical Processes
    What do we do? (6–10 primary functions)
    ↓

Current Situations
    Where are we now?
        Needs of population
        Needs of community
        Culture

      ↓ → → → → →
               ↓

        Gap
            What is the gap between our vision and
            the current situation?
            ↓

        Focus Issues
            Which issues will we focus on first?
            Which processes are involved?
            ↓

        Measurable Goals
            How will we know we've improved?
            ↓

        Action Plan
            One- to two-year plan to begin

APPENDIX D:
STRATEGIC PLAN OUTLINE

<u>Strategic Goals</u>

<u>Key Participant Needs</u>

<u>Key Realities (internal and external)</u>

<u>Strategy</u>

<u>Action Priorities</u>

APPENDIX E:
COMMON DEFINITIONS FOR
DEVELOPING THE STRATEGIC PLAN

Strategic Planning

The process by which we envision the future and develop explicit action plans to achieve that future.

Mission Statement

An expression of who we are, what we're all about, and whom we serve. Following are some fundamental reasons for developing a mission statement:

- To help achieve unanimity of purpose
- To lay the foundation for allocating resources
- To serve as a focal point for individuals to identify with our purpose and direction
- To facilitate the translation of objectives into an appropriate work plan or structure
- To help translate our purposes into objectives that can be measured over time

In short, a mission statement provides the foundation for the development of objectives, strategies, tactics, and priorities contained in the strategic plan. It specifies the fundamental reasons for which the organization exists.

Vision Statement

A statement that describes in bold and broad terms what we hope to become, in terms of the "best or preferred future"; provides an overall framework with which to evaluate the appropriateness and relevance of our mission and objectives; and creates an energizing focus for our communication, participation, empowerment, and commitment.

Philosophy

The belief system and principles by which our group operates.

Goal

A statement of the general results.

Objectives

Specific statements of the degree of quantitative results expected over a defined period of time. Objectives include descriptions of (1) the results to be accomplished, (2) who or what will display the results, (3) the conditions under which the results will be observed, and (4) the criteria that will be used to measure success.

Strategy

A set of well-coordinated action programs aimed at securing long-term sustainable goals and objectives.

Tactic

A short-term, focused technique (six to eight months in duration) used to secure an objective.

Operational Plan or Action Plan

A plan that emphasizes the autonomy of each unit as it defines the unit's individual strategy for achieving the vision. The plan includes the unit's objectives as they relate to the goals and subgoals.

Living Document

A document that has the flexibility to withstand changes based on the dynamics of our environment, given how internal and external forces influence the work of the group.

Evaluation

The process of making judgments as to the degree of success achieved at some predetermined point after implementation of the strategic plan.

APPENDIX F: INTERVIEW SCHEDULE FOR A STUDY OF CONTEMPORARY ALTERNATIVE SCHOOLS

I. Educational Goals

(Q1) Which of the following types of goals generally characterize your school?

Exploratory goals: Characterized by student-initiated activities, project learning, stress on creativity and natural growth, and terms like *open education*

Preparatory goals: Characterized by career education; vocational training; acquisition of basic reading, writing, and arithmetic skills; and preparation for socially acceptable targets

Revolutionary goals: Characterized by ideological commitments, radical curriculum content, and preparation for targets that are not acceptable to the general population

Participatory goals: Characterized by a dedication to democratic school government, town meetings, and student decision making

Therapeutic goals: Characterized by stress on self-exploration, group process, personal growth, and affective development

Academic goals: Characterized by unusual courses, college-style learning experiences, seminars, and student independent study

Demonstrative goals: Characterized by emphasis on the school as a lab for the development of new techniques, teacher training, and educational experimentation

No primary goals

II. Pedagogical Dimensions

(Q2) How is age-grouping accomplished in your school?

Grades corresponding to chronological years

Mixed-age units of two or three years

No age-grouping at all

(Q3) How is ability-grouping accomplished in your school?

Students are grouped heterogeneously

Students are grouped homogeneously

Students are grouped homogeneously on a limited basis (e.g., in reading only)

(Q4) How is instructional grouping accomplished in your school? (Indicate only the mode[s] used frequently.)

Large-group instruction

Small-group instruction

Individualized instruction

Independent study

(Q5)   How is the curriculum structured in terms of required and elective courses?

Elementary level—No requirements

Requirements in reading and mathematics only

Additional requirements

Secondary level—No elective courses

Some electives

All electives

(Q6)   How do the curriculum offerings compare to those in a conventional public school?

Generally equivalent

Less variety

More variety

(Q7)   Which of the following instructional features can be found in your school?

In-and-outness (extensive use of extra-classroom environments)

School-without-walls

School-within-a-school

Learning centers

Creative room arrangement

Work-study programs

Simultaneous use of various learning materials

Integrated day (undivided by specific periods)

Modular scheduling

Multiple staffing

Team teaching

Cross-age tutoring

(Q8)   How can teacher-student relations be characterized in your school?

Professional (formal, superordinate-to-subordinate)

Democratic (informal, as equals)

(Q9)   What are the bases for evaluation of student progress in your school?

Standardized tests

Fixed scales and grades

Individualized judgments of performance

Criterion-referenced measures

No consistent form of evaluation

(Q10)   How is student progress reported in your school?

Report cards
Portfolios of student work
Parent-teacher conferences
Student-teacher conferences
Parent-teacher-student conferences
No method of reporting progress

III. Administrative Organization

(Q11) How would you characterize the administrative organization of your school? (Choose only one.)

Parent cooperative
Parent-teacher operated
Parent-teacher-administrator operated
Teacher-administrator operated
Headmaster operated
Teacher operated
Student operated
Student-teacher cooperative
Student-teacher-administrator operated

(Q12) Which of the following decision-making roles, processes, or groups exist in your school?

Town meeting
Committees
Faculty meetings
Advisory groups
Elected Board of Trustees
Appointed Board of Trustees
Coordinator
Headmaster or director
Autonomous teachers
Teacher planning teams
Consultants

IV. Composition

(Q13) What is the estimated educational background of the students in your school? (You can choose more than one.)

More than 25 percent with successful previous experience in conventional public schools
More than 25 percent with unsuccessful previous experience in conventional public schools
Some students with nonpublic school experience
Some with day-care or preschool experience

(Q14) Which of the following characteristics best fit the parents of the students in this school?

        50 percent or more from intact families
        50 percent or more middle class
        25 percent or more working class
        25 percent or more upper-middle or upper class
        50 percent or more white
        25 percent or more nonwhite
        25 percent or more working mothers
        25 percent or more engaged in new lifestyles
        25 percent or more with liberal political beliefs
        25 percent or more professionals (at least one in the family)

(Q15)   Which of the following characteristics best fit the teachers in the school?

        At least three years of teaching experience
        Between one and three years of teaching experience
        No teaching experience
        Teacher training courses in college
        College degree but not teacher training courses
        Unemployed just prior to getting the present job
        Children of teacher in the school
        Teacher engaged in alternative lifestyles

V. Impetuses to the Development of Alternative Schools

(Q16)   Which of the following factors influenced the emergence of this alternative school?

        Desire for improved instruction
        Desire for a different curriculum
        Tense racial situation
        Threat of forced school integration
        Federal grants
        Private grants
        Student discontent in local public schools
        Closing of an existing alternative school
        Threat to close an existing public school
        Need for day-care facilities
        Availability of unused building facilities
        Desire for a "neighborhood school"
        University influence
        Second-generation alternative school arising out of
           dissatisfaction with previous alternative school
        Offshoot of a social service program
        Influence of a commune or collective
        Teacher frustration in local public school
        Other: (Please specify.)

APPENDIX G:
SOME QUESTIONS YOU MIGHT ASK
OF ALTERNATIVE EDUCATION PROVIDERS

1. What programs/services do you offer?
2. Who are your students? (Describe their demographics.)
3. What are the goals of your services? (Examples include credit retrieval, return to traditional school environment, GED.)
4. How do you measure your success?
5. Describe your school/classroom environment.
6. What is your teacher/student ratio?
7. How do you create and support smaller class sizes?
8. Do you offer all curriculum areas? If not, which do you offer?
9. What is the students' average length of stay in your program?
10. What objectives are most important in terms of meeting your students' needs?
11. What have you done as a staff-school to address the state content standards? (Examples include curriculum alignment and how data have been interpreted.)
12. How do you prepare your students to meet these standards?
13. What is your biggest hurdle in preparing students to meet these standards? How have you cleared that hurdle so far?
14. What factors account for the high percentage of students who have met benchmarks in the current year?
15. What kinds of support do students have in your program? (Examples include access to counselors and student support groups.)
16. What makes your program unique?

APPENDIX H: MISSION STATEMENTS

What a Mission Statement Should Look Like

It should capture the essence of why the project or program exists, and it should be short enough for everyone in the organization to know and understand it.

Process for Developing a Mission

Whose Mission Is This?

Define the program covered by this mission. Is it part of a larger organization? If so, what is the mission of the larger organization?

Mission as a Product

What will you use it for? Where will it appear? Who will see it? How will it serve your organization? What purpose will it serve?

Developing the Mission

The group should work together to examine and develop the following:

> *Aim:* What is the purpose of the program? Why does it exist? If your unit is part of a larger organization, what is the mission of the larger organization? What is the role of your unit in carrying out that mission?
> *Audience:* Who is impacted? What population will you serve?
> *Action:* What will the program do to accomplish the aim for the audience?

Brainstorm (Appendix K) and discuss the above items. If there are many, prioritize them.

Then use that information to develop a draft statement that captures the essence of the reason the program exists. Make it short and to the point, something everyone in the group can know and understand.

Moving the Mission on Down

Each person in the group is likely to be a key participant in the process. Each should take the draft statement and solicit feedback and comments from trusted friends and colleagues. Others' perspectives may prove helpful, particularly those of people who know something about what you are attempting to do.

Each group member should talk about his or her role in carrying out the mission and spend time reflecting on the content; then reconvene with the comments and develop the mission/vision statement.

Evaluation: How will you determine that the mission is being carried out?

Guiding Principles

What Are Guiding Principles?

Guiding principles are the values that guide decision making in any group.

The Purpose of Guiding Principles

As we are caught up in the stresses and conflicts inherent in group work, we can easily forget the values that we want to drive our decision making. Deciding those as a group can help group members develop an understanding that will provide a basis for working together and making consensus decisions that reflect those values.

Guiding Principles as Product

Who will see these? You may choose to make them an internal list that the group uses in its activities. Or you may choose to communicate them to groups who will make decisions about your program.

You may even choose to make them public knowledge by including them in your promotional materials. Your guiding principles may be important to your ability to deliver the program you are developing.

Examples

Examples of guiding principles are the very characteristics that many believe should be present in alternative schools.

Developing Your Guiding Principles

1. Brainstorm (Appendix K): "What values should your group possess?"
2. Use an affinity diagram (Appendix J) to group your values. Then use a multi-voting process to prioritize them.
3. Hold an open discussion of the prioritized elements. (This can be done before multi-voting, if preferred.)
4. Then discuss: "What principles will guide our actions as a group and as individuals?" (This may or may not involve language different from that used to discuss your values.)

5. Develop one or more statements that are concise and understand-
able to your audience.

Vision

What Is a Vision?

A vision is a mental picture of a desired future state.

It can consist of one phrase or several statements. It should be concise
and clear to everyone in the group and to the audience the group intends to
serve. Everyone in the group should know and understand the vision.

It should be a real stretch to get to the vision. Consider setting it beyond
the point of attainable goals. Reach far.

The Purpose of a Vision

A vision gives everyone in the group a clear sense of the organization's main
thrust. It serves as a grounding when daily decisions are being made. It guides
our activities toward an agreed-upon future state. It can be a driving force for innovative actions and a commitment to purpose.

Without vision, people tend to maintain their current status, and mediocrity is the norm.

How Does It Fit with Other Components?

The vision builds on the mission. The mission is the reason we exist. But to exist is not enough. The vision gives us direction to strive for, to develop and improve, to exceed the needs of those we serve.

The vision provides a picture of the planning that follows. Issues, critical
processes, and measurable goals are derived from the vision.

Passing It Down: Developing Ownership at All Levels

The vision will take on real power when it is owned by everyone in the group. To
feel that sense of ownership, everyone needs to be involved in developing the vision and included in the efforts to attain it.

Developing a Vision

1. Ask all group members to silently list their thoughts on the following
question: "What makes this group strong and distinctive now?"
2. Share those thoughts and put them on movable cards. Group them
and notice common themes.

3. Discuss the future. What trends will be affecting this group? Consider economic, social, demographic, technological, and other trends. How will these affect the needs of your population? How will they directly affect your group?

4. Ask all group members to silently list their thoughts on this question: "In five or ten years, what should be the strengths of our group? How can it remain distinctive? In what ways will it be known as the best? How is it exceeding the needs of the population we serve?" (For this last question, you might imagine that a team of news reporters is featuring your group. What are they focusing on? What is newsworthy about the group?)

5. Again, share each person's thoughts, capture them on movable cards, and do an affinity diagram (Appendix J). Notice common themes.

6. Discuss and decide on key descriptors. Begin to create a vision statement using those key descriptors.

7. Create a draft version of the vision statement, and have each member spend time away from the group reflecting on it.

8. Meet again and discuss other ideas they come up with. Refine and agree on your vision statement.

9. Determine how to communicate this vision statement throughout the group. Discuss how to develop ownership of the vision by all group members.

10. Plan your next steps. Without a plan to attain the vision, it is no more than a dream.

11. Discuss how you will know if the vision is being realized. Discuss meaningful measures of success. Discuss how and when this will be evaluated.

Current Situation

A vision is a stretch for the future. From where? In order to get from one place to another, you have to know where you have started. Even a map is useless without knowing where you are now. Before developing a plan, you must have a clear picture of the current situation. This is not as we wish it to be but, rather, a true, clear picture of reality as it is. You will make few measurable gains in the future without an honest picture of the present.

Defining the Current Situation

Are participants' needs now being met? How do you know? How can you find out? What are the baseline measures?

Describe the current culture of the population being served.

Define your burning issues (the ones that keep you awake at night).

What are your strengths, weaknesses, and opportunities? What threats are confronting you?

What trends and major events are affecting your group?

The Gap

So now you know where you want to go.

And now we know where we are.

Let's compare them and define the gap.

What are the differences? What is in good shape? What needs improvement? Capture ideas on:

> The gap
> Improvement needs
> Developmental needs
> Maintenance needs
> Learning needs

Key Results Areas

What Are Key Results Areas?

Once you have acknowledged the gap between the vision and the current situation, you can begin to identify areas on which to focus major development and/or improvement efforts over the next year or more.

You will want to choose only one to three key result areas. In order to do them justice, dedicate sufficient resources and energy to each of them.

The key results areas are additional to managing all of the other tasks that need to be done to complete development and maintenance of the program. Management must be ongoing, and you will want to continue making improvements in the procedures on which you rely.

The key results areas are the breakthrough development. They go above and beyond regular improvement and daily maintenance.

Why Have Key Results Areas?

You have probably generated ideas on many major development and improvement areas in this planning process—in addition to all the ideas you had before you started.

But you cannot do it all and do it well. Having key results areas allows you to identify the most important opportunities and focus your resources.

Once this focus is achieved, new areas can be identified and developed.

Identifying Key Result Areas

1. Brainstorm (Appendix K) all the issues or key result areas that are derived from the comparison of your vision with the current situation (the gap).
2. Do an affinity diagram (Appendix J) to group the areas.
3. Discuss the groupings.
4. Decide on one to three key results areas for major development or improvement.

Critical Processes and Measurable Goals

What Are Critical Processes?

Critical processes are processes at the base of the key results areas. *Example:* If increased diversity is a key result area, then the processes for recruitment and retention might be your critical process.

What Are Measures of Success?

Measures of success are the way you determine whether or not improvement is being attained. How will you know the situation is getting better? How will you measure and monitor?

Measurable Goals

Once you know what you will measure, determine your goals. How much better do you want to strive to be? By when?

Developing Your Critical Processes and Measurable Goals

1. Examine your key results areas. What processes are critical to their success?
2. Do a Pareto chart to determine which processes are the most important. Choose a few to focus on.
3. For each critical process chosen, develop measurable goals (a) What is the baseline of the process now? (b) What do we need the process to be able to do to exceed participant needs? (c) Set goals for each.

APPENDIX I:
EVALUATING A MISSION/VISION STATEMENT

The following questions provide useful criteria for evaluating a mission/vision statement.

1. Is it written? The very process of writing this statement helps to sharpen issues and clarify positions. Although putting a mission/vision statement in writing does not ensure that it will be effective in influencing individuals within the organization, the lack of a written statement suggests inattention to this important aspect of organizational life.
2. Is it widely disseminated? If a mission/vision statement is to influence the decisions and behavior of individuals within the organization, they must be aware of it. Efforts should constantly be made to call attention to the statement.
3. Is it widely supported? The effect of the mission/vision statement will be directly correlated to the level of support that it has within the school community. Once again, it must reflect the hopes, aspirations, and personal visions of those who are called on to make it a reality.
4. Is it used in day-to-day operations? An effective mission/vision statement serves as a blueprint for school improvement. It cannot simply be filed away and forgotten. It should serve as a constant reference point, a guiding star in the establishment of goals, programs, procedures, and priorities. Effective organizations are characterized not by high-sounding mission/vision statements floating in space but, rather, by a relentless willingness to examine current conditions in light of an explicitly stated desired future. The drafting of a statement does not bring about a shared vision. It can become a reality only as a direct result of the efforts of committed individuals who make the advancement of that vision central to their daily work.

APPENDIX J:
AFFINITY DIAGRAM

Uses of an Affinity Diagram

An affinity diagram is used for

1. Adding structure to large or complicated issues (*examples:* What are the issues relative to implementing a thematic approach to teaching? What are the central issues in the development of a particular new product?)
2. Breaking down a complicated issue into broad categories (*examples:* Which departments are more likely to implement Total Quality Management [TQM] in this school? What are the major steps in the completion of a complex project?)
3. Gaining agreement on an issue or situation (*examples:* Which direction should the school take to restructure its curriculum? How should a new product be marketed?)

Steps in Constructing an Affinity Diagram

1. State the issue or problem to be explored. Start with a clear statement of the problem or goal and provide a time limit for the session. (Usually forty-five to sixty minutes are sufficient.)

2. Brainstorm (Appendix K) ideas for the issue or problem. Each participant should think of ideas and write them individually on index cards or sticky tags, or have a recorder write them on a flip chart.

3. Collect the cards or sticky tags, mix them up, and spread them out (or stick them) on a flat surface such as a desk or wall. Index cards can easily be secured to a wall with a putty-type adhesive.

4. Arrange the cards or sticky tags into related groups. For approximately fifteen minutes, allow participants to pick out cards that list related ideas and set them aside until all cards are grouped.

5. Create a title or heading for each grouping that best describes its theme.

APPENDIX K:
BRAINSTORMING

Definition

Brainstorming is a systematic way to involve all group members in generating a large number of ideas.

Goals (Why do we brainstorm?)

- Generate many ideas
- Involve everyone
- Increase creativity
- Build understanding and ownership
- Break down barriers
- Expand the range of options
- Build teamwork
- Prevent put-downs, impasses, and groupthink

Techniques

Materials

- Flipchart pad or blackboard
- Felt pens and masking tape
- Wall space on which to post each page generated

Methods

- Free-for-all
  Ask for ideas from anyone in the group.
- Round-robin
  Ask each person to share one idea.
  A person may pass if he or she does not have an idea.
  Go from person to person until there are no new ideas.
- Write and share
  Ask each person to spend five minutes writing down his or her ideas.
  Use the round-robin technique as a way to share ideas.
- Storyboarding
  Ask each person to write ideas on sticky tags. Then organize the notes in a variety of sequences to arrive at the most effective plan.

Roles and Responsibilities

Facilitator/Recorder

- Encourage sharing
- Create a safe environment
- Record all ideas *exactly as stated*
- Write visibly and legibly
- Print, abbreviate
- Respect all ideas
- Don't rephrase ideas
- Protect all members
- Uphold the ground rules with absolute conformity
- Challenge the group's creativity
- Ask open-ended questions
  "What do you mean by that?"
  "Can you say more about that?"

Participants

- Be free-wheeling
- Strive for many ideas
- Combine, expand, and build on others' ideas
- Listen to the ideas of others
- Check the accuracy of the recorder's record
- Assume responsibility for the success of the group
- Uphold the ground rules

Brainstorming Ground Rules

- No criticism
- Do not judge or evaluate ideas
- Everyone gets a turn
- One idea per turn
- Be respectful
- Don't interrupt
- Don't interpret

APPENDIX L:
STAGES OF CONCERN ACCORDING TO
THE CONCERNS-BASED ADOPTION MODEL (CBAM)

Stage 0: Awareness Concerns

("What is the innovation?")

- If possible, involve teachers in discussions and decisions about the innovation and its implementation.
- Share enough information to arouse interest, but not so much that it overwhelms.
- Acknowledge that a lack of awareness is expected and reasonable, and that no questions about the innovation are foolish.
- Encourage unaware persons to talk with colleagues who know about the innovation.
- Take steps to minimize gossip and inaccurate sharing of information about the innovation.

Stage 1: Information Concerns

("I need to know more about the innovation.")

- Provide clear and accurate information about the innovation.
- Use a variety of ways to share information—through speech, writing, and available media. Communicate with individuals as well as with small and large groups.
- Ask persons who have used the innovation in other settings to visit with your teachers. Visits to users' schools can also be arranged.
- Help teachers see how the innovation relates to their current practices, in regard to both similarities and differences.
- Be enthusiastic, and enhance the visibility of others who are excited.

Stage 2: Personal Concerns

("How will the innovation affect me?")

- Legitimize the existence and expression of personal concerns. Knowing that these concerns are shared can be comforting.
- Use personal notes and conversations to provide encouragement and reinforce personal adequacy.

•• Connect the teachers with others whose personal concerns have diminished and who will be supportive.

•• Show how the innovation can be implemented sequentially rather than in one big leap. It is important to establish expectations that are attainable.

•• Do not push innovation use, but encourage and support it while maintaining expectations.

Stage 3: Management Concerns

("How will I find time to do this?")

•• Clarify the steps and components of the innovation.

•• Provide answers that address the small, specific "how-to" issues that are so often the cause of management concerns.

•• Demonstrate exact and practical solutions to the logistical problems that contribute to these concerns.

•• Help teachers sequence specific activities, and set timelines for their accomplishments.

•• Focus on the immediate demands of the innovation, not on what will be or could be in the future.

Stage 4: Consequence Concerns

("How is my use of the innovation affecting kids?")

•• Provide staff members with opportunities to visit other settings in which the innovation is in use and to attend conferences on the topic.

•• Provide them with positive feedback and needed support.

•• Find opportunities for them to share their skills with others.

•• Share information pertaining to the innovation with them.

Stage 5: Collaboration

("I would like to discuss my findings and ideas with others.")

•• Provide staff members with opportunities to develop the skills necessary for working collaboratively.

•• Bring together persons, both within and outside the school, who are interested in collaboration.

• Help the collaborators establish reasonable expectations and guide-lines for their collaborative efforts.
• Ask the collaborators to provide technical assistance to others who need assistance.
• Encourage the collaborators, but do not attempt to force collabora-tion on those who are not interested.

Stage 6: Refocusing Concerns

("I have an idea for improving upon the innovation.")

• Respect and encourage the staff members' interest in finding a better way.
• Help channel their ideas and energies in ways that will be produc-tive rather than counterproductive.
• Encourage them to act on their concerns for program improvement.
• Help them access the resources they need to refine their ideas and put them into practice.
• Be aware of and willing to accept the fact that these staff members may replace or significantly modify the existing innovations.

Chapter 9

☙ Evaluating Alternative Schools and Programs

This chapter completes the program development cycle by addressing tasks associated with the *L* in the IDEAL model. In Chapter 8, we Identified the challenge (*I*), Defined the challenge (*D*), Explored alternatives (*E*), and Acted on the plan (*A*). Now it is time to consider a process that permits us to Look at and reflect on the results (*L*).

Program evaluation is the process of systematically assessing the quality of a program and determining how it can be improved. Evaluation gives direction to all facets of the process when you are developing, changing, and/or improving a program. It is perhaps one of the toughest aspects of program development and implementation. Successful program development cannot occur without evaluation. It is the process used to identify needs. It is the process used to set priorities among needs and to translate needs into program objectives or to modify existing objectives. It is the process used to identify and select among different program approaches, organizations, assignments, materials and equipment, facilities, schedules, and other elements in order to build a program that has a high likelihood of success. It is the process used to monitor and adjust programs as they are implemented. And, finally, it is the process used to determine whether a program is resulting in desired outcomes and why the outcomes are as they are.

When evaluating alternative programs, you need to set specific goals for the evaluation process. The evaluation should, at a minimum, provide feedback on the purpose, the approaches, who is involved, who is excluded, the costs, the accomplishments, and the short- and long-term features of the program. According to James Sanders (1992), there are three aspects of good program evaluation: "communication, communication, communication." Program evaluation decisions that must be made early on are as follows:

1. Who will do the evaluation?
2. Who are the stakeholders in the evaluation?

3. What is to be evaluated?
4. What resources and personnel are available for the evaluation?

David Stufflebeam (cited in Worthen and Sanders, 1987) suggests that the following five tasks should be completed when conducting program evaluation:

1. Focusing the evaluation
2. Collecting information
3. Organizing and analyzing information
4. Reporting information
5. Administering the evaluation

FOCUSING THE EVALUATION

A list of purposes can serve as a focal point for your evaluation. Having the group identify program needs, individual needs, resource allotments and strategies, and monitoring requirements is one way to begin the process. It is important during this phase to be sure that all group members understand the difference between formative and summative evaluation and the value of each in identifying and sharing results of program implementation. Group members or others working in the program can conduct formative evaluation; the purpose is to gather feedback on aspects of the program that are undergoing review and possible revision. Summative evaluation is best conducted in a way that is external to the program. Programs with evaluations conducted by a third party often enjoy a higher degree of credibility than those with evaluations conducted internally.

In this phase of the evaluation process it is also extremely important to clarify what is to be evaluated. Evaluation can be clear and accurate only if there is agreement on exactly what is being reviewed.

A basic evaluation worksheet like the one shown in Appendix M can be used to organize the process. The six columns in this worksheet identify the information needed to complete the process: evaluation questions, why each question is important, information needed to answer each questions, when and how the information will be collected, and data analysis and interpretation procedures.

At this point, the evaluation questions should be identified. Once that is done, you will have completed step 1—focusing the evaluation.

You will have clarified the evaluation purposes, clarified what is to be evaluated, and identified the evaluation questions to be answered.

COLLECTING INFORMATION

To complete the next two columns of the worksheet, you must identify the information needed to answer each question. It would be helpful during this phase to brainstorm a list of sources of information as well as methods and instruments to be used for collecting information. Feedback from an experienced evaluator would also be helpful. Some of the data collection strategies listed in Chapter 8—especially observations, interviews, and focus groups—can be used for program evaluation as well as for program development. For each evaluation question, you need to determine the way in which the information will be analyzed.

ORGANIZING AND ANALYZING INFORMATION

The process used in this phase depends on the kind of data collected. If you have conducted observations, interviews, or focus groups, you will want to organize the data in a way that generates common themes on which to focus your analysis of the information. Alternatively, if you have collected quantitative data from surveys or questionnaires, the statistical procedures discussed earlier in the book will prove helpful.

REPORTING INFORMATION

It is wise to keep participants and stakeholders informed throughout the entire evaluation process. Interested parties should know the status of the evaluation at all times. Once the draft report of the evaluation is completed, it should be circulated to all key stakeholders for review and comment. At that point, reviewers can be asked to comment on factual errors, typing errors, missing interpretations, missing evidence, and any other problems that compromise the writing style or appearance of the report. Last, but not least, share the results. After all, your reason for doing the evaluation is to use the data for program improvement and appropriate follow-up action. Determine the audience that should receive information about the program, and follow up to ensure that the evaluation data are translated into an action plan.

ADMINISTERING THE EVALUATION

An evaluation cannot be effectively completed without a management plan. This plan must include a description of the task to be completed, a list of the personnel to be involved, a budget, and a time schedule. A review of evaluation standards from an appropriate professional association is also recommended, as it can provide guidance at all levels of the evaluation process. One source to consider is the Joint Committee on Standards for Education Evaluation (1981).

REFERENCES

Frechtling, J. (Ed.) (1997). *User-Friendly Handbook for Missed Method Evaluations.* Arlington, VA: National Science Foundation.

Joint Committee on Standards for Educational Evaluation (1981). *Standards for Evaluations of Educational Programs, Projects, and Materials.* New York: McGraw-Hill.

Owens, T. R., and Evans, W. E. (1977). *Program Evaluation Skills for Busy Administrators.* Portland, OR: Northwest Regional Educational Laboratory.

Sanders, J. (1992). *Evaluating School Programs: An Educator's Guide.* Newbury Park, CA: Corwin Press.

Worthen, B. R., and Sanders, J. R. (1987). *Educational Evaluation: Alternative Approaches and Practical Guidelines.* New York: Longman.

APPENDIX M:
EVALUATION INFORMATION COLLECTION
AND ANALYSIS WORKSHEET

Evaluation Questions	Why Each Question Is Important	Information Needed to Answer Each Question	When and How the Information Will Be Collected	Data Analysis and Interpretation Procedures

Chapter 10
●✦ The Future of
Public Alternative Education

The American school system was designed in the early national period under the leadership of school reformers such as Horace Mann. It reflected the influence of the old New England colonial district and catered to the needs of a new democracy. The nation then was dominated by agriculture, making a common school with summer vacations and local control quite acceptable. With the rise of industry, standardization of the curriculum and a delivery system based on a Newtonian mechanistic model was adopted. The school system became a closed machine with top-down administration, predetermined standards, lock-step definitions of content by grade, and fixed rules of behavior. Obviously, the system worked well to prepare students for the factory or the office. With its emphasis on assimilation, conformity, and traditional values, it was able to handle the masses of European immigrants and the growing American population.

New needs began to emerge with the onset of the world wars, the Great Depression of the 1930s, social unrest, the rising affluence of the middle class, the human rights movement, and the demands of minorities for status. Superimposed upon these changes were the new requirements of the information age, a service economy, and a global culture. New programs were tried in an effort to cope with changing life conditions, social mobility, and new expectations. These included open classrooms, individualized instruction, alternative schools, nongraded schools, team teaching, and magnet schools. In general, these innovations were added to the existing system, but they did not become the dominant pattern. Many were simply tried for a time and then withdrawn, allowing the old system to emerge again.

Most of the current reform movement is aimed at modifying the basic traditional schools. There are those who think a piecemeal approach is not adequate and that it is now time for a holistic redesign of the whole structure. Some who would restructure education have moved their children outside the system.

The home school movement of the mid-1980s is an example. With individual computers, communications networks, and many parents working at home, it became possible to give children a basic education without recourse to the schools. The home school movement is growing among well-educated citizens who prefer to provide their own educational programs for their children.

Public schools have been the target of reform and improvement initiatives for several decades. That pattern is unlikely to change in the future. The alternative school movement is gaining momentum even now. The Supreme Court, in 2002, heard arguments for and against school vouchers. This case is considered one of the most important the Court will hear this term because the outcome could significantly reshape American education policy. The Edison Project, which is about to take control of a yet to be determined number of schools in Philadelphia, is just another example of the strength of privatization movements in the country today. According to the Council for American Private Education, one in four of the nation's schools is a private school and 11 percent of all students attend them. That translates into 27,000 schools and nearly 6 million students. In January 2001, President Bush presented his K–12 education proposal entitled "No Child Left Behind" to Congress. On May 23, 2001, the House passed H.R. 1, the "Leave No Child Behind Act of 2001," and sent it to the Senate. On June 14, 2001, the Senate passed S. 1, the "Better Education for Students and Teachers Act." A Conference Committee worked on the bill from June through December 2001. On December 13, 2001, the House approved the Conference Committee Report by a vote of 381 to 41. On December 18, 2001, the Conference Committee Report was approved in the Senate by a vote of 87 to 10. President Bush signed the bill on January 8, 2002. It is now known as P.L. 107-110. Title V of the law has specific language about charter schools. Authorized at $300 million in 2002, the program provides aid to help states and localities support charter schools, including money to assist with the planning and design of charter schools, the evaluation of their effectiveness, and the costs of facilities. With the passage of the "No Child Left Behind" legislation in January 2002, that number will likely increase as parents are given the option to remove their children from failing schools. Even though the law, which brings about a transformation of the federal role in education, is rooted in what George W. Bush calls bipartisan politics, it has the potential to significantly impact the development of alternative schools and alternative programs. The push for an end to the public school monopoly continues to surface as advocates for competition and choice continue to call for more freedom and quality in school selection. They propose a number of ways to achieve school choice, specifying tax credits, vouchers, and charter schools as just a few examples of options within our reach.

A review of alternative education requires an examination of our views about the aim and purpose of public education. It has become virtually impossible, over the last decade, to separate alternative education from school reform. Yet, as noted in earlier chapters, alternative education was once defined simply as a program for misfits, students who did not fit into the mainstream environment.

The number and types of alternative schools will increase significantly during this decade, in both the public and private sectors. There is now a significant knowledge base on which to support maintenance and expansion of alternative schools. Because the Bush administration is "choice friendly," alternative schools will satisfy the need to provide choice and diversity within a monopolistic bureaucratic giant of public education. A very large majority of people across the nation are interested in developing options for all students.

Given alternatives' proven track record for unusually positive effects on their students and teachers, along with the dramatic increase in the number of children being taught at home and the availability of technology, we are likely to see many more entrepreneurial efforts focused on options for schooling.

More than twenty years ago Vern Smith of Indiana University identified over 150 types of alternative schools. Such schools have stimulated reform in public schools and offer a cost-effective way to provide education in today's pluralistic society. In the face of alarming statistics indicating that one in every four students quits before receiving a traditional high school diploma, availability of expanded options for choice is almost certain.

Recall, however, that most alternative schools in the United States have been developed without state or national leadership. Laboratory schools, schools-without-walls, and magnet schools intended to draw students to a superior and specialized program were created by school districts. Larger school districts, in particular—especially those with considerable resources, highly professional staff members, and active community leaders—have been able to establish models of excellence in education. John Dewey insisted that the school and the community must work as a unit for high-quality education. John Goodlad stated many times that the community should be the major educator of the child. Lawrence Cremin argues that the community should serve to interlock all educative agencies within and outside of the school. The "No Child Left Behind" legislation does address some of these issues.

The statement of principles developed in 1990 by the steering committee of the Network of Progressive Educators (Appendix N) describes the components and characteristics of an alternative school for the twenty-first century. To be prepared and responsive to the needs of children and communities, any provider of an alternative program can use these principles as an assessment of effectiveness.

We see now, and will continue to see, a proliferation of alternative programs cropping up all over the country. For example, community colleges in Oregon and California, as well as several state universities (e.g., University of North Carolina, Louisiana State University, Ball State) operate alternative schools as learning laboratories for colleges of education. We also continue to see private foundations taking a civic and financial interest in schools across the country. The Parkway School in Philadelphia, one of the nation's first alternative schools, was started with support from Ford Foundation. And the Baltimore City school system recently received a $20 million award from eight foundations to support high school reform, with the Bill Gates Foundation listed as one of the major contributors. These are just a few examples of nationwide efforts that support the initiation and expansion of alternative schools and alternative programs. There are certainly many more to come.

REFERENCES

Bennet, J. (1978). *The Alternative School Network: Its Schools, Its Genesis and Its Maintenance.* (ERIC Document Reproduction Service No. ED151947.)

Cooper, B. (1971). *Freedom Schools: A National Survey of Alternative Programs.* (ERIC Document Reproduction Service No. ED058499.)

Fantini, M. (1973). *The What, Why, and Where of the Alternatives Movement.* (ERIC Document Reproduction Service No. EJ078625.)

Howe, H. (1990). "Thinking About the Forgotten Half." *Teachers' College Record,* *92*(2), 293–305.

Mintz, J. (Ed.). (1994). *Handbook of Alternative Education.* New York: Macmillan.

Pulliam, J., and Van Patten, J. (1999). *History of Education in America.* Upper Saddle River: NJ: Merrill.

No Child Left Behind, Executive Summary. Available online at http://www.ed.gov/inits/nclb/part2.html.

The Secretary's Commission on Achieving Necessary Skills (1991). *What Work Requires of Schools: A SCANS Report for America 2000.* Washington, DC: U.S. Department of Labor.

APPENDIX N: STATEMENT OF PRINCIPLES OF THE STEERING COMMITTEE OF THE NETWORK OF PROGRESSIVE EDUCATORS, Drafted on November 10, 1990

1. Education is best accomplished where relationships are personal and teachers design programs that honor the linguistic and cultural diversity of the local community.
2. Teachers, as respected professionals, are crucial sources of knowledge about teaching and learning.
3. Curriculum balance is maintained by a commitment to children's individual interests and developmental needs, as well as a commitment to community within and beyond the school's walls.
4. Schools embrace the home cultures of children and their families. Classroom practices reflect these values and bring multiple cultural perspectives to bear.
5. Students are active constructors of knowledge and learn through direct experience and primary sources.
6. All disciplines—the arts, sciences, humanities, and physical development—are valued equally in an interdisciplinary curriculum.
7. Decision-making within schools is inclusive of children, parents, and staff.
8. The school is a model of democracy and humane relationships, confronting issues of racism, classism, and sexism.
9. Schools actively support critical inquiry into the complexities of global issues. Children can thus assume the powerful responsibilities of world citizenship.

Cited in Network of Progressive Educators, "Statement of Principles," *Pathways*, 7(2), 1991, p. 3.

Chapter 11

⮞ Directory of Organizations, Associations, and Government Agencies Associated with Alternative Schools, Alternative Programs, and Alternative Education

A+ Research Foundation
William E. Smith, Jr., Chairman
Cathy Gassenheimer, Managing Director
P.O. Box 4433
Montgomery, AL 36103
Telephone: 334-279-1886
Email: bill@aplusala.org
Web site: http://www.aplusala.org

A+ organizes town meetings that have enabled more than 23,000 people to have a voice in school improvement and develop a blueprint for school reform, which eventually was drafted into a legislative plan, the Alabama First Plan. A+ also provides support to state policy makers and leadership training for school principals and superintendents.

Achievement Council
4055 Wilshire Blvd., Suite 350
Los Angeles, CA 90010
Telephone: 213-487-3194

The Achievement Council in Los Angeles has developed tools and approaches to gathering and using data that bring the focus of equity to the forefront of school reform. Its strategy helps schools respond with a heightened sense of urgency about establishing new expectations and opportunities for their students.

AERO—The Alternative Education Resource Organization

Jerry Mintz, Director
417 Roslyn Road
Roslyn Hgts., NY 11577
Telephone: 516-621-2195
Toll-free: 800-769-4171
Fax: 516-625-3257

The Alternative Education Resource Organization (AERO) is a nonprofit organization sponsored by the School of Living, which was founded in 1934. Director Jerry Mintz has worked with hundreds of alternative schools and home school programs, and is an expert on educational alternatives. AERO helps people who want to change education to a more empowering and holistic form. It helps individuals and groups of people who want to start new community schools, public and private, or change existing schools. It also provides information to people interested in home schooling their children, or finding private or public alternative schools. The organization provides a message board, a catalog of educational products, an instructional magazine, and consulting services.

The Alfie Kohn Organization provides supplies, products, and advice for improving school curriculums and enriching the learning experience.

The Algebra Project

Robert Moses, Founder
Bethany Allen, President
99 Bishop Allen Drive
Cambridge, MA 02139
Telephone: 617-491-0200

The Algebra Project is a nationwide network of projects designed to equip students with a new mathematics literacy required for full participation in our changing technological society. There are currently eighteen projects in twelve states.

Alliance Organizing Project

Gary Rodwell
152 West Lehigh Avenue
Philadelphia, PA 19133
Telephone: 215-739-5702

Founded in 1995, the Alliance Organizing Project (AOP) educates and funds professional community organizers to train parents to be able to hold all parts of the community accountable for maintaining and improving a quality public education system. AOP believes that parents and community organizing is the key component to creating and sustaining deep parental involvement in schools.

The Alliance for Parental Involvement in Education (AllPIE) is a non-profit organization that assists and encourages parental involvement in education, wherever that education takes place: in public school, in private school, or at home.

The Alternative Learning Exchange, based in the Netherlands, was created to facilitate communication between adults and children of different countries and cultures who are interested in alternatives to tradiional systems of education, and perhaps also interested in participating in the creation of such alternatives.

Alternative Public Schools, Inc.
28 White Bridge Road
Suite 311
Nashville, TN 37205
Telephone: 615-356-6975
Fax: 615-352-2138

APS is a for-profit school-management company based in Nashville, TN. The company currently manages one 375-student public elementary school in Wilkinsburg, PA. It seeks additional contracts with local school districts and other government entities to manage existing and newly created public schools. APS's fundamental purpose is to provide better education, particularly for high-needs children in urban areas.

Alternative Schools Network
1807 West Sunnyside—Suite 1D
Chicago, IL 60640
Telephone: 773-728-4030
Fax: 773-728-3335
Email: AltSchools@aol.com

The Alternatives Schools Network (ASN) is a not-for-profit organization in Chicago working to provide quality education for everyone, with specific emphasis on inner-city children, youths, and adults. Since 1973, the

ASN has been active in supporting community-based and community-run programs to develop and expand needed education, training, and support services, particularly in Chicago's inner-city neighborhoods.

American Association of Christian Schools (AACS)
P.O. Box 2189
Independence, MO 64055
Telephone: 816-795-7709
Fax: 816-795-7462

AACS is a national association of fundamentalist and theologically conservative Christian schools. Its member schools enroll about 120,000 students. AACS offers various services to member schools and lobbies for Christian education at the national level. Many states have state-level AACS, from which parents can get information about local schools.

American Educational Research Association (AERA)
1230 Seventeenth Street, NW
Washington, DC 20036-3078
Telephone: 202-223-9485
Web site: www.aera.net

AERA is the nation's most prominent educational research organization. Its web site includes links to research institutes, clearinghouses, and think tanks.

American Federation of Teachers (AFT)
555 New Jersey Avenue, NW
Washington, DC 20001
Telephone: 202-879-4400
Web site: www.aft.org

The mission of the American Federation of Teachers (AFT), which provides resources and information to teachers and other educators, is to improve the lives of its members and their families; to give voice to their legitimate professional, economic, and social aspirations; to strengthen academic institutions; to improve the quality of the services provided; and to bring together all members to assist and provide support to promote democracy, human rights, and freedom in the union, in the nation, and throughout the world.

American Homeschool Association
P.O. Box 3142
Palmer, Alaska 99645-3142

Email: AHA@americanhomeschoolassociation.org
Web site: http://www.americanhomeschoolassociation.org

The American Homeschool Association (AHA) is a service organization created in 1995 to network home schoolers on a national level and to provide news and information about home schooling relevant to any concerned parent, media writer, academic researcher, education professional, or home schooler.

American Montessori Society
281 Park Avenue South, 6th floor
New York, NY 10010
Telephone: 212-358-1250
Fax: 212-358-1256
Web site: www.amshq.org

The American Montessori Society is a national association that accredits teacher trainings and schools, publishes *Montessori Life Magazine,* and helps place teachers. It is not affiliated with the Association Montessori Internationale.

Annenberg Institute for School Reform
Brown University
P.O. Box 1985
Providence, RI 02912
Telephone: 401-863-7990
Fax: 401-863-1290
Email: AISR_Info@brown.edu

The Annenberg Institute for School Reform at Brown University is designed to support the needs of urban communities and schools that serve disadvantaged children. It shares knowledge and research-based information that will improve conditions and outcomes for students in these urban communities.

Arkansas Advocates for Children and Families
Amy Rossi
931 Donaghey Building
Little Rock, AR 72201
Telephone: 501-371-9678

Arkansas Advocates for Children and Families is a policy-oriented think tank that aims to get more parents involved in schools. To engage parents, they hire a coordinator and use ideas and materials from the National Coalition of Advocates for Students. "Super Saturday" meetings have been developed to convene parents and administrators to talk about issues facing the schools for Title I parents.

Arkansas Friends for Better Schools
Judy Wilmouth White, Coordinator
1111 West Capitol, Suite 1096
Little Rock, AR 72201
Telephone: 501-373-5882
Web site: rayw@arkansas.net

Arkansas Friends for Better Schools is an alliance of fourteen statewide organizations that support public schools. Arkansas Friends helped to develop "Arkansas Public Schools Week" to encourage schools to welcome members of the community to visit schools and to take part in school activities. Arkansas Friends also collaborated with the *Arkansas Times* to initiate "Arkansas Public School heroes," an annual cover feature that profiles administrators, principals, teachers, parents, community members, and volunteers who are making a difference in the lives of school children.

Artists for Humanity
Susan Rodgerson, Founder
188-300 A Street
South Boston, MA 02210
Telephone: 617-737-2455

Artists for Humanity was founded as an after-school program in Boston. Students participate in an apprenticeship program where they are paid to create artwork that is then marketed to the business community. There are forty students on the staff, and the sale of the students' art generates $100,000 in revenue each year. Students must maintain a 2.5 grade-point average to stay in the program. Ninety-eight percent of the students in the program go on to college.

Association of Christian Schools International
P.O. Box 35097
Colorado Springs, CO 80935-3509
Telephone: 719-528-6906

The Association of Christian Schools International is the largest of the Christian school associations. It publishes a directory of schools, which includes 3,100 schools with about 540,000 students. It also publishes a survey of textbooks, which reviews textbooks and curricula of Christian as well as secular publishers in the full range of elementary and high school subjects.

Association for Experiential Education
2305 Canyon Blvd., Suite 100
Boulder, CO 80302
Telephone: 303-440-8844
Web site: http://www.aee.org

This association promotes experiential learning in numerous settings, especially through outdoor adventure programs. It publishes books, directories, and the *Journal for Experiential Education*. The group also sponsors conferences.

Association Montessori Internationale—USA (AMI-USA)
170m West Schofield Road
Rochester, NY 14617
Telephone: 716-544-6709

AMI-USA is the American branch of the international Montessori organization that is based in the Netherlands. Its services include accreditation of Montessori teacher training and Montessori schools, school consultations, national conferences and teacher refresher courses, teacher placement assistance, publications, and research assistance.

Association of Waldorf Schools of North America
3911 Bannister Road
Fair Oaks, CA 95628
Telephone: http://www.waldorfeducation.org

The Association of Waldorf Schools of North America is the major organization linking Waldorf (Steiner) schools, teachers' education programs, publications, and other resources. The organization publishes *Renewal: A Journal for Waldorf Education*.

Baltimoreans United in Leadership Development (BUILD)
Leslie McMillan
2521 North Charles Street
Baltimore, MD 21218
Telephone: 410-467-9770

BUILD is the largest African American community organization in the country. It mobilizes community members to ensure a quality education for all children. BUILD helped found the Child First Authority, a public authority with the ability to issue bonds and raise capital. With support from the mayor, ten after-school programs were created in Baltimore schools on a pilot basis. These after-school programs are partnerships between schools and BUILD. Parents serve as volunteer staff at these programs.

The Brookings Institution
1775 Massachusetts Ave., N.W.
Washington, DC 20036
Telephone: 202-797-6000
Fax: 202-797-6004
e-mail: brookinfo@brook.edu
Web site: http://www.brook.edu/

The Brookings Institution, a private, independent, nonprofit research organization, seeks to improve the performance of American institutions, the effectiveness of government programs, and the quality of U.S. public policies. It addresses current and emerging policy challenges and offers practical recommendations for dealing with them.

California Continuation Education Association (CCEA)
Web site: http://www.cceanet.org

Continuation high schools have been in operation in California since 1991 as a mandated alternative for students who need a more flexible school day or week and a program different from that of the traditional high school. The California Continuation Education Association (CCEA) represents the interests of the more than 500 continuation high schools in the state. The association advocates for the betterment of continuation education and promotes the development of quality schools for students. It also provides professional development for the improvement of instruction that leads to student achievement of high standards, completion of a high school diploma, effective preparation for work, positive community involvement, and a foundation for life-long learning.

California Homeschooling Association
P.O. Box 868
Davis, CA 95617
Toll-free: 888-HSC-4440
Email: info@hsc.org
Web site: http://www.hsc.org

The Homeschool Association of California has been around for more than a decade. It started in 1987, when a small group of Bay Area home schooling moms got together to establish what was then called the Northern California Homeschool Association.

Carden Educational Foundation
P.O. Box 659
Brookfield, CT 06894-0659
Telephone: 860-350-9885
Fax: 860-354-9812
Web site: http://www.cardenschool.org

The Carden Educational Foundation is the central organization for the Carden movement. It maintains a list of Carden schools around the country, promotes Carden education, and sells the Carden readers and other books and educational materials related to the Carden method. It also provides training for teachers and administrators.

Center for the Advancement of Ethics and Character
Boston University
School of Education
605 Commonwealth Avenue
Boston, MA 02215
Telephone: 617-353-3262
Fax: 617-353-3924

The Center for the Advancement of Ethics and Character was founded in 1989. Its mission is to promote character education in the nation's elementary and secondary schools, and its approach emphasizes the curriculum as the primary vehicle for transmitting moral values to the young. The Center sees the school as a social environment where students can gain the enduring habits that make up strong character. Its strong connection to the "Character Education Network" helps keep parents and school personnel informed. It also provides services to school districts, universities, and other agencies, and publishes the newsletter *Character.*

The Center for Civil Leadership at the Institute for Education Reform
Mike Kiefer, Director
2000 Huron River Drive, Suite 102
Ypsilanti, MI 48197
Telephone: 313-484-3232

The Center for Civil Leadership, created in 1997, uses community dialogue as a lever for effective change within schools. The Center has developed a diagnostic tool to benchmark the behavior of school governance teams and to identify training needs. This tool will be used on an ongoing basis to monitor changes in the behavior of governance teams and the degree to which collaboration between school and community has increased.

The Center for Collaborative Education
1573 Madison Avenue, Room 201
New York, NY 10029-3899
Telephone: 212-348-7821
Fax: 212-348-7850

The Center of Collaborative Education is the New York City affiliate of the Coalition of Essential Schools. It promotes Coalition concepts in New York City.

The Center for Education Reform
1001 Connecticut Avenue, NW
Suite 204
Washington, DC 20036
Telephone: 202-822-9000
Toll-free: 800-521-2118
Fax: 202-822-5077
Email: cer@edreform.com
Web site: http://www.edreform.com

The Center for Education Reform, the nation's leading authority on school reform, opened its doors in 1993 to provide one-stop shopping for people, groups, and policy makers working in education. It considers itself the nerve center for the reform movement and supports distribution of information to parents who want change and choices. Leadership, products, and services are made available to people who represent every class, creed, and color to galvanize support for shared reform efforts.

Center for Law and Education
Paul Weckstein, Co-Director
Kathleen Boundy, Co-Director
Anne T. Henderson, Consultant
1875 Connecticut Avenue, N.W.
Suite 510
Washington, DC 20009
Telephone: 202-986-3000

Email: cledc@erols.com

The Center for Law and Education (CLE) is a national, nonprofit organization that seeks to advance the rights of all students, especially low-income students and their families. CLE helps community and school-based initiatives to increase parent and student involvement in education. It also conducts and publishes research on parent involvement, including its report titled *Urgent Message: Families Crucial to School Reform.*

Center for School Change
Hubert H. Humphrey Institute of Public Affairs
University of Minnesota
301 19th Avenue
South Minneapolis, MN 55455
Telephone: 612-626-8910

The mission of the Center for School Change is to work with educators, parents, businesspeople, students, policy makers, and other concerned people throughout the United States to increase student achievement, raise graduate rates, improve students' attitudes toward learning in schools and their communities, and strengthen communities by building stronger working relationships among educators, parents, students, and other community members.

The Center for Teaching and Learning
3605 Cross Point Road
Edgecomb, ME 04556
Telephone: 207-882-9706

The Center for Teaching and Learning is a demonstration school with an internship program, utilizing whole language and related approaches to learning.

Center on Education and Work
1025 W. Johnson St., Room 964
Madison, WI 53706-1796
Telephone: 608-262-3696
Toll-free: 800-466-0399
Email: cewmail@education.wisc.edu

The Center on Education and Work (CEW) was established in 1964 to enable educators to engage youth and adults in learning and career development that leads to productive careers.

Character Education Partnership (CEP)
809 Franklin Street
Alexandria, VA
Telephone: 703-739-9515
Fax: 703-739-4967

The Character Education Partnership (CEP), founded in 1992, is a broad-based, nonpartisan, nonprofit coalition of individuals and organizations dedicated to developing civic virtue and moral character in the nation's youth as a way of creating a more compassionate and responsible society. CEP campaigns against sex and violence in the media and opposes values clarification programs, and while it does not support prayer in schools, it does support teaching about religion in the public schools. Several public school systems—in Los Angeles, Baltimore, St. Louis, and elsewhere—have adopted a character education program, and CEP promotes similar programs for public and private schools.

Charter Friends National Network is a national network for supporters of charter schools that provides a directory of state contacts and network publications.

Child Achieving Challenge
Vicki Phillips, Executive Director
1818 Market Street, Suite 3510
Philadelphia, PA 19103
Web site: http://www.philsch.k12.pa.us

The Children Achieving Challenge is a public-private partnership, created with a $50 million grant from the Annenberg Foundation, to support Philadelphia's school improvement plan. Public engagement is one component of the Philadelphia Public Schools' ten-part Children Achieving plan. The Challenge has promoted the development of school councils to enable parents to take part in site-based management.

Children First America
P.O. Box 330
Bentonville, AR 72712
Telephone: 501-273-6957
Fax: 501-273-9362
Web site: http://www.childrenfirstamerica.org

Children First America promotes parental choice in education through private tuition grants and tax-funded options, giving all families the power to choose the K–12 school that best fits their needs. It is also a national clearinghouse of information on privately funded voucher programs, providing support services ranging from administrative training and programmatic consulting to technical support.

Christian Schools International
3350 East Paris Avenue, SE
Grand Rapids, MI 49512-3054
Telephone: 800-635-8288; 616-957-1070
Fax: 616-957-5022

This is an association primarily of Christian schools affiliated with the conservative wing of the Presbyterian Church, although it increasingly has member schools that are connected with other conservative Protestant groups. Many states have state associations of Christian schools.

Coalition of Essential Schools
Brown University
Box 1969
Providence, RI 02912
Telephone: 401-863-3384
Web site: http://www.essentialschools.org.

The Coalition of Essential Schools, a reform movement that links hundreds of schools around the nation and was founded by Theodore Sizer, is currently based at Brown University in Providence, Rhode Island. Sizer has written about the ideas behind the Coalition in *Horace's Compromise: The Dilemma of the American High School* (Boston: Houghton Mifflin, 1985), *Horace's School: Redesigning the American High School* (Boston: Houghton Mifflin, 1991), and *Horace's Hope: What Works for the American High School* (Boston: Houghton Mifflin, 1996). The web site includes a link to the Annenberg Institute for School Reform.

The Core Knowledge Foundation
2012-B Morton Drive
Charlottesville, VA 22903
Telephone: 804-977-7550

E. D. Hirsch started the Core Knowledge Foundation, which provides information on the Core Knowledge approach and helps schools wishing to adopt the program. It also publishes a newsletter called *Common Knowledge* and holds regular conferences dealing with Core Knowledge curricula.

Council for American Private Education
13017 Wisteria Drive, #457
Germantown, MD 20874
Telephone: 301-916-8460
Fax: 310-916-8485
Email: cape@capenet.org
Web site: http://www.capenet.org

The Council for American Private Education (CAPE) is a coalition of national organizations and state affiliates serving private elementary and secondary schools. Founded in 1971 to provide a coherent voice for private education, CAPE is dedicated to fostering communication and cooperation within the private school community and with the public sector to improve the quality of education for all of the nation's children. CAPE member organizations represent about 80 percent of private school enrollment nationwide.

Council for a Better Louisiana
Harold Suire, Chairman and CEO
P.O. Box 4308
Baton Rouge, LA 70821
Telephone: 504-344-2250

Founded in 1962, the Council for a Better Louisiana (CABL) is a statewide citizens-advocacy organization. CABL engages voters to help them become informed and make better decisions. Its People's Agenda project utilizes scientific research, surveys, and focus groups to better understand the concerns of voters. CABL's work in education has centered on the development, since 1990, of nine permanently endowed local education funds across the state. CABL has received a grant from the BellSouth Foundation to initiate school-board leadership training programs across the state. CABL also serves as a resource for the state department of education in helping it communicate with citizens.

Council of Great City Schools
1301 Pennsylvania Avenue, NW
Suite 702
Washington, DC 20004
Telephone: 202-393-2427
Fax: 202-393-2400
Web site: www.cgcs.org

The Council of the Great City Schools is a coalition of nearly sixty of the nation's largest urban public school systems. Founded in 1956 and incorporated in 1961, the Council is located in Washington, DC, where it works to promote urban education through legislation, research, media relations, instruction, management, technology, and other special projects designed to improve the quality of urban education.

Cross City Campaign for Urban School Reform
Anne Hallett
407 South Dearborn Street, Suite 1725
Chicago, IL
Telephone: 312-322-488
Email: ahallett@compuserve.com

The Cross City Campaign is an active, strategic national network supporting urban school reform leaders, both inside and outside school districts, through information, shared strategies, joint work, and support of local reform agendas.

Down to Earth Books
72 Philip Street
Albany, NY 12202
Telephone: 518-432-1578

Down to Earth Books is run by members of The Free School community. It publishes *SKOLE: A Journal of Alternative Education* and the *Journal of Family Life.*

Education Commission of the States
707 17th Street #2700
Denver, CO 80202-3427
Telephone: 303-299-3600
Fax: 303-296-8332
Email: ecd@ecs.org
Web site: www.ecs.org

The Education Commission of the States (ECS) helps state leaders develop and carry out policies that promote improved performance of the education system, reflected by increased learning by all citizens. The ECS formed in the late 1960s when participants at a national governor's conference called for a nationwide alliance for the improvement of education, with the active leadership and participation of the governors. Each member state or territory appoints, usually through the governor's office, seven ECS commissioners who represent all segments of education. These commissioners meet three times a year to discuss important education issues affecting their states. These discussions, in turn, guide the commission's work.

Education Law Center
Steve Block
155 Washington Street, Room 209
Newark, NJ 07120-3106
Telephone: 201-624-1815, ext 18

The Education Law Center is a school-finance reform group that focuses on litigation. The Center's Parent Representation Project takes calls from parents, identifies their problems with schools, and works to improve those areas of concern.

Education Leaders Council
1225 19th St., Suite 400
Washington, DC 20036
Telephone: 202-261-2600
Fax: 202-261-2638
Email: info@educationleaders.org
Web site: http://www.educationleaders.org

The Education Leaders Council (ELC) was formed in 1995 to create an organization that represents leaders in education committed to the kinds of fundamental reforms demanded by millions of parents, yet often ignored by national organizations. The purpose of the organization is to focus on students, not the school system. Its members believe that the system exists to serve students, and that student achievement and performance should be reported in a way that is easily understood by parents and taxpayers. Its mission is to serve education leaders who share these same beliefs. The ELC provides a national voice for state leaders who are transforming public education and a strategic network for reform-minded leaders that is independent and nonpartisan.

Educators for Social Responsibility
23 Garden Street
Cambridge, MA 02138
Telephone: 800-370-2515
Fax: 617-864-5164

Educators for Social Responsibility (ESR) offers books, videos, curricula, and teacher and administrator trainings on conflict resolution, violence prevention, character education, diversity education, and social responsibility.

Florence Crittenton School/Human Services, Inc.
2880 West Holden Place
Denver, CO 80204
Telephone: 303-825-9696
Fax: 303-825-0922

The Florence Crittenton School/Human Services, Inc., provides a wide range of comprehensive and integrated services for pregnant and parenting teens. Founded as a residential home for unwed mothers, the Florence Crittenton School has evolved into a multiservice day program that is now the largest provider of services to teen parents.

The Foxfire Fund, Inc.
Post Office Box 541
Mountain City, GA 30562-0541
Telephone: 706-746-5828
Fax: 706-746-5829
Email: foxfire@foxfire.org
Web site: http://www.foxfire.org

Foxfire (The Foxfire Fund, Inc.) is a not-for-profit, educational, and literary organization based in Rabun County, Georgia. Foxfire's learner-centered, community-based educational approach is advocated through both a regional demonstration site grounded in the Southern Appalachian culture that gave rise to Foxfire and a national program of teacher training and support that promotes a sense of place and appreciation of local people, community, and culture as essential educational tools.

The Fratney School (Escuela Fratney)
3255 North Fratney Street
Milwaukee, WI 53212
Telephone: 414-264-4840

The Fratney School, a pioneer in the application of multicultural principles, focuses on urban schools and issues of equity and social justice. In this school, classroom issues are linked to broader policy concerns.

The Free School
8 Elm Street
Albany, NY 12202
Telephone: 518-434-3072

The Free School has been operating in Albany for more than thirty years. It is committed to helping parents and teachers apply its principles and ideals.

The Friends Council on Education
1507 Cherry Street
Philadelphia, PA 19102
Telephone: 215-241-7245

The Friends Council on Education is the central source of information on Friends education. It publishes a list of the schools, colleges, and study centers under its care.

The George Lucas Educational Foundation
Mark Sargent, Communications Director
P.O. Box 3494
San Rafael, CA 94912
Telephone: 415-662-1641
Email: msargent@glef.org
Web site: http://glef.org/welcome.html

The George Lucas Educational Foundation, located in Nicasio, California, was established as a tax-exempt charitable organization in 1991 based on the filmmaker's belief that education is the most important investment we can make to secure the future of our democracy. To help the public revitalize the nation's schools, the Foundation gathers, synthesizes, and disseminates information and other resources through various media to promote and share the latest strategies to change the K–12 educational system, especially those that integrate technology with teaching and learning. In 1997, the Foundation completed *Learn and Live*, a documentary film (hosted by Robin Williams), with a companion resource book, that illustrates ways in which innovative schools and communities are using technology to enhance teaching and learning.

The Georgia Partnership for Excellence in Education
Tom Upchurch, President
233 Peachtree Street, Suite 200
Atlanta, GA 30303
Telephone: 404-223-2280
Web site: http://www.gpee.org

The Georgia Partnership for Excellence in Education was founded in 1990 with the mission to be Georgia's foremost change agent and a significant leader in the journey to higher standards and increased academic achievement for all students. Since 1993, Georgia's education, business, and government leaders have traveled by bus in various tours of schools to highlight innovative education approaches. The Georgia

Partnership also works with communities across the state, through the Ambassadors for Education program, to build awareness about education issues.

Gesell Foundation
310 Prospect Street
New Haven, CT 06511
Telephone: 203-777-3481
Fax: 203-776-5001

Since 1918, this foundation has been promoting developmental education. Based on the work of Arnold Gesell, workshops are conducted to help teachers, counselors, administrators, and other professionals involved with children understand and meet their developmental needs. It sells books for parents and teachers interested in learning about the typical behavior of children from birth to sixteen years of age. It also provides psychological and developmental evaluations of individual children.

Global Alliance for Transforming Education (GATE)
P.O. Box 21
Grafton, VT 05146
Telephone: 802-843-2382

The Global Alliance for Transforming Education (GATE) is an organization committed to holistic education. According to GATE, holistic education's vision "fosters personal greatness, social justice, peace, and a sustainable environment." GATE works with teachers, educators, educational organizations, United Nations organizations, child advocates, local communities, business leaders, and government officials as well as with schools and families to promote holistic education.

Heritage Foundation
214 Massachusetts Ave., N.E.
Washington, DC 20002
Telephone: 202-546-4400
Fax: 202-546-8328
e-mail: info@heritage.org
Web site: http://www.heritage.org/

Founded in 1973, the Heritage Foundation is a think tank whose mission is to formulate and promote conservative public policies based on the principles of free enterprise, limited government, individual freedom, traditional American values, and a strong national defense. Heritage's staff pursues this mission by performing research that addresses key policy issues and marketing these findings to its primary audiences: members of Congress, key congressional staff members, and policy makers in the executive branch, the nation's news media, and the academic and policy communities. Heritage's products include publications, articles, lectures, conferences, and meetings.

Home School Legal Defense Association
P.O. Box 3000
Purcellville, VA 20134
Telephone: 540-338-5600
Fax: 540-338-2733
Web site: www.hslda.org

This organization provides legal advice to home schooling parents. Upon request, parents can receive a free one-page synopsis of the home schooling laws in their state.

Hudson Institute
5395 Emerson Way
Indianapolis, IN 46226
Telephone: 317-545-1000
Fax: 317-545-9639
Email: grantp@hudson.org
Web site: http://www.hudson.org/

The Hudson Institute is a private, nonprofit research organization that analyzes and makes recommendations about public policy for business and government executives and for the public at large. The institute describes itself as having a viewpoint that embodies skepticism about the conventional wisdom, optimism about solving problems, a commitment to free institutions and individual responsibility, an appreciation of the crucial role of technology in achieving progress, and an abiding respect for the importance of values, culture, and religion in human affairs.

Institute for Democracy in Education (IDE)
College of Education
313 McCracken Hall
Ohio State University
Athens, OH 45701
Telephone: 614-593-4531

The Institute for Democracy in Education (IDE) was founded by a group of teachers dismayed that the debate over public school reform had disregarded the historic purpose of public schooling—namely, the development of responsible citizens. IDE is a partnership among all those who play a role in teaching and learning—classroom teachers, administrators, parents, and students. It offers a forum for sharing ideas, a support network of people holding similar values, and opportunities for professional development. The Institute publishes a quarterly journal, *Democracy and Education.*

Institute for Educational Leadership, Inc.
Mike Usdan, President
Jacqueline Danberger, Director, Governance Programs
1001 Connecticut Avenue, NW
Suite 310
Washington, DC 20036
Telephone: 202-822-8405
Email: iel@icl.org
Web site: iel@icl.org

The mission of the Institute for Educational Leadership (IEL) is to improve individual lives and society by strengthening educational opportunities for children and youth. IEL accomplishes this mission by connecting leaders from every sector of our increasingly multiethnic and multiracial society and by reconnecting the public with educational institutions. IEL collaborates with public agenda on "Engaging Americans in Education Reform" to involve Americans at the grassroots level in civic dialogue among themselves and with educators.

Institute for Responsive Education
Tony Wagner, President
Northeastern University
50 Nightingale Hall
Boston, MA 02115
Telephone: 617-373-4479
Email: twagner@nunet.neu.edu
Web site: http://www.dac.neu.edu/ire

Founded in 1973, the Institute for Responsive Education (IRE) promotes family and community involvement in schools and new approaches to elementary and secondary education that are responsive to the changing needs of students, families, communities, and the larger society. IRE's Responsive School Project was launched in 1994 and now involves clusters of K–12 schools in eight school districts across the country. Responsive Schools seek to develop and demonstrate new strategies for creating locally based, "bottom-up" systematic changes in schools' service to economically disadvantaged families. IRE provides site grants, part-time facilitators, and training and resources on gathering data on the community's needs and concerns.

Institute for Study of the Liberal Arts and Sciences
Web site: http://www.islas.org

The Institute for Study of the Liberal Arts and Sciences (ISLAS) is a college preparatory institute that offers online distance-learning to high school students. It sponsors two online college preparatory schools: Scholars' Online Academy and Regina Coeli Academy. The idea for ISLAS began in 1994 in Baton Rouge, Louisiana. Both programs provide opportunities for students to excel in specialized studies or to enroll in a complete academic curriculum.

The International Association for the Study of Cooperative Education
Box 1582
Santa Cruz, CA 95061-1582
Telephone: 408-426-7926
Fax: 408-426-3360

The International Association for the Study of Cooperative Education is a nonprofit organization dedicated to the study and practice of cooperative education. It offers individual/household and institutional memberships. Member benefits include a subscription to *Cooperative Learning: The Magazine for Cooperation in Education.*

International Baccalaureate North America (IBNA)
200 Madison Avenue, Suite 2007
New York, NY 10016
Telephone: 212-696-4464
Fax: 212-889-9242

The International Baccalaureate North America, which is the main administrative organization of the International Baccalaureate (IB) in North America, publishes an information packet that includes a directory of all schools in North America that offer an IB program. The organization also helps school prepare to initiate IB programs and sells study guides and other materials.

International Baccalaureate Organization
15, route des Morillons
1218 Grand-Sacconnex

Geneva, Switzerland
Telephone: 41-22-791-0274
Fax: 41-22-791-0277

The International Baccalaureate Organization publishes a magazine called *IB World* and also distributes a list of the United World colleges around the world. Three of these world colleges are listed next:

United World College of the American West
P.O. Box 248, Route 65
Montezuma, NM 87731
Telephone: 505-454-4217
Fax: 505-454-4274
United World College of the Pacific
R. R. 1, Victoria, British Columbia V9B5T7
Canada
Telephone: 604-391-2411
Fax: 604-391-4212
United World College of the Atlantic
Saint Donat's Castle, Llantwit Major
South Glamorgan, Wales CF61 1WF
United Kingdom
Telephone: 44-1446-792-345
Fax: 44-1446-794-163

Iowa Association of Alternative Education
EXCEL Alternative High School
Marshalltown, IA
Telephone: 641-752-4645, Ext. 283
Email: hungerfo@iavalley,cc.ia.us

The Iowa Association of Alternative Education provides assistance to educators who wish to establish and maintain alternatives for students. Consultations and printed materials are available to both members and nonmembers.

Islamic Circle of America
166-26 89th Avenue
Jamaica, NY 11432
Telephone: 718-658-1199
Fax: 718-658-1255

The Islamic Circle of America is a resource center for information about Islam that provides free brochures and information.

Jewish Education Service of North America (JESNA)
730 Broadway, 2nd Floor
New York, NY 10003-9540
Telephone: 212-529-2000
Fax: 212-529-2009
Email: jesna@ix.netcom.com
Web site: http://www.users.aol.com.jesna/jesna.htm

JESNA publishes a directory of the central agencies for Jewish education, Jewish education resource centers, and Jewish schools and school systems, which provide some central agency services. Four other organizations that provide information about Jewish day schools are listed next:

> **Solomon Schechter Day Schools**
> 155 Fifth Avenue
> New York, NY 10010
> Telephone: 212-260-8450
> **Jewish Community Day School Network**
> 15749 N. E. 4th Street
> Bellevue, WA 98008
> Telephone: 206-641-3335
> **Torah Umesorah**
> The National Society of Hebrew Day Schools
> 160 Broadway
> New York, NY
> Telephone: 212-249-0100
> **PARDeS (Reform Day Schools)**
> Union of American Hebrew Congregations
> 633 Third Avenue
> New York, NY 10017
> Telephone: 212-650-4000

Joint Venture: Silicon Valley Network's 21st Century Education Initiative
Tim Cuneo
99 Almaden Boulevard, Suite 620
San Jose, CA 95113
Telephone: 408-938-1510
Email: jvvoffice@aol.com
Web site: http://www.jointventure.rog

The Joint Venture: Silicon Valley Network includes people in business, government, education, and the community who have joined together to act on regional issues affecting economic vitality and quality of life. In 1995, the Network agreed to raise more than $20 million and launch the 21st Century Education Initiative to spark a renaissance in public education in Silicon Valley. The Initiative's Challenge 2000 program, using a venture capital model, works with "Renaissance teams" of educators, businesspeople, and community members to implement systematic improvement programs focused on student performance and involving continuous evaluation. The Initiative made commitments of more than $1 million over three years to Renaissance teams in the form of financial, human, and technological resources. Continued support is dependent upon the achievement of measurable results toward world-class standards.

Knowledge Network
Dr. Kent Lloyd, Chairman and President
Dr. Diane Ramsey, Vice President
1511 Lincoln Way, Suite 304
McLean, VA 22102
Telephone: 703-356-5009

In the spring of 1997, the Knowledge Network published a resource book, *Reclaiming Our Nation at Risk: Lessons for Reforming Our Elementary Schools,* to kick off a nationwide public engagement campaign. The information, strategies, and models of successful reform contained in the book were drawn from interviews with forty-four nationally recognized school reformers and educational leaders. The idea for this guide came from an April 1995 summit, sponsored by the Network, that involved 150 educational, political, business, parent, and community leaders.

Lancaster Mennonite Historical Society
2215 Millstream Road
Lancaster, PA 17602
Telephone: 717-393-9745

The Lancaster Mennonite Historical Society is one of many organizations around the country that supplies information about Mennonite history and Mennonite education.

Los Angeles Educational Alliance for Restructuring Now (LEARN)
Michael Roos, President and CEO
300 South Grand Avenue, Suite 1160
Los Angeles, CA 90071
213-255-3276

Email: learnla@aol.com
Web site: http://www.lausd.K12ca.us/lauds/offices/learn/learn.html

A working group of thirteen community leaders formed LEARN in 1991. More than 600 civic, education, and business leaders help LEARN to build supportive, student-focused learning communities with the autonomy to define and realize their student achievement outcomes in new and imaginative ways best suited to their unique needs. The principal and one teacher from each LEARN school take part in an eighteen-month applied management training course with UCLA's Graduate Schools of Management and Education. Additionally, partnerships are formed with school communities and educational organizations.

Magnet Schools of America
Dr. Judith S. Stein, Executive Director
P.O. Box 600490
North Miami Beach, FL 33160
Fax: 954-262-3988

Magnet schools are based on the premise that not all students learn in the same ways, and that if we find a unifying theme or a different organizational structure for students with similar interests, those students will learn more in all areas. Magnet Schools of America welcomes individuals, schools, and/or school districts to join to (1) promote goals of desegregation, equity, and excellence through the expansion and improvement of magnet schools; (2) encourage the passage of legislation at both the state and national levels that will promote the development and improvement of magnet schools; (3) explore and establish linkages with other professional groups with similar interests; and (4) promote networking among magnet schools.

Maryland Business Roundtable
June Streckfus, Executive Director
111 South Calvert Street, Suite 2250
Baltimore, MD 21202
Telephone: 410-727-0448

The Maryland Business Roundtable for Education (MBRT) is a coalition of eighty companies that have made a ten-year commitment to support education reform and improve student achievement in Maryland. MBRT used a 1993 gap analysis that identified nine components missing from Maryland's school reform effort as the framework for an Education Summit in January 1996 with 250 of the state's key education stakeholders. That conversation sparked local conversations in communities across the state. In addition, MBRT's Speaker's Bureau identifies and trains well-known people, chiefly business leaders, to make presentations on education reform throughout the state.

Mennonite Board of Education
500 South Main Street, Box 1142
Elkhart, IN 46515
Telephone: 219-294-7523

The Mennonite Board of Education is the central information resource for Mennonite education in North America. As such, it can supply information about Mennonite elementary and secondary schools and colleges.

Michigan Alternative Education Organization (MAEO)
204 East Muskegon Street
Cedar Springs, MI 49319
Telephone: 616-696-1203
Fax: 616-696-3755

The Michigan Alternative Education Organization (MAEO) was formed in 1975 to provide services and networking opportunities for alternative educators across the state. The purpose of the organization is to advocate quality alternative education for Michigan's youth, to provide a network of support for alternative educators and students, and to promote awareness of alternative education at local, state, and national levels. MAEO hosts annual fall and spring conferences, as well as regional activities for students and alternative educators around the state. Additionally, MAEO publishes a quarterly newsletter, maintains a web site, and recognizes outstanding contributions to alternative education with annual awards.

Minnesota Association of Alternative Programs (MAAP)
Northfield ALC
1651 Jefferson Parkway
Northfield, MN 55057
Telephone: 507-664-3750
Fax: 507-664-3751
Email: david.bly@nfld.k12.mn.us

The Minnesota Association of Alternative Programs (MAAP) is an organization of 900 members from more than 700 alternative school programs of choice serving some 100,000 students in Minnesota. MAAP is dedicated to the improvement of alternative education in Minnesota by meeting the needs of students, parents, and educators.

Minnesota Association of Christian Home Educators
P.O. Box 32308
Fridley, MN 55432-0308
Telephone: 763-717-9070
Email: mache@isd.net
Web site: http://www.mache.org

MACHE functions as a support umbrella for individual home schooling families and local support groups in Minnesota. It focuses on a Christian worldview and values, and provides national and statewide information and connectedness to what would otherwise be a large but diverse and fragmented group. There are no restrictions on membership.

Minnesota Homeschoolers Alliance
P.O. Box 23072
Richfield, MN 55423
Telephone: 612-288-9662; 888-346-7622
Email: mha@homeschoolers.org

The Minnesota Homeschoolers Alliance (MHA) is a nonprofit 501c(3), nonpolitical, nonsectarian organization committed to encouraging and enabling home schooling families through education, networking opportunities, activities, and guidance on home schooling issues. It provides information to families considering the home schooling option and raises community awareness about the legal option of home education.

National Association for Core Curriculum
1640 Franklin Avenue, Suite 104
Kent, OH 44240
Telephone: 330-677-5008

The National Association for Core Curriculum is a network of innovative educators influenced by the principles of progressive education. It promotes integrative interdisciplinary studies, team teaching, block scheduling, and other learning-centered approaches.

National Association for Legal Support of Alternative Schools (NALSAS)
P.O. Box 2823
Santa Fe, NM 87504-2823
Telephone: 505-471-6928

NALSAS is a sister organization of the National Coalition of Alternative Community Schools (NCACS) that accredits Coalition member schools. It offers legal information and services to alternative schools.

National Association for Mediation in Education (NAME)
1726 M. Street, NW, Suite 500
Washington, DC 20036-4502
Telephone: 202-466-4764
Fax: 202-466-4769

Founded out of a concern about the epidemic of violent and disruptive behavior in the nation's schools, NAME is a part of the National Institute for Dispute Resolution. It seeks to promote conflict resolution programs in schools and colleges. NAME offers various conflict resolution curricula, as well as videos, tapes, books, and articles about conflict resolution. It publishes a newsletter titled *The Fourth R,* holds national conferences, and promotes networking at the national, state, and local levels for educators and others interested in conflict resolution.

National Association for Year-Round Education
P.O. Box 711386
San Diego, CA 92171
Telephone: 619-276-5296
Web site: http://www.NAYRE.org

The National Association for Year-Round Education (NAYRE) presents an alternative way of thinking about the school's relationship to the community as a whole, encouraging experimental programs and life-long learning. NAYRE also publishes books, articles, and monographs, and sponsors an annual conference.

National Association of Independent Schools
1620 L Street, NW
Washington, DC 20036-5695
Telephone: 202-973-9700
Fax: 202-973-9790
Web site: http://www.nais.org

The National Association of Independent Schools, which represents over 1,100 independent schools and associations in the United States and abroad, offers a broad variety of services to its member schools and associations. Its mission is to serve and strengthen the member schools and associations by "articulating and promoting high standards of educational quality and ethical behavior; working to preserve their independence to serve the free society from which that independence derives; and advocating broad access for students by affirming the principles of diversity, choice, and opportunity."

National Association of Partners in Education, Inc. (NAPE)
Sara Melnick, Director of Development
901 N. Pitt Street, Suite 320
Alexandria, VA 22314
Telephone: 703-836-4880
Email: napehq@napehq.org
Web site: http://www.napehg.org

Formed in 1988, the National Association of Partners in Education (NAPE) provides leadership in the growth and formation of educational partnerships between businesses, schools, and the community to ensure success for all students. Its Ambassadors for Education program aims to raise the level of awareness around education. NAPE trains people at the national level who, in turn, train "ambassadors" in their state and locality to get involved with schools and the issues facing them.

National Catholic Education Association (NCEA)
Suite 100
1077 30th Street, NW
Washington, DC 20007-3852
Telephone: 202-337-6232
Fax: 202-333-6706

The National Catholic Education Association is the national association of teachers in Roman Catholic schools. Its main mission is to promote Catholic education. It publishes a journal called *Momentum* and a newsletter for Catholic schools. It also publishes and sells books and audiotapes.

National Center for Fair and Open Testing
342 Broadway
Cambridge, MD 02139
Telephone: 617-864-4810
Fax: 617-497-2224
Email: info@fairtest.org
Web site: http://www.fairtest.org

The National Center for Fair and Open Testing (FairTest) is an advocacy organization working to end the abuses, misuses, and flaws of standardized testing and to ensure that evaluation of students and workers is fair, open, and educationally sound.

National Center for Innovation
1201 16th St., NW
Washington, DC 20036

Launched by the National Education Association, the National Center for Innovation sponsors a number of programs to restructure and revitalize public education. Its teacher-education initiative is a collaborative partnership with colleges, universities, and schools designed to improve the quality of teacher-preparation programs.

National Center on Education and the Economy
700 Eleventh Street, NW, Suite 750
Washington, DC 2001
Telephone: 202-783-3668
Fax: 202-783-3672
Web site: http://www.ncee.org

The National Center on Education and the Economy, a not-for-profit organization based in Washington, DC, believes it is possible for almost everyone to learn far more and develop far higher skills than most of us have thought possible. The hallmark of the National Center's work is standards-based reform. Its staff members believe that education and training systems work best when clear standards are set for student achievement, accurate measures of progress against those standards are devised, and the people closest to the students are given the authority for figuring out how to get them to the standards and are then held accountable for their progress.

National Center on Restructuring Education, Schools, and Teaching (NCREST)
Columbia University
Teachers College
Telephone: 212-678-3432
Fax: 212-678-4170

Established at Columbia University's Teachers College in 1990, the National Center on Restructuring Education, Schools, and Teaching (NCREST) provides support and assistance to the twenty-one-member Middle High School Consortium. NCREST is credited with helping the consortium devise a "critical friends" review system in which schools are evaluated for effective practices. Currently, NCREST is involved in a variety of projects including Professional Development Schools, teacher learning, assessment, the documentation of successful school reform efforts in elementary and secondary schools, educational technology in schools, and the development of local, state, and national policies based on practice.

National Coalition of Advocates for Students (NCAS)
100 Boylston Street, Suite 737
Boston, MA 02116-4610
Telephone: 617-357-8507

The National Coalition of Advocates for Students (NCAS) is an umbrella organization that has member organizations all over the county. NCAS publishes a wide variety of periodicals and books, sponsors various projects, and is active with immigrant groups and in the movement for HIV/AIDS awareness and education. NCAS also has a National Center for Immigrant Students, which publishes a newsletter called *New Voices*.

National Coalition of Alternative Community Schools (NCACS)
1266 Rosewood, Unit 1
Ann Arbor, MI 48104-6205
Telephone: 888-771-9171
Fax: 734-668-9171
Email: ncacs1@earthlink.net

The mission of the National Coalition of Alternative Community Schools (NCACS) is to unite and organize a grassroots movement of learners and learning communities dedicated to participant control and the elimination of human and ecological oppression. The organization serves its members through networking, conferences, newsletters, a directory, and student-staff-school exchanges and visits. Its major objectives are to inform the general public about alternative schools with a proven record of success, advocate for educational alternatives, and support educational change.

National Coalition of Education Activists (NCEA)
P.O. Box 679
Rhineback, NY 12572-0679
Telephone & Fax: 845-876-4580
Email: ncea@aol.com
Website: http://members.aol.com/nceaweb

The National Coalition of Education Activists (NCEA) is a multiracial network and membership organization of parents, school staff, union and community activists, and children's advocates working for equitable and excellent public schools.

National Community Education Association
3929 Old Lee Highway, #91A
Fairfax, VA 22042
Telephone: 703-359-8973
Web site: http://www.ncea.com

The National Community Education Association (also abbreviated NCEA) supports schools (primarily public schools) and community leaders working to provide expanded learning opportunities in response to individual and community needs. After-school and extended day programs, social services, alternative schools, and lifelong learning approaches are among the models it promotes. Its work is based on principles of local control and self-determination.

National Dropout Prevention Center
Clemson University
209 Martin Street
Clemson, SC 29634-0726
Telephone: 864-656-2599
Email: ndpc@clemson.edu
Web site: http://www.dropoutprevention.org

The National Dropout Prevention Center provides resources that enable a new or enhanced appreciation for the importance of a quality education and a high school diploma. Comprehensive, up-to-date information about critical K–12 youth in at-risk situations along with strategies and solutions are focused on keeping youth in school.

National Education Association (NEA)
1201 16th Street, NW
Washington, DC 20036
Telephone: 202-833-4000
Website: http://www.nea.org

The National Education Association (NEA) is America's oldest and largest organization committed to advancing the cause of public education. Founded in 1857, the NEA now claims 2.6 million members who work at every level of education. It has affiliates in every state and in more than 13,000 local communities across the country.

National Education Commission on Time and Learning
1255 22nd Street, NW
Washington, DC 20202-7591
Web site: http://www.ed.gov/pubs/PrisonersOfTime

The *Prisoners of Time* report of the National Commission on Time and Learning sparked national interest. The Commission concluded that consideration of the effects of time was a crucial missing element in the national debate about learning and high standards. It urged states to convene groups to analyze the impact of time on education and to develop action plans identifying possible ways to reinvent schools around learning, not time.

National Home Education Network
Email: info@nhen.org
Web site: http://www.nhen.org

The National Home Education Network (NHEN) encourages and facilitates the vital grassroots work of state and local home schooling groups and individuals by providing information, fostering networking, and promoting public relations on a national level.

National Home Education Research Institute
Box 13939
Salem, OR 97309
Telephone: 503-364-1490

The National Home Education Research Institute conducts research into the effects of home schooling on academic performance and collects the results of other research in the field. A bimonthly newsletter is distributed along with a fact sheet summarizing important recent research.

The National Research Center on the Gifted and Talented
OERI Project Liaison: Beverly Coleman
Office of Educational Research and Improvement
United States Department of Education
Room 611A, Mail Stop 5521
555 New Jersey Avenue, NW
Washington, DC 20208-5521

The National Research Center on the Gifted and Talented (NRC/GT) is supported under the Educational Research and Development Centers Program, PR/Award Number R206R000001, as administered by the Office of Educational Research and Improvement (OERI), U.S. Department of Education.

National Society for Experiential Education (NSEE)
9001 Braddock Road, Suite 380
Springfield, VA 22151
Telephone: 703-933-0017
Fax: 703-426-8400
Email: info@nsee.org
Web site: http://www.nsee.org

The National Society for Experiential Education (NSEE), a membership association committed to all forms of experiential learning, is a strong advocate of partnerships that contribute to more dynamic classrooms, a stronger workforce, and thriving communities. Members are offered ongoing professional development, which includes an annual conference, cutting-edge publications and research on all forms of experiential learning, and access to colleagues from around the world.

New Horizons for Learning
4649 Sunnyside North
Seattle, WA 98103
Telephone: 206-524-1710

New Horizons for Learning is a nonprofit, international human resources network, founded in 1980 to offer an expanded vision of possibilities in human development. It provides group advocacy programs for educational reform and focuses on synthesizing and communicating leading-edge educational research, theory, and practice through its newsletter *On the Beam*, annual international conferences, network meetings, and seminars throughout the world.

North American Division of the Seventh-Day Adventists
Education Department
12501 Old Columbia Pike
Silver Spring, MD 20904
Telephone: 301-680-6442

The North American Division of the Seventh-Day Adventists is responsible for fostering work in behalf of the spiritual interests of its members and maintaining a strong program of evangelism.

North American Montessori Teacher's Association
11424 Bellflower Road, NE
Cleveland OH 44106
Telephone: 216-421-1905

The North American Montessori Teacher's Association is an affiliate of the Association Montessori Internationale that provides information, books, and educational materials about the Montessori method.

Northeast Foundation for Children
71 Montague City Road
Greenfield, MA 01301
Telephone: 800-360-6332

Northeast Foundation for Children is an organization dedicated to the improvement of classroom teaching through professional development programs, summer workshops, long-term collaboration, and internships. It publishes a newsletter called *The Responsive Classroom;* sells books and classroom materials relating to classroom management, conflict resolution, and developmental education; and provides resources to help teachers develop their professional skills.

Oregon Association for Alternatives in Education
OME
P.O. Box 69486
Portland, OR 97201
Web site: http://www.oaae.org

The Oregon Association for Alternatives in Education was formed in 1984. The association's purpose is to promote and coordinate alternative education in Oregon. Members advocate for alternative instruction in the state's schools and provide a support network for teachers, parents, and students.

Outward Bound National Office
Route 9D-R2, Box 280
Garrison, NY 10524
Telephone: 800-243-2141

The Outward Bound movement began in England after World War II and came to the United States in the early 1960s. Outward Bound courses use wilderness environments to help students develop certain character traits, including commitment, cooperation, a positive approach to physical and mental challenges, honesty, and generosity. The standard Outward Bound course is about four weeks long. There are five Outward Bound schools in North America; these offer courses in a variety of natural environments, ranging from eight days to three months in length.

Partners for School Success
Carole Parkins

Regional Office of Education
DuPage County
421 N. County Farm Road
Wheaton, IL 60187
Telephone: 630-682-6955
Email: cparkins@dupage.k12.il.us
Web site: http://www.dupage.k12.il.us

Partners for School Success provide multiple learning environments that utilize a variety of strategies. Their curriculum includes partnerships with families, home schools, social service agencies, educational communities, businesses, and mentors.

Partnership for Learning
William Porter, Executive Director
Washington Mutual Bank
1201 3rd Avenue, 12th Floor
Seattle, WA 98161-1007
Telephone: 206-625-9655
Email: pfl@eskimo.com

After the Washington School Improvement Act passed in 1993, the Washington Business Roundtable helped to form the Partnership for Learning (PFL). PFL's main goal is to promote public awareness about the state's efforts to raise student standards and enhance student achievement. It works primarily with opinion leaders and policy makers and develops print materials for a database of 20,000 to 25,000 people.

Pathfinders
11011 Tyler Foote Road
Nevada City, CA 95959-9309
Telephone: 916-292-1000; 800-200-1107

Using the work of its developers, Sambhava and Josette Luvmour, Pathfinders is an organization that works with children and families. Its approach to child rearing is called "Natural Learning Rhythms." Throughout this innovative approach to child rearing and education, the importance of the family as a healthy, communicating unit is emphasized. The organization's work is based on theories presented by Piaget, Gesell, and Steiner.

Phi Delta Kappa
Dr. Ron Joekel, Executive Director
P.O. Box 789

Bloomington, IN 47402
Telephone: 812-339-1156
Web site: http://www.pdkintl.org

Phi Delta Kappa (PDK), in collaboration with the National Parent Teacher Association, has sponsored discussions across the country as part of the Civic Forum on the Future of Public Schools. These forums focus on three questions: What is the purpose of public schools? How effective are our public schools? And what changes must be made to attain these purposes?

The Philadelphia Yearly Meeting Library
1515 Cherry Street
Philadelphia, PA 19102
Telephone: 215-241-7220

The Philadelphia Yearly Meeting Library provides books and pamphlets about Friends education. Information and materials are available by mail.

Powerful Schools
Greg Tuke, Executive Director
3301 South Horton
Seattle, WA 98144
Telephone: 206-722-5543
Email: gtuke@cks.ssd.ke12.wa.us
Web site: http://www.seatleantioch.edu/students/jdobmeier.p

Begun in 1989, Powerful Schools is a coalition of elementary schools in Seattle that is partnered with two community organizations. Its mission is to improve student performance for all children, to strengthen the community by establishing schools that serve as community hubs, and to create an effective and cost-efficient model for school reform that can be replicated elsewhere. Its parent-incentive program has hired twenty-five to thirty low-income parents to work in schools and classrooms as tutors and aides or in other positions.

Program for Academic and Cultural Enhancement of Rural Schools (PACERS)
Dr. Jack Shelton
University of Alabama
Box 870372
Tuscaloosa, AL 35487
Telephone: 205-348-6432

Web site: http://www.pacers.pacespg.htm

The Program for Academic and Cultural Enhancement of Rural Schools (PACERS) is an association of twenty-nine small public schools in rural communities throughout Alabama. PACERS schools seek to improve and change the nature of learning through the active participation of the community. Projects include hands-on, interdisciplinary exercises for building on indigenous skills and resources. Each PACERS school has a newsletter that demonstrates student work and publicizes and reports on community activities. Twenty of these papers now have a readership of over 125,000 people.

Project Zero
Harvard Graduate School of Education
Longfellow Hall, 2nd Floor
Appian Way
Cambridge, MA 02138

Project Zero directs Howard Gardner's various projects and research initiatives. Upon request, it will send a list of public and private schools that are using the multiple intelligences approach.

Public Education Network
Wendy Puriefoy, President
601 Thirteenth Street, NW
Suite 900 North
Washington, DC 20001
Telephone: 202-628-7460
Web site: http://www/publiceducation.org

The Public Education Network is a national association of local education funds committed to achieving high-quality public education for all American children, especially those who are disadvantaged. Its mission is to link and unite these funds and to mobilize the energy and resources of communities to build effective and successful public schools.

Regional Education Laboratories, a network of ten Laboratories serving geographic regions that span the nation, works to ensure that those involved in educational improvement at the local, state, and regional levels have access to the best available information from research and practice. These Laboratories operate as vital partners with state and local educators, community members, and policy makers in using research to tackle the difficult issues of education reform and improvement.

Congress implemented the concept of Regional Educational Laboratories as a national resource for local and state benefits over three decades ago under the Elementary and Secondary Education Act. While each Laboratory has distinctive features tailored to meet the special needs of the geographic region it serves, all ten Laboratories have characteristics in common. Guided by a governing board representing stakeholders in its region—educators, business leaders, state officials, and community members—each Laboratory's work is shaped by the concerns, issues, opportunities, and special attributes of its region. Specifically, the Laboratories (1) conduct development and applied research resulting in models for implementing systemic reform and for achieving improvement on a broad scale; (2) provide information, training, and technical assistance to help states, schools, and communities to implement comprehensive school improvement strategies; (3) promote widespread access to information regarding research and best practice; (4) create communities of learners who collaborate with the Laboratories in development and dissemination; (5) cooperate with other agencies and programs to deliver services that support the efforts of educators and policy makers to improve education; and (6) forge strong links to the research community to promote the creation of new knowledge to improve education.

In addition, each Laboratory brings particular expertise in Specialty Areas designated by the Office of Educational Research and Improvement (OERI), making that expertise widely and readily available to all schools and communities throughout the nation.

The ten Laboratories in the Regional Education Laboratories network are listed next:

Appalachia Educational Laboratory (AEL)
Dr. Allen Arnold, President and CEO
Post Office Box 1348
Charleston, WV 25325-1348
Telephone: 304-347-0400
Fax: 304-347-0487
Email: aelinfo@ael.org
Web site: http://www.ael.org

National Leadership Area: Educational Technology
Region Served: Kentucky, Tennessee, Virginia, and West Virginia

Laboratory for Student Success (LSS)
Dr. JoAnn Manning, Interim Executive Director

Temple University/Center for Research in Human Development
   and Education
933 Ritter Annex, 13th Street and Cecil B. Moore Avenue
Philadelphia, PA 19122-6091
Telephone: 215-204-3030, 800-892-5550
Fax: 215-204-5130
Email: lss@vm.temple.edu
Web site: http://www.temple.edu/lss

National Leadership Area: Educational Leadership
Region Served: Delaware, Maryland, New Jersey, Pennsylvania,
   and Washington, DC

Mid-Continent Research for Education and Learning (McRel)
Dr. J. Timothy Waters, Executive Director
2550 South Parker Road, Suite 500
Aurora, CO 80014-1678
Telephone: 303-337-0990
Fax: 303-337-3005
Email: info@mcrel.org
Web site: http://www.mcrel.org

National Leadership Area: Standards-Based Instructional
   Practice
Region Served: Colorado, Kansas, Missouri, Nebraska,
   North Dakota, South Dakota, and Wyoming

North Central Regional Educational Laboratory (NCREL)
Dr. Gina Burkhardt, Executive Director
1120 East Diehl Road, Suite 200
Naperville, IL 60563-1486
Telephone: 630-649-6500
Fax: 630-649-6700
Email: info@ncrel.org
Web site: http://www.ncrel.org

National Leadership Area: Educational Technology
Region Served: Illinois, Indiana, Iowa, Michigan, Minnesota,
   Ohio, and Wisconsin

**Northeast and Islands Regional Educational Laboratory
at Brown University**
Dr. Mary-Beth Fafard, Interim Executive Director

222 Richmond Street, Suite 300
Providence, RI 02903-4226
Telephone: 401-274-9548
Fax: 401-421-7650
Email: info@lab.brown.edu
Web site: info@lab.brown.edu

National Leadership Area: Teaching Diverse Students
Region Served: Connecticut, Maine, Massachusetts,
    New Hampshire, New York, Rhode Island, Vermont,
    Puerto Rico, and the Virgin Islands

Northwest Regional Educational Laboratory
Dr. Carol F. Thomas, Chief Executive Officer
101 S. Main, Suite 500
Portland, OR 97204-3297
Telephone: 503-275-9500
Fax: 503-275-0448
Email: info@nwrel.org
Web site: http://www.nwrel.org

National Leadership Area: Re-engineering Schools
Region Served: Alaska, Idaho, Montana, Oregon, and
    Washington

Pacific Resources for Education and Learning (Prel)
Dr. John W. Kofel, President and CEO
1099 Alakea Street, 25th Floor
Honolulu, HI 96813-4513
Telephone: 808-441-1300
Fax: 808-441-1385
Email: askprel@prel.org
Web site: http://www.prel.org

National Leadership Area: Curriculum and Instruction Related
    to Reading and Language Mastery
Region Served: American Samoa, Commonwealth of the
    Northern Mariana Islands, Federated States of Micronesia,
    Guam, Hawaii, Republic of Marshall Islands, and the
    Republic of Palau

The Regional Educational Laboratory SERVE
P.O. Box 5367
Greensboro, NC 27435

Telephone: 336-334-3211
Fax: 336-334-3268
Email: info@serve.org
Web site: http://www.serve.org

National Leadership Area: Expanded Learning Opportunities
Region Served: Alabama, Florida, Georgia, Mississippi,
    North Carolina, and South Carolina

Southwest Educational Development Laboratory (SEDL)
Dr. Wesley A. Hoover
211 East Seventh Street
Austin, TX 78701-3281
Telephone: 512-476-6861, 800-476-6861
Fax: 512-476-2286
Email: info@sedl.org
Web site: http://www.sedl.org

National Leadership Area: Family and Community Involvement
Region Served: Arkansas, Louisiana, New Mexico, Oklahoma,
    and Texas

West Ed
Dr. Glen Harvey, Executive Director
730 Harrison Street
San Francisco, CA 94107-1242
Telephone: 415-565-3000
Fax: 415-565-3012
Email: dtorres@wested.org
Web site: http://www.wested.org

National Leadership Area: Assessment of Educational
    Achievement
Region Served: Arizona, California, Nevada, and Utah

Resource Center for Redesigning Education
P.O. Box 298
Brandon, VT 05733-0298
Telephone: 800-639-4122
Fax: 802-247-8312

The Resource Center for Redesigning Education publishes *Great Ideas in Education*, a book and video catalogue that also reviews new books and videos. It features materials concerning holistic education, Montessori education, whole language, and alternative education.

School Change Collaborative
Northwest Regional Educational Laboratory
101 SW Main, Suite 500
Portland, OR 97204
Telephone: 503-275-9500

The School Change Collaborative is a national association of regional laboratory staff, school practitioners, and other education stakeholders that has been meeting since 1996 to help schools involve students in their efforts to become professional learning communities. It operates as a professional learning community whereby members pool their expertise as they engage in discourse about the most effective means to achieve results, identify techniques that can strengthen reform efforts, and test approaches in real-world school settings.

School of Ethical Education
1000 Lafayette Blvd.
Bridgeport, CT 06604
Telephone: 203-330-5052
Email: Ethics@wisy.com

Founded in 1995, the School of Ethical Education is dedicated to promoting character education and to helping schools create effective character education programs.

The Self-Education Foundation
P.O. Box 30790
Philadelphia, PA 19104
Telephone: 215-235-4379
Email: info@selfeducation.org
Web site: http://www.selfeducation.org

The Self-Education Foundation funds communities that are initiating their own education. It gives small grants/awards to groups working across cultures and disciplines to build more resources for self-education, including independent media, inspired home schooling/ unschooling groups, self-educating prisoners, and student-led reform. It also publishes pamphlets and a newsletter to facilitate networking.

Society for Developmental Education
Route 202, Box 577
Peterboro, NH 03458
Telephone: 603-924-9621

The motto for the Society for Developmental Education is "Childhood should be a journey, not a race." To promote developmental education and the multi-age classroom, it offers workshops and customized training programs, which can be used by parents as well as teachers. The Society sponsors an annual national conference on "Multi-age Continuous Progress Practices." It also publishes an information packet that includes an extensive bibliography on developmental education.

Southern Regional Council
Marcia Klenbort, Director of Education Programs
133 Carnegie Way, NW
Suite 900
Atlanta, GA 30303-1024
Email: 73251.2024@compuserve.com
Web site: http://www.gpee.org

Founded in 1919, the Southern Regional Council (SRC) is a nonpartisan, nonprofit organization that works to achieve racial equality and economic and social justice in the southern United States through research and action that engage and transform individuals, communities, and institutions.

Sudbury Valley School
2 Winch Street
Framingham, MA 01701
Telephone: 508-877-3030
Fax: 508-788-0674

The Sudbury Valley School is one of the first and most successful of the democratic and libertarian schools in the country. The school's press publishes and sells books, pamphlets, and audio and video cassettes. It also offers a "New School Starter Kit."

Teacher Union Reform Network (TURN)
30 N. Union Street, Suite 301
Rochester, NY 14607
Telephone: 716-546-2681
Fax: 716-546-4123
Email: urbanski@servtech.com
Web site: www.turnexchange.net

The Teacher Union Reform Network (TURN) is a union-led effort to restructure the nation's teachers' unions to promote reform that will ultimately lead to better learning and higher achievement for America's children. Adam Urbanski, president of the Rochester Teachers Association and vice-president of the American Federation of Teachers, is the director of TURN. He is also a trustee of the National Center for Education and the Economy.

Thomas B. Fordham Foundation
1627 K Street, NW
Suite 600
Washington, DC 20006
Telephone: 202-223-5452
Fax: 202-223-9226
Email: fordham@dunst.com
Web site: http://www.edexcellence.net/

The Thomas B. Fordham Foundation supports research, publications, and action projects of national significance in elementary/secondary education reform, as well as significant education reform projects in and around Dayton, Ohio. It has taken over the work of the Educational Excellence Network and is affiliated with the Manhattan Institute for Policy Research.

Whole Language Umbrella
100 Heritage
Bloomington, IN 47408
Telephone: 812-336-6925
Fax: 812-856-8287

Whole Language Umbrella is an organization that promotes and distributes information on whole language. Its location changes according to the home base of the current director.

The Yale Child Study Center/School Development Program
55 College Street
New Haven, CT 06510
Telephone: 800-811-7775
Web site: http://www.info.med.yale.edu/comer

The Yale Child Study Center/School Development Program is part of Yale University. It provides information to and support for parents, teachers, and administrators interested in implementing James Comer's principles and approaches in their schools.

Zephyr Press
3316 North Chapel Avenue
P.O. Box 66006

Tucson, AZ 85728
Telephone: 602-322-5090
Fax: 602-323-9402

This company sells books, videos, and education materials related to multiple intelligences. It also organizes conferences with multiple intelligences as the theme.

Chapter 12
◆ Selected Print and Nonprint Resources

MAJOR EDUCATIONAL REFORM REPORTS
(LISTED BY DATE)

The Paideia Proposal: An Educational Manifesto, Mortimer J. Adler, on behalf of the members of the Paideia Group, 1982.

The Troubled Crusade: American Education 1945–1980, Diane Ravitch, 1983.

A Place Called School: Prospects for the Future, John Goodlad, 1983.

Academic Preparation for College: What Students Need to Know and Be Able to Do, Educational Equality Project, The College Board, 1983.

Action for Excellence: A Comprehensive Plan to Improve Our Nation's Schools, Task Force on Education for Economic Growth, Education Commission of the States, 1983.

High School: A Report on Secondary Education in America, Ernest L. Boyer, The Carnegie Foundation for the Advancement of Teaching, 1983.

Making the Grade, Report of the Twentieth-Century Fund Task Force on Federal Elementary and Secondary Education Policy, 1983.

Horace's Compromise: The Dilemma of the American High School, Theodore R. Sizer, 1984.

A Study of High Schools, Theodore R. Sizer, co-sponsored by the National Association of Secondary School Principals and the National Association of Independent Schools, 1984.

In Search of Excellence: Lessons from America's Best-Run Companies, Thomas Peters and Robert Waterman, 1984.

Investing in Our Children, Report of the Committee for Economic Development, 1985.

A Nation Prepared: Teachers for the 21st Century, Report of the Carnegie Task Force on Teaching as a Profession, 1986.

Time for Results, National Governors' Association, 1986.

Cultural Literacy: What Every American Needs to Know, E. D. Hirsch, Jr., 1987.

The Forgotten Half: Non-College Youth in America: An Interim Report on the School-to-Work Transition, Report of William T. Grant Foundation's Commission on Work, Family and Citizenship, 1988.

Teachers for Our Nation's Schools, John Goodlad, 1990.

Horace's School: Redesigning the American High School, Theodore R. Sizer, 1991.

Results in Education: 1990, Report of the National Governors' Association, 1991.

Savage Inequalities: Children in America's Schools, Jonathan Kozol, 1991.

Shared Vision: Policy Recommendations for Linking Teacher Education to School Reform, Calvin Frazier, 1993.

Prisoners of Time, Report of the National Education Commission on Time and Learning, April 1994.

The Basic School, Ernest Boyer, 1995.

The Schools We Need and Why We Don't Have Them, E. D. Hirsch, Jr., 1996.

What Matters Most: Teaching for America's Future, National Commission on Teaching and America's Future, 1996.

Horace's Hope: The Future of the American High School, Theodore R. Sizer, 1996.

The Public Purpose of Education and Schooling, edited by John I. Goodlad and Timothy J. McMannon, 1997.

Report of the SREB High Schools That Work, 1998: Secondary School Teacher Survey, Gene Bottoms, 1998.

Pursuing Excellence: A Study of U.S. Twelfth-Grade Mathematics and Science Achievement in an International Context, U.S. Department of Education, NCES/OERI, Initial Findings from the Third International Mathematics and Science Study (TIMMS), 1998.

Small Schools, Big Imaginations: A Creative Look at Urban Public Schools, Cross City Campaign for Urban School Reform, Michelle Fine and Janis Somerville, 1998.

Whole School Restructuring: The Urban Comprehensive High Schools, Nettie Legters for CRESPAR School and Classroom Intervention: Middle and High School, Report #31, 1999.

Raising Our Sights: No High School Senior Left Behind, National Commission on the High School Senior Year, 2001.

REFERENCE PUBLICATIONS

After School Programs: Good for Kids, Good for Communities

Available by mail from
Northwest Regional Education Laboratory
101 S. W. Main Street, Suite 500
Portland, OR 97204
Telephone: 503-275-9515
Email: info@nwrel.org

***Results-Based Programs Directory, Kentucky Department of
Education, Division of School Improvement***

Available by mail from
Windy Newton, Communication Services
Kentucky Department of Education
500 Mero Street, 19th Floor
Frankfort, KY 40601
Telephone: 502-564-3421
Email: wnewton@kde.state.ky.us

***The Three-Year Effect of 10 Promising Programs on the Academic
Achievement of Students Placed at Risk,*** Sam Stringfield, Mary Ann
Millsap, Elois Scott, Rebecca Herman (NCBE#BE020583,
ERIC#ED369854)

Available by mail from
Sam Stringfield
C.S.O.S.
The Johns Hopkins University
3505 N. Charles Street
Baltimore, MD 21218

***What Do We Know? Widely Implemented School Improvement
Programs,*** Margaret C. Wang, Geneva D. Haertel, and Harbert J.
Walberg

Available by mail from
Temple University Center for Research in Human Development
    and Education
1301 Cecil B. Moore Avenue
Philadelphia, PA 19122-6091
Telephone: 800-892-5550
Fax: 215-204-5130
Web site: http://www.temple.edu/LSS/csr_info.htm

Schoolwide Reform Models: What Works?, Olatokunbo S. Fashola and Robert E. Slavin, Phi Delta Kappan.

Web site: www.pdkintl.org/kappan/ksla9801.htm#4a

Catalog of School Reform Models, Northwest Regional Education Laboratory

Available by mail from
Northwest Regional Education Laboratory
101 S. W. Main Street, Suite 500
Portland, OR 97204
Telephone: 503-275-9515
Email: info@nwrel.org
Web site: http://www.nwrel.org/csrdp

Creating Learning Communities: Models, Resources, and New Ways of Thinking about Teaching and Learning

Coalition for Self-Learning, Catalog Number 4171
Great Ideas in Education
Box 328, Brandon, VT 05733-0328
Telephone: 800-639-4122

Charter Schools: Creating and Sustaining Family Friendly Schools

Charter Friends National Network
Produced under a grant from the Annie E. Casey Foundation, November 2000

BOOKSTORES, PUBLISHING COMPANIES, AND NETWORKS

Abeka Books
Box 18000
Pensacola, FL 32523-9160
Telephone: 800-874-2352

Abeka Books distributes curricula, books, and education materials for Christian schools and Christian home schoolers.

American School Directory
Web site: http://www.asd.com

The American School Directory (ASD) is the Internet guide to all 108,000

K–12 schools, providing information as well as communication and payment tools for teachers, students, parents, local communities, and families planning to move. ASD is sponsored by Computers for Education, IBM, and Innisbrook Wraps.

Ask ERIC
Web site: http://ericir.syr.edu

The Educational Resources Information Center (ERIC) is a national information system designed to provide ready access to an extensive body of education-related literature. Established in 1966, ERIC is supported by the U.S. Department of Education's Office of Educational Research and Improvement and is administered by the National Library of Education (NLE).

Autodidactic Press
Wasilla, AK 99687
Telephone: 907-376-2932
Web site: http://www.autodidactic.com

Autodidactic Press is a small publishing company dedicated to the proposition that lifelong learning is the lifeblood of democracy and a key to living life to its fullest.

Bob Jones University Publishers
Bob Jones University
Greenville, SC 29614-0001
Telephone: 800-845-5731

Bob Jones University Publishers is a major distributor of textbooks and educational materials for Christian schools. Its available materials now include curricula as well as books designed specifically for Christian home schooling.

Designs for Learning
1745 University Avenue
St. Paul, MN 55104
Telephone: 651-649-5400, ext. 3009

The Designs for Learning organization provides research on principles of learning and charter school designs, relevant to creating alternatives in both the private and public sectors. It is coordinated by Wayne Jennings, director of five charter schools and the originator of the St. Paul Open School.

Directory of Resources for Educational Alternatives
Alliance for Parent Involvement in Education
P.O. Box 59
East Chatham, NY 12060-0059
Telephone: 518-932-6900
Email: allpie@taconic

Services include a catalog of resources, workshops, and conferences, a mail-order lending library, phone consultations, and AllPIE mailings.

Down to Earth Books
P.O. Box 488
Ashfield, MA 01330
Email: maryskole@aol.com
Web site: http://www.spinninglobe.net

This publisher provides an online bookstore specializing in education psychology, spirituality, poetry, and other topics. Back issues of *SKOLE*, a journal of alternative education, are available, as are current issues of the newly titled publication *Paths of Learning*.

Education Futures Project
P.O. Box 2977
Sacramento, CA 95812
Telephone: 916-393-8701

This clearinghouse has information on the original philosophy of alternatives and on the history of the movement. It also provides publications on how to create alternative programs.

Education Week on the Web
Telephone (toll-free): 800-728-2790
Fax: 301-280-3250
Web site: www.edweek.org

Education Week on the Web is a comprehensive guide to education news nationwide. It includes a searchable index of past issues.

Educational Heretics Press
113 Arundel Drive
Bramcote Hills, Nottingham, N693FQ, U.K.
Telephone (international): +44115-925 7261
Telephone (within U.K.): 0115-9257561

Education Heretics Press, a not-for-profit, research, writing, and publishing company, was founded in 1991. Its purpose is to question the dogmas of schooling in particular and education in general, and to develop the logistics of the next new learning system.

Educational Research Service
200 Clarendon Boulevard
Arlington, VA 22201
Telephone: 703-243-2100; 800-791-9308
Fax: 703-243-1985; 800-791-9308
Email: crs@ers.org
Web site: http://www.ers.org

The Educational Research Service (ERS) is a not-for-profit, independent research organization. It was established in 1973 by four national associations of school administrators to fill a pressing need in education for an independent organization to provide reliable, unbiased information to local school districts. Today, seven national associations of school administrators are recognized as ERS founders, with the executive directors of each comprising its board of directors: the American Association of School Administrators, the American Association of School Personnel Administrators, the Association of School Business Officials, the Council of Chief State School Officers, the National Association of Elementary School Principals, the National Association of Secondary School Principals, and the National School Public Relations Association.

EnCompass
11011 Tyler Foote Road
Nevada City, CA 95960
Telephone: 530-292-1000
Web site: http://www.encompass-nir.org

EnCompass, a nonprofit holistic learning center, teaches and models the Natural Learning Rhythms (NLR) approach, developed by Ba and Josette Luvmour. It does so through an integrated program of workshops, classes, internships, retreats, family camps, outdoor education, special programs, conferences, and publications.

The Grandfather Economic Reports
Website: http://mwhodges.home.att.net

The Grandfather Economic Reports are a series of reports showing, in picture form, threats to the economic future of families and their children, compared to prior generations. These reports cover such issues as education quality, debt, savings, voting, health care, and international competition. They are based on the premise that unacceptable education quality is a very real and serious threat facing our young generation. Some call this site one of the very best concerning education quality issues.

Great Ideas in Education
Box 328
Brandon, VT 05733-0328
Telephone: 800-639-4122
Fax: 802-247-8312
Email: info@great-ideas.org
Web site: http://www.great-ideas.org

Great Ideas in Education is the home of both the Holistic Education Press (HEP) and the Psychology Press (PP). HEP publishes the *Holistic Education Review* and other books on educational renewal; PP publishes educational tests. The web site includes a catalog of almost 100 books and videos on educational transformation.

Heinemann
361 Hanover Street
Portsmouth, NH 03801-3912
Telephone: 800-793-2154
Web site: http://www.heinemann.com

This publisher provides numerous titles on whole-language approaches to literacy and other student-centered methods of teaching, including several books on alternative education.

***Home Education* Magazine**
P.O. Box 159
Tonasket, WA 98855
Telephone: 509-486-2477

Home Education is a bimonthly magazine with useful articles and information.

Home Educators and You (HEY)
Web site: http://www.home-school.com

This web site provides a wide range of information on home schooling, including an easily accessed worldwide directory of home school organizations. It is the official web site of the Practical Home Schooling Magazine.

Islamic Publications International
P.O. Box 247
Teaneck, NJ 07666
Telephone: 201-599-9708; 800-568-9814
Fax: 201-599-1169; 800-466-8111

Islamic Publications International is a source of books, videos, and brochures about Islam.

John Dewey Project on Progressive Education
535 Waterman Building
University of Vermont
Burlington, VT 05405
Telephone: 802-856-1355

The John Dewey Project on Progressive Education is a policy research institute promoting ideas such as justice, equity, human development, creativity, care, ethics, and community in public discussion of educational issues. Its ideas are communicated through workshops, forums, and the publication of studies and position papers.

John Holt's Bookstore
2269 Massachusetts Avenue
Cambridge, MA 02140
Telephone: 617-864-3100
Fax: 617-864-9235

This bookstore offers a variety of books, videos, and home schooling materials. Holt's organization also publishes a bimonthly journal titled *Growing Without Schooling*. Each year the December issue includes a directory of home schoolers covering all fifty states.

Jola Publications
2933 N. 2nd Street
Minneapolis, MN 55411
Telephone: 612-529-5001

This company publishes the periodical *Public School Montessorian* as well as the annual *Montessori Community Directory*, a comprehensive listing of hundreds of Montessori schools across the United States. It also provides information on organizations, teacher education centers, publications, materials, suppliers, and other resources of Montessori education.

The Merrow Report
Learning Matters, Inc.
6 E. 32nd Street, 8th floor
New York, NY 10016
Telephone: 212-725-7000
Toll Free: 877-263-7769
Fax: 212-725-2433
Email: merrow@merrow.org
Web site: http://www.pbs.org/merrow

The Merrow Report looks at issues that shape the ways we live and work and learn. John Merrow's TV and radio documentaries on education issues are considered among the best, and his web site has links to video and audio clips as well as rich collections of resources. Learning Matters, Inc., is the production company that produces the Merrow Report.

MiddleWeb
Web site: http://www.middleweb.com

MiddleWeb is a project supported by the Edna McConnell Clark Foundation, which is dedicated to reform and innovation in middle schools, with an emphasis on urban issues. It provides resources for educators and parents and includes good links to other online resources.

Minnesota Coalition for Authentic Reform in Education (MNCARE)
Web site: http://www.mncare.homestead.com/

The goal of MNCARE is to provide a network for students, parents, teachers, and others interested in the issue of authentic reform in education, particularly as it relates to fair and equitable assessment and the uses of standardized testing to make important decisions about students' educational opportunities.

Muslim Journal
910 West Van Buren, #100
Chicago, IL 60637
Telephone: 312-243-7600

The *Muslim Journal* is a weekly newspaper published by the African American Islamic community. The organization also publishes an annual Muslim Resource Directory, which includes a list of Islamic schools in North America.

National Commission on High School and the Senior Year
Web site: http://www.commissiononthesenioryear.org

The National Commission on High School and the Senior Year is a twenty-nine-member panel set up by former U.S. Secretary of Education Richard W. Riley to examine how high schools can be improved. Its forty-six-page report is replete with the Commission's descriptions of ways that high schools have failed graduating seniors.

National Parent Information Network
Anne Robertson
ERIC Clearinghouse on Elementary and Early Childhood Education
University of Illinois at Urbana-Champaign
Children's Research Center
51 Gerty Drive
Champaign, IL 61820-7469
Telephone (toll-free): 800-583-4135
Email: arobrtsn@uiuc.edu
Web site: http://npin.org

The mission of the National Parent Information Network (NPIN) is to provide access to research-based information about the parenting process and family involvement in education. This mission is based on the belief that well-informed families are likely to make good decisions about raising and educating their children.

New Horizons for Learning
P.O. Box 15329
Seattle, WA 98115
Telephone: 206-547-7936
Web site: http://www.newhorizons.org

This online resource for educators explores ideas not yet in mainstream educational practice. Online journals, books, and other materials are provided for individuals as well as organizations.

Partnership Education Consultants
Center for Partnership Studies
P.O. Box 30538
Tucson, AZ 85728

Telephone: 502-547-0176
Web site: http://www.partnershipway.org

Partnership Education Consultants is a network of professional development/school reform consultants who help schools implement the principles of Partnership Education presented in Riane Eisler's book *Tomorrow's Children*. Partnership Education is a comprehensive approach to the content, structure, and process of teaching, emphasizing values of caring, community, inclusiveness, and cooperation.

Pathfinder Center
P.O. Box 804
Amherst, MA 01004
256 North Pleasant Street
Amherst, MA 01002
Telephone: 413-253-9412
Email: plc@valinet.com
Web site: http://www.pathfindercenter.org

The Pathfinder Center supports teenaged unschoolers and their families. It offers strategic consultations for families either considering unschooling for their teens or interested in improving their unschooling. The Center publishes *Liberated Learners*, which provides a forum for teen home schoolers to tell their stories.

Paths of Learning: Options for Families and Communities
P.O. Box 328
Brandon, VT 05733
Telephone: 800-639-4122

This quarterly magazine is a guide to the diverse ways of educating young people in schools and alternative settings. The publication shows how educators and parents can nourish children's development and help them become caring, resourceful citizens in the twenty-first century.

Rethinking Schools
1001 E. Keefe Avenue
Milwaukee, WI 53212
Telephone: 414-964-9646
Toll Free: 800-669-4192
Fax: 414-964-7220
Email: webrs@excps.com

Web site: http://www.rethinkingschools.org

Founded in 1986 by activist teachers, Rethinking Schools is a nonprofit, independent publisher of educational materials that advocate the reform of elementary and secondary education, with a strong emphasis on issues of equity and social justice. Its activist publication encourages teachers, parents, and students to become involved in building quality public schools for all children.

Sudbury Valley School Press
2 Winch Street
Framingham, MA 01701
Telephone: 508-877-3030

Sudbury Valley School (SVS) has educated young people in a free, democratic environment for over thirty years, and educators associated with the school have written numerous essays and books on the philosophy and concrete results of the school's distinctive approach. SVS Press distributes these thought-provoking writings, along with audio and video tapes, periodicals, and planning kits for starting new democratic schools.

The Teaching Home
Editorial and Advertising Departments
P.O. Box 2029
Portland, OR 97294
Telephone: 503-253-9633

The Teaching Home is a bimonthly magazine that focuses on Christian home schooling. Each issue lists currently operating state Christian home schooling organizations and advertises suppliers of Christian curricula, books, and educational materials.

Zephyr Press
P.O. Box 66006
Tucson, AZ 85728-6006
Telephone: 800-232-2187
Web site: http://www.zephyrpress.com

Zephyr Press publishes books exploring "new ways of teaching for all ways of learning," including multiple intelligences, brain-based learning, and integrated curricula. The company also sponsors workshops and an annual conference.

RECOMMENDED READING LIST

Bagley, M., and Hess, K. (1984). *2000 Ways of Using Imagery in the Classroom.* New York: Trillium Press.

Bennis, W., and Nanus, B. (1985). *Leaders.* New York: Harper and Row.

Bloom, B. (1980). *All Our Children Learning.* New York: McGraw Hill.

Bowles, S., and Gintis, H. (1976). *Schooling in Capitalist America.* New York: Basic Books.

Bracey, G. W. (1991). "Why Can't They Be Like We Were?" *Phi Delta Kappan* (October): 105–117.

Brain Research and Learning (1978). Washington, DC: National Education Association.

Burns, M. (1976). *The Book of Think.* Boston: Little, Brown.

Butler, K. (1984). *Learning and Teaching Style: In Theory and Practice.* Maynard, MA: Gabriel Systems, Inc.

Byham, W. C. (1992). *Zapp in Education.* New York: Fawcett Columbine, 1992.

Canfield, J., and Wells, H. (1976). *100 Ways to Enhance Self-Concept in the Classroom.* Englewood Cliffs, NJ: Prentice-Hall.

Clark, B. (1986). *Optimizing Learning.* Columbus, OH: Charles E. Merrill.

Colfax, D., and Colfax, M. (1989). *Home Schooling for Excellence.* New York: Warner Books.

_____. (1992). *Hard Times in Paradise.* New York: Warner Books.

Conant, J. (1959). *The American High School Today.* New York: McGraw-Hill.

Cordes, H. (2000). "Battling for the Heart and Soul of Home Schoolers." Available online at www.salon.com.mwt/feature/2000/10/02/home schooling battle/

Costa, A. (Ed.). (1985). *Developing Minds: A Resource Book for Teaching Thinking.* Washington, DC: Association for Supervision and Curriculum Development.

Covey, S. (1989). *Seven Habits of Highly Effective People.* New York: Simon and Schuster.

Deal, T., and Kennedy, A. (1982). *Corporate Cultures.* Reading, MA: Addison-Wesley.

Dennison, G. (1969). *The Lives of Children.* New York: Random House.

De Pree, M. (1989). *Leadership Is an Art.* East Lansing, MI: Michigan State University Press.

Featherstone, J. (1968). *Schools Where Children Learn.* New York: Liveright Press.

Gardner, H. (1984). *Frames of Mind.* New York: Basic Books.

Gardner, J. (1961). *Excellence: Can We Be Equal and Excellent Too?* New York: Harper and Row.

Garfield, C. (1986). *Peak Performances.* New York: W. Morrow.

Glasser, W. (1968). *Schools Without Failure.* New York: Harper and Row.

Guilford, J. (1986). *Creative Talents.* Buffalo: Pearly Limited.

Holt, J. ((1964). *How Children Fail.* New York: Pitman.

_____. (1970). *What Do I Do Monday?* New York: Dutton.

_____. (1972). *Freedom and Beyond.* New York: Dutton.

Horton, M., and Freire, P. (1990). *We Make the Road by Walking: Conversations on Education and Social Change.* Philadelphia: Temple University Press.

Illich, I. (1971). *Deschooling Society.* New York: Harper.

Johnson, D., and Johnson R. (1984). *Circles of Learning.* Washington, DC: Association for Supervision and Curriculum Development.

Kohl, H. (1967). *36 Children.* New York: New American Library.

_____. (1969). *The Open Classroom.* New York: Vintage Books.

Kozol, J. (1967). *Death at an Early Age: The Destruction of the Hearts and Minds of Negro Children in the Boston Public Schools.* Boston: Houghton Mifflin.

_____. (1972). *Free Schools.* Boston: Houghton Mifflin.

_____. (1985). *Illiterate America.* Garden City, NY: Anchor Press/ Doubleday.

Llewellyn, G. (1991). *The Teenage Liberation Handbook: How to Quit School and Get a Real Education.* Eugene, OR: Lowry House.

_____. (1993). *Real Lives: Eleven Teenagers Who Don't Go to School.* Eugene, OR: Lowry House.

Matthews, D. (1997). *Is There a Public for Public Schools?* Dayton, OH: Kettering Foundation Press.

McCarthy, B. (1983). *4-Mat in Action: Creative Lesson Plans for Teaching to Learning Styles with Right/Left Brain Mode Techniques.* Arlington Heights, IL: Excel.

McCune, S. (1986). *Guide to Strategic Planning for Educators.* Alexandria, VA: Association for Supervision and Curriculum Development.

Moss Kanter, R. (1983). *The Changemasters.* New York: Simon & Schuster.

Naisbitt, J., and Aburdene, P. (1985). *Reinventing the Corporation.* New York: Warner Books.

Novak, J., and Gowin, B. (1984). *Learning How to Learn.* Cambridge, MA: Cambridge University Press.

Olsen, L. (1994). *The Unfinished Journey: Restructuring Schools in a Diverse Society.* Oakland, CA: California Tomorrow.

Peters, T., and Austin, N. (1985). *A Passion for Excellence.* New York: Random House.

Peters, T., and Waterman, R. (1982). *In Search of Excellence.* New York: Harper and Row.

Ravtich, D. (1985). *The Schools We Deserve: Reflections on the Educational Crisis of Our Times.* New York: Basic Books.

Roszak, T. (1970). *A Man for Tomorrow's World.* Berkeley, CA: University of California Press.

_____. (1972). *Where the Wastelands End.* Berkeley, CA: University of California Press.

_____. (1995). *The Making of a Counter Culture.* Berkeley, CA: University of California Press.

Senge, P. (1990). *The Fifth Discipline.* New York: Doubleday.

Silberman, C. (1970). *Crisis in the Classroom.* New York: Random House.

Sund, R. (1976). *Piaget for Educators.* Columbus, OH: Charles E. Merrill.

Waterman, R. (1987). *The Renewal Factor.* New York: Bantam Books.

_____. (1990). *Adhocracy.* New York: W. W. Norton.

Wenk, E. (1987). *Tradeoffs: Imperatives of Choice in a High-Tech World.* Baltimore, MD: Johns Hopkins University Press.

Williams, L. (1983). *Teaching for the Two-Sided Mind.* Englewood Cliffs, NJ: Prentice-Hall.

ᴥ Glossary

Achievement: Performance as determined by some type of assessment or testing.

Affective: Relating to emotions, feelings, and attitudes.

Affinity Diagram: A creative process, used with or by a group, to gather and organize ideas, opinions, issues, and so on.

Alternative schools: A term that broadly refers to public schools set up by states or school districts to serve populations of students who are not succeeding in the traditional public school environment. Alternative schools offer students who are failing academically or may have learning disabilities or behavioral problems an opportunity to achieve in a different setting. There are many different kinds of alternative schools, but most are characterized by flexible schedules, small teacher-student ratios, and modified curricula.

Assessment: A term often used as a synonym for *evaluation*, referring to processes that are focused on quantitative testing approaches.

At risk: A phrase describing students with socioeconomic challenges, such as poverty or teen pregnancy, that may place them at a disadvantage in achieving academic, social, or career goals. Such students are deemed "at risk" of failing, dropping out, or "falling through the cracks" at school.

Authentic assessment: An alternative to traditional testing, using indicators of student task performance.

Behavioral objectives: Specifically stated terms of attainment to be checked by observation or test/measurement.

Bell-shaped curve: A curve produced from a distribution of numbers called a *normal distribution*. When the distribution is normal, then the mean = median = mode.

Carden schools: Schools that use a curriculum method developed by Mae Carden, currently numbering more than eighty in the United States. While a student at Columbia, Miss Carden found herself disagreeing with her professors about children and how they learn. She rejected the progressive methods proposed by Dewey and others and developed her own education technique based on phonetics and other methods. Miss Carden found that she could teach virtually every child to read, spell, and express him- or herself in writing and in speech, clearly and correctly. She said, "If a child has failed to learn, it is because the teacher had failed to teach." Many private schools, most of them in Florida, Texas, and California and other western states, have adopted the Carden method. A number of independent schools were founded specifically as Carden schools.

Certificates: Mechanisms for dispersing funds to children in school choice plans, whereby parents have a designated dollar amount that they may "spend" to enroll their child at the educational institution of their choice. (Such mechanisms also include *scholarships* and *vouchers.*)

Charter school: Schools that are independent of the traditional public school system but receive public funding, run by groups such as teachers, parents, or foundations. Charter schools are free of many district regulations and are often tailored to community needs. In some states, existing public schools may convert to charter status. Charter schools differ from magnet schools in terms of autonomy and the way they are created.

Christian schools: Schools founded in the 1960s as religiously based but nondenominational schools. The Christian school movement is the fastest-growing movement in the country. As of the late 1970s there were still only a handful of these schools, but in the early 1980s the movement began to grow at a very rapid pace. Hundreds of schools were founded each year. Second only to the Roman Catholic school system, the Christian school movement encompasses the largest group of schools outside the public school system. Conservative Christians (fundamentalists, evangelicals, and charismatics) are the driving force behind the Christian school movement. Most Christian schools follow traditional teaching methods, using classes in which a single teacher instructs same-age children as a group. Caucasian parents who wanted to avoid sending their children to newly integrated public schools founded many of the first Christian schools. Today, however, Christian schools admit virtually all students regardless of race, color, or national origin. Christian schools are based on strongly held views of the world, human nature and destiny, the aims of education, and the present-day public school system. The movement is especially strong in the Bible belt, which stretches across the southern part of the nation through the Southwest and into southern California.

Comer schools: Schools and school systems that have adopted the Comer model. The program that James Comer developed, known both as the School Development Program (SDP) and as the "Comer process," helps parents, teachers, school staff and officials, and community members to make schools places for children to learn and to develop as whole human beings. Over 600 schools in the United States and abroad have adopted the program. The Comer process is based on an innovative vision of what a school should be and do. Comer himself maintains that a school must minimize the effects that societal problems have had on the teaching and learning process. His approach brings school, parents, and community together in the collective enterprise of raising and educating children.

Constructivism: A psychological theory of learning that "construes learning as an interpretive, recursive, building process by active learners interacting with the physical and social world."

Controlled choice: School choice that is limited by court-ordered desegregation guidelines. Because choice programs limit parents to choices that do not upset the racial balance of a particular school, school districts with these programs can control parental choices based on race and space limitations.

Cooperative education: A program that allows students to receive credit for career work done in their field of study. Some businesses create cooperative education plans for training and evaluation of students.

Cooperative learning programs: Programs in which students are divided into small, heterogeneous groups and each group member is charged to learn the material or master the skill, to ensure that everyone else in the group masters the material, and, ultimately, to ensure that everyone in the class has mastered it. Roger Johnson and David Johnson, two leading theorists of cooperative learning, believe that there are three patterns of classroom life— the competitive, the individualistic, and the cooperative—and the cooperative is the most effective of the three. Research indicates that students in cooperative learning situations have more self-esteem and develop more positive interpersonal relations.

Developmental education: A developmental approach in education based on the belief that the child is a unique being who unfolds and develops according to a specific pattern and timetable. Advocates of developmental education believe that if certain types of learning are introduced before the child is ready for them, healthy and well-rounded development will be impeded.

Education Reform Network: A communications network connecting schools, educators, and education advocates so that they can share ideas, relate new approaches to improving teaching and learning, and discuss education reform topics. This network was introduced by the Eisenhower Regional Alliance for Mathematics and Science Education Reform.

Enrichment programs: Programs originally designed primarily for gifted students but now widely used with at-risk children as well. Enrichment programs are intended to supplement the regular academic curriculum for students who might otherwise be bored with their classwork. For the gifted they are an alternative to acceleration, whereby even the cleverest students can remain in class with children their own age and maturity, yet be adequately challenged. Sometimes run as pull-out programs, enrichment programs are also an alternative to creating entirely separate gifted classrooms. Enrichment is intended to add value to the curriculum, often in a fun way, through such activities as special projects, guest speakers, concerts, and museum visits. Many educators have found that what was originally considered enrichment is actually worth incorporating into the regular curriculum.

Essentialism: A view of education based on the belief that a main purpose of schooling is to transmit a cultural heritage from one generation to another.

Evaluation planning: Planning that is required before a program begins, both to get baseline data and to evaluate the program plan, at least for evaluability. Through evaluation planning, one is able to avoid designing a program that cannot be evaluated.

Experiential education: Education that stresses hands-on experience (accomplished through field trips, internships, or activity-oriented projects) as opposed to traditional classroom learning.

Focus group: A group selected for its relevance to an evaluation and engaged by a trained facilitator in a series of discussions designed for sharing insights, ideas, and observations on a topic related to the evaluation.

Formative evaluation: Evaluation designed and used to improve an intervention, especially while it is still being developed.

Friends Schools: Schools organized and run by the Religious Society of Friends. Friends Schools are known for their academic excellence and for the moral and spiritual values they embody. They educate both Quaker and non-Quaker students.

Full choice: School choice that includes private as well as public schools.

Functionalism: A view of society that holds that society is functioning well and that schools are necessary to help maintain and improve the "well-oiled machine" of our country.

Gifted students: Pupils who are considered to have the capacity to achieve beyond the norm—because of either their IQ scores, their demonstrated ability in the classroom, or both. Once limited to academic skills, the definition of giftedness in many schools has been expanded to include children with a wide variety of talents.

Holistic education: Education that includes most or all of the elements of classical progressive education as well as the recent neo-progressive addenda. Holistic education is child centered and largely experiential. Cooperative learning, the use of developmental models of childhood, multicultural education, and democratic and consensual decision making typically are incorporated into holistic schools.

Impact evaluation: An evaluation focused on outcomes or payoff.

Inclusion: A controversial practice—sometimes called "full inclusion"—in which children with disabilities are educated alongside their non-disabled peers, often in a regular classroom in their neighborhood school. The Individuals with Disabilities Education Act requires that disabled children be educated in the "least restrictive environment" possible.

Independent schools: Private or nonpublic schools that are not part of a school system. Independent schools are governed by a board of trustees instead of by the state board of education and are funded by tuition and private donations and grants. They must hold a nonprofit status and be accredited by an approved state or regional association. They must also be nondiscriminatory, and can be either religious or nonreligious.

In-depth interview: A guided conversation between a skilled interviewer and an interviewee that seeks to maximize opportunities for the expression of the respondent's feeling and ideas through the use of open-ended questions and a loosely structured interview guide.

Interdistrict choice: School choice in which students are permitted to cross district lines to attend schools. Some states allow interdistrict choice among a limited number of districts.

Intradistrict choice: Open enrollment among schools within a district.

Islamic schools: Schools that uphold the principles of Islam, one of the world's great religions. The Muslim community in the United States consists of three principal groups. One is an immigrant group composed of first- and second-generation immigrants from countries such as Egypt, Jordan, India, and Pakistan. Another group consists of African American Muslims who are followers of W. Deen Mohammed. The third is the Nation of Islam. Muslim immigrant groups have established and support about fifty schools around the country. Sister Clara Muhammad, the wife of Elijah Mohammad, founded the first African American Muslim school in the 1930s.

Jewish day schools: Full-time Jewish schools largely run by Orthodox Jews. The first Jewish day school was an academy located in Philadelphia in the late 1700s. There are now about 600 Jewish day schools in the country. All Jewish schools provide a double education: In addition to teaching Hebrew, the Torah, and Jewish history, they offer a general education curriculum similar to that used in public schools including English, mathematics, American and world history, geography, and science.

Kentucky Education Reform Act: The nation's most sweeping state school reform law. Passed by the Kentucky General Assembly in 1990, it enacted new curriculum, governance, finance, and technology initiatives. The law grew out of a 1989 state supreme court decision.

Labeling theory: A broad theory of social behavior that describes how attaching labels to a person (such as deviant, disabled, high-risk) can shape both the person's self-perception and the expectations and behavior of others toward the labeled person in ways that reinforce the label.

Magnet schools: Public schools offering specialized programs to attract students. Once used as a voluntary method of achieving racial balance in districts under court order to desegregate, magnets are now offered to students as an optional substitute for their location-based school assignment.

Mandatory statewide choice: The right of parents to decide which public school their children attend anywhere in the state, rather than having children irrevocably assigned to a school based on location. With *voluntary open enrollment*, the district is not required to offer choice among its schools, but it can allow parents to choose a school. With *mandatory open enrollment*, the district must allow parents this option.

Mean: The arithmetic average of a series of numbers.

Median: The middle number in a series of numbers.

Mennonite and Amish schools: Schools that uphold the beliefs and values of Mennonite and Amish families. Today there are about 400,000 Mennonites in the United States and Canada, with substantial communities in Indiana, Ohio, Maryland, Virginia, and Pennsylvania. Each is distinguished by the degree to which it accepts and rejects the trappings of modern American life. There are several hundred Mennonite schools in the country. The schools are small, both in size and in number of students. Parent involvement is very high. Students live close to the school, usually within walking distance. There is a correlation of beliefs and values between the community, the family, and the school. The teacher shares the beliefs, values, and lifestyle of the families served. The teacher's relationship to the school and the parents is not a business relationship. The teacher is considered to have been called to a religious "vocation." The teacher lives in the community and has frequent contact with the children outside the school. Religious activities, prayer, and the reading of the Bible frame the school day. Moral education is an important part of learning. The basic academic skills of reading, writing, and arithmetic are emphasized. Older children help younger children with lessons.

Mixed-method evaluation: An evaluation for which the design includes the use of both quantitative and qualitative methods for data collection and data analysis.

Mode: The number occurring most frequently in a series of numbers.

Montessori Education: The legacy of Maria Montessori, a physician who became interested in the educational problems of mentally retarded children. The Montessori method is one of the best-known and most widespread approaches in the world to early childhood education. Most of the Montessori schools in the United States are private institutions. The Montessori movement did not become firmly established in the United States until Dr. Montessori's death in 1952. Today the Montessori movement in the United States is large, well organized, and influential.

Multicultural education: An educational method that deals with the culture, history, heroes, literature, and traditions of African Americans, Hispanics, Native Americans, and other minorities in the United States. Advocates for multicultural education believe that the aim of education is to prepare all students equally for full participation in a pluralistic society.

Multiple intelligences education: An educational method based on the principles of Howard Gardner, originator of the theory of multiple intelligences. In 1983, Gardner, a professor at Harvard University's School of Education, published *Frames of Mind: The Theory of Multiple Intelligences.* In this book, he challenged the existing definition of intelligence, suggesting that intelligence is the ability to solve problems and difficulties in a particular domain and to create products in that domain that are valued in the culture. Gardner's theory posits that there are at least eight distinct intelligences, each with its own developmental history in the child, its own way of acquiring information, and its own way of expressing itself and creating products. The eight intelligences are linguistic, logical-mathematical, spatial, bodily-kinesthetic, musical, interpersonal, intrapersonal, and naturalistic.

Objective: A specific description of an intended outcome.

Observation: The process of direct sensory inspection involving trained observers.

Outcome: A term referring to post-treatment or post-intervention effects.

Outcomes-based education: An education theory that guides curriculum by setting goals for students to accomplish. Outcomes-based education focuses more on these goals, or outcomes, than on "inputs," or subject units. This theory has drawn intense criticism from parent groups who fear that, by focusing on outcomes, schools are inflicting values onto students.

Pareto chart: A chart that is used to graphically summarize and display the relative importance of differences between groups of data.

Parochial school: A school that is church-related. Most parochial schools are related to the Roman Catholic Church, but some are linked to other Protestant denominations. Hebrew day schools can also be termed *parochial.*

Percentile number: A numerical expression of ranking that is represented as a percentage.

Perennialism: A view of education based on the thought that students should study the classics in order to touch the minds of the greatest writers and philosophers of all time.

Post-secondary enrollment options: Options that permit high school students (usually juniors or seniors) to enroll in courses at state universities or community colleges at government expense and to receive high school graduation credits and college credits toward future enrollment. Public money allocated for the students' high school education is used to pay for the post-secondary courses, thereby forcing high schools to compete with colleges for student funds.

Private contracting: An arrangement whereby school districts contract with a private company to run some or all of the schools in their district; to provide specific academic programs, such as remedial, at-risk, or special education programs; or to cover certain parts of the curriculum, such as foreign languages, science, or math. Under private contracting, districts also contract out support services such as transportation, maintenance, or food services.

Private scholarship programs: Scholarship programs set up by private corporations or foundations to provide low-income parents with assistance for their children to attend the public, private, or parochial school of their choice. Such programs offer anywhere from half to full tuition to allow these children to attend their school of choice, including religiously affiliated schools.

Private school: Independent schools that are controlled by an individual or agency other than the state or district. They are usually supported by private funds and are not controlled by publicly elected or appointed officials.

Privatization: Transfer of the management of public schools to private or for-profit education organizations. Privatization emphasizes typical business-oriented concepts such as customer satisfaction and managerial autonomy in running schools.

Progressive schools: Independent schools dating back to the 1920s that were founded on the basis of John Dewey's experiential and child-centered approach to education. Some private schools have also adopted many of Dewey's ideas. The characteristics of progressive schools include the following: The curriculum is strongly influenced by the students' interests; learning is self-motivated, self-directed, and experiential; the teacher is a guide and facilitator of learning; theme-based projects are a primary approach to learning; the students play a role in making and enforcing the rules of the classroom; there are few if any written tests and probably no letter grades; arts, crafts, music, and drama are important; and development in the student of an inquiring, critical, and curious mind is a high priority. Current progressive school programs include whole language, cooperative learning, the social curriculum, multicultural education, and developmental education.

Progressivism: A view of education based on the belief that teachers should focus on children first and on the subject matter second.

Protestant schools: Parish schools that are operated around the country by Protestant denominations such as Lutherans, Presbyterians, and Seven-Day Adventists. Protestant schools are noted for their strong traditional academic education, which includes moral and religious instruction. They serve a range of children in the community because church membership and belief are not required of either students or parents.

Public school choice: School choice that pertains only to public schools.

Recommendations: Suggestions for specific actions derived from analytic approaches to program components.

Reform network: An association of educators, schools, or districts joined together to provide mutual support as they work on common plans for improving education. Popular reform networks include Theodore Sizer's Coalition of Essential Schools and James Comer's School Development Program.

The Responsive Classroom Program: A program developed by the Northeast Foundation for Children (NFC) in Greenfield, Massachusetts. The NFC is a teacher education and outreach organization that includes a consulting teachers division, a publishing division, and a laboratory/demonstration school. It presents the Responsive Classroom Program in staff development workshops around the country.

Roman Catholic schools: Schools established by the Roman Curia in response to concerns about morality in education. The first Roman Catholic school in the United States was founded in 1784 in Philadelphia. Several such schools were started in 1875. Nine years later, in 1884, the American Catholic bishops decreed that every parish should establish a school and that parents should give their children a good Catholic education. Roman Catholic schools, whether run by the diocese, a parish, or a religious order, are controlled by a given diocese. Each diocese has an office of education.

Scholarships: Mechanisms for dispersing funds to children in school choice plans, whereby parents have a designated dollar amount that they may "spend" to enroll their child at the educational institution of their choice. (Such mechanisms also include *certificates* and *vouchers*.)

School-based management: The shift in decision-making authority from school districts to individual schools. Such proposals vary, but they usually give control of a school's operation to a school council composed of parents, teachers, and local administrators. *See also* Site-based management.

School choice: Any proposal that allows children to attend schools outside their local district boundaries. Such schools may be public institutions other than the school assigned in their district or they may be private and/or religious schools. Often these proposals include public funding for all or some of the tuition costs.

School-community links: Efforts made by school administrators to reach out to parents, families, community leaders, and human-services professionals to improve community life and address social issues that impede learning. Examples range from making school space available for before- and after-school programs to connecting a family to services in the community to planning better long-range coordination of services.

School reform: A generic term encompassing the variety of efforts being made to improve schools. Reform efforts focus on all aspects of schooling, from the way schools are governed to the curriculum taught in the classroom.

School-to-work transition: Any of a host of programs from on-the-job training to apprenticeships to cooperative agreements between high schools and community colleges designed to prepare students not bound for college to enter the job market.

Site-based management: The shift in decision-making authority from centralized bureaucracies to local individual establishments. Such proposals vary, but they usually give control of an organization's operation to local administrators. *See also* School-based management.

Social curriculum: A series of teacher-directed classroom lessons and exercises through which children learn manners and commonly accepted standards of behavior.

Stakeholder: A person who has credibility, power, or other capital invested in a project and thus assumes a degree of risk in connection with it.

Standard deviation (SD): A number that tells us how spread out a group of scores are. If the scores are closely bunched together, we have a small SD number. If the scores are highly spread out, we have a large SD number.

Strategy: A systematic plan of action to reach predefined goals.

Structured interview: An interview in which the interviewer asks questions from a detailed guide that lists the questions to be asked as well as the specific areas for probing.

Summative evaluation: An evaluation designed to present conclusions about the merit or worth of an intervention and recommendations about whether it should be regained, altered, or eliminated.

Tax credits: A funding method for educational choice in which parents receive a credit against income or property taxes for money spent on school tuition, books, or other expenses associated with sending their child to school.

Triangulation: In an evaluation, an attempt to get a fix on a phenomenon or measurement by approaching it via several (three or more) independent routes. Triangulation essentially provides redundant measurement.

Vouchers: Documents or chits, usually issued by the state, that can be used by parents to pay tuition at an out-of-district public school, a private school, and/or a religious school. The term *vouchers* is also used more broadly to refer to school choice proposals in which states would help pay tuition for children attending private or religious schools.

Whole language: An approach to reading and writing that was developed in Australia and New Zealand in the 1970s and introduced in the United States in the early 1980s. Whole language is now used in virtually all public and independent schools that have a progressive inclination. The whole-language approach assumes that children are natural learners—that they love to learn and can motivate and direct themselves.

✎ Index

⦿ About the Author

Dr. Brenda Edgerton Conley is an associate professor and chair of Teacher Education programs in the graduate school at the University of Maryland University College. Prior to Dr. Conley's university appointment, the Baltimore City Public School System employed her for twenty-nine years. In addition to spending ten years as a classroom teacher, she served as assistant superintendent for Professional Development, Organizational Development, and Attitudinal Reform; director of Policy Development and Leadership Support; and director of Human Resources. She also served as director for the Performance-Based Teacher Evaluation Project and director of Project SITE SUPPORT, a United States Department of Education Title II–funded partnership among three universities: Johns Hopkins University, Morgan State University, and the University of Maryland–Baltimore County.

Dr. Conley earned both a bachelor's and a master's degree at Morgan State University in Baltimore, MD. She received her doctorate in education from The George Washington University in Washington, DC.